D0126843

MAYOR FOR LIFE

THE INCREDIBLE STORY OF MARION BARRY, JR.

MAYOR FOR LIFE

THE INCREDIBLE STORY OF MARION BARRY, JR.

MARION BARRY, JR.
AND OMAR TYREE

SBI

STREBOR BOOKS

NEW YORK LONDON TORONTO SYDNEY

Strebor Books
P.O. Box 6505
Largo, MD 20792
http://www.streborbooks.com

This book is a work of nonfiction.

© 2014 by Marion Barry, Jr. and Omar Tyree

All rights reserved. No part of this book may be reproduced in any form or by any means whatsoever. For information address Strebor Books, P.O. Box 6505, Largo, MD 20792.

ISBN 978-1-59309-505-5
ISBN 978-1-4767-3056-1 (ebook)
LCCN 2013933645

First Strebor Books hard cover edition June 2014

Cover design: www.mariondesigns.com
Cover photograph: © Keith Saunders Photos

10 9 8 7 6 5 4 3 2 1

Manufactured in the United States of America

For information regarding special discounts for bulk purchases, please contact Simon & Schuster Special Sales at 1-866-506-1949 or business@simonandschuster.com

The Simon & Schuster Speakers Bureau can bring authors to your live event.
For more information or to book an event, contact the Simon & Schuster Speakers Bureau at 1-866-248-3049 or visit our website at www.simonspeakers.com.

*This memoir is dedicated to my one and only son, Marion Christopher Barry—
the hallmark of my life—and all of the many friends and supporters
who have been with me through the best of times and the worst of times.
It's been an incredible journey, and I never could have done it without you.
Thank you for everything! I love you all!!*

ACKNOWLEDGMENTS

Over the years, I figured there was so such written about me that I started thinking about writing a book to tell my own story and without pretense. I'm tired of other people in the media trying to tell my story. So I started thinking that it was time for me to tell it myself and the way I want to tell it.

And finally, we're here. There are so many, many people who I want to thank for touching my life. Unfortunately, I'm not afforded the time, nor space, to thank you all, but just know that you will always be embedded in my heart, and that's what matters most.

First, I want to begin by thanking God, for without his grace and mercy, none of this would have been possible. Never in a million years could I have imagined the life that God had in store for me when I was picking cotton in Itta Bena, Mississippi, once again proving that with God, anything is possible.

I want to thank my mother, the late Mattie Cummings. My mother was the first person who taught me courage. It was courage that helped me fight through the Civil Rights Movement. It was courage that helped me change the face of the nation's capital. It was courage that led me to create opportunities that ultimately changed the lives of thousands of men, women and youth. Thank you, Mama, for the greatest life lesson ever.

The late Effi Barry, my wife, friend, and mother of my only child, you changed my life in ways you will never imagine. When you entered my life, it changed forever. And when God called you home, it changed my life forever. You were a heaven-sent angel.

I want to thank my dear friend Greg Holloway for introducing me to my publisher, Zane, and for your many years of friendship.

To Zane, thank you for believing in this project and bringing my life to bookshelves all across the country. Because of you, generations will learn the real story of Marion Barry, Jr.

I also want to thank Charmaine Roberts Parker of Strebor Books. You had your work cut out for you, and you rose to the occasion. Thank you for the many, many hours that you devoted to making this book a success.

To my coauthor, *New York Times* Bestselling Author Omar Tyree. Who would have thought that many years later, after interviewing me for *The Capitol Spotlight* newspaper when I first returned to Washington, D.C. politics in 1992 that you would receive the opportunity of a lifetime? After a year of arguing back and forth over all of the details of my life, inside and outside of politics, and how to tell it, we finally got it done. You told my story well, Omar. Thank you for all of those trips back and forth from North Carolina to Washington, D.C. It was a labor of love, and we knocked the ball out of the park. And for the record, I'm not doing a second or a third book, buddy! LOL!!

I had no idea that writing a book would be such a long and challenging process. I want to thank LaToya Foster, my spokeswoman and Director of Communications, for the nights, weekends, and many long hours of assistance. I don't think Omar or I could have finished this book without her. In fact, I know we couldn't have. LaToya was inseparable from the process, and she showed great patience, reserve, tolerance and professionalism to deal with both of us. So I want to thank her and Omar from the bottom of my heart, for pushing me so effectively to get this book done.

To Cora Masters Barry—my wife and friend of forty-five years. What would I have done without you?! You've been a supportive friend during the mountain highs and valley lows of my life. Thank you for everything.

To my legal advisers, Fred Cooke and David Wilmot—the legal dynamic duo. You are amazing. Thank you so very much for your friendship and legal counsel over the years.

To Sandy Bellamy, my special companion. You've been an amazing asset in my life. I love you dearly.

To my Council staff (Joyce Clements-Smith, Mary Thompson, Chan Tei Durant, Charles Lindsay and Danielle Greenfield), thank you so very much for all your hard work.

I also want to thank my cabinet during my sixteen years as mayor of the District. We worked hard, and look at what we accomplished.

To my dear friend Kim Dickens. Your kindness demonstrates the epitome of true friendship. You sacrificed a kidney so I could have life. I can't even find a word that describes how eternally grateful I am for you. I love you much!

I want to give a very special thanks to the late Herbert O. Reid for his tremendous legal work, and Dr. Robert Williams, M.D., for keeping me healthy while I ran the city government.

I also want to thank my good friend Ivanhoe Donaldson, my very first campaign manager. Together, we made a spectacular difference.

To Elijah Rogers, Carol Thompson, Tom Downs, and Michael Rogers—my four City Administrators. Thank you for your contributions to the city.

I want to give special thanks to Maudine Cooper, who served as my Chief of Staff during one of the most difficult moments of my life. I also want to acknowledge the late Barry Campbell, who also served as my Chief of Staff.

I also want to express a very special thanks to Reverend Jesse Jackson, my good friend who I nominated for President of the United States.

I also want to acknowledge Reverend Willie Wilson, my pastor and political supporter of Union Temple Baptist Church, as well as Bishop Glen Staples, my pastor at Temple of Praise Church.

David Eaton, you were one of the early visionaries of my political career. Thank you for your support.

To Carlise Davenport, owner of TOTS Education Center. Thank you for the wonderful care that you gave to Christopher, and your friendship to the Barry family.

Raymone Bain, my longtime friend, former press secretary and publicist. Thank you for your many years of friendship, and your invaluable expertise.

To Rock Newman. Thank you for your many years of friendship.

I can never forget my good friend Cathy Hughes, CEO of Radio One, Inc. I am so proud of you. Thank you for giving me a voice on your airwaves during one of the most challenging moments in my life.

Special thanks to Mayor Vincent Gray, the Council of the District of

Columbia, and all of the extraordinary political minds that I've worked with over the years.

And last, but certainly not least, I want to extend a very special thanks to all of the many people who supported me over the years. I am so grateful to the thousands of Washingtonians and all of the many people across the country who've been with me through the best of times and worst of times. I could have NEVER done this alone. I can never thank you enough. I love you all!!!!!

INTRODUCTION
HAVING BIG VISIONS
A MARION BARRY, JR.

Most people don't know me. They don't know my work ethic, and they don't know me as a person. They know me from ten-second sound bites. They don't know about all of the fighting I've done to manage a government that was progressive and more oriented to uplift the people rather than to suppress them. That's what I want my legacy to be. I was a freedom fighter, and a fighter for the economic livelihood of not only black people but all people. However, I recognized that black people, my people, needed the most help, so I created government policies to help them. And it wasn't about favoritism or corruption; it was about providing an equal opportunity for more people to make a living and to be successful.

More white people, and some black people, only remember me from the Vista Hotel twenty years ago. And it's important that I impart and draw attention to the things that I've done to develop more knowledge, skills and professional experience in the Washington community.

I want people to gather the truth from me rather than from a T-shirt. I want them to gain knowledge about all of the things I was able to do and the challenges that I was able to overcome.

It took a lot of courage to achieve in the community what I call big dreams and big vision. I've always been a big vision person. The promise is too great to think small. You have to think big. With small vision you have a small effect, small solutions and small successes. But with big visions and big dreams, you have big changes and big successes.

So I used these big dreams and visions that God gave me as a tool to create strategies to assist people. I built bigger programs to help the community learn job skills and to create more employment. And not only did I create opportunities for one color of people, I worked for all of the people who needed help: women, gays, Jews, the underprivileged and the educated. Whether you are poor or have money or don't have money, your kids still need milk and food. So there had to be some programs and things that I could do, using the political structure, to help the people whom I represent.

I would say that God has given me a lot of gifts, and I have taken those gifts and used them for the benefit of a whole bunch of people.

In the Christian Church, we learn that God doesn't anoint everybody the same way. So if God gives you these gifts, you have a responsibility to give them back instead of holding on to them. What's the point in that? If God gives them to you, you don't keep them to yourself; you use them!

The correct way to serve people with these gifts is to be more of a giver than a taker. You want to be more selfless than selfish. You want to be more helpful, rather than deprive people of things. And you want to be a loving person rather than being one who spends time hating people. Love is better than hate.

These are all character traits of good leadership. It's also good to have tenacity, courage, accountability, integrity, and a love of people. It's all about the people. You want to lead those people who don't have a voice, or don't know how to use their voices. You want to lead the people who won't stand up, or don't know how to stand up. Or people who don't know how to fight or won't fight.

You have to possess that desire and strength to lead inside of you, especially as a black man, to withstand allowing your past or cultural history to hold you back. You should never allow your future to be determined by your past. I continued to teach people that, and I still do. Black people are the only group who arrived in the U.S. in chains during slavery. And there are many of us who remain psychologically enslaved.

When I came to Washington in 1965, black people's minds were still psychologically confined to a certain extent. We still needed to learn how to develop the type of skills to effect politics and to make a difference. But when I got here, we weren't even allowed to be elected officials. Once we changed that and were elected, we had to do what we were supposed to do. You couldn't promise people things that you were not trying to give them.

You had to give them what you promised; otherwise, you were merely blowing hot air.

When I first won office as mayor in 1978, the District of Columbia government had about 4,000 youth working during the summer months. I grew up in segregated Memphis, Tennessee, selling newspapers, rags, wallets, pop bottles, and washing cars; anything to get a dollar. I told myself, if I ever got any power, I would do something about that. I understood that these young people had nothing to do with politics; they simply wanted a job. So they would stand on the corners and do whatever they could do to survive.

When I took office, I told my work team that I needed 25,000 young workers. I told them, "Let's go out there and find them, and sign them up all over Washington." I didn't discriminate. I promised and delivered meaningful jobs to anyone who wanted to work.

But my team was more concerned about what 25,000 young workers were going to do, and how were we going to do it. So they told me they would think about it.

We thought about it and set it up, and it was a nightmare for the first two years. We didn't have computers or any type of organized methods in place. When we finally got it all together, it became the biggest thing, where thousands more of these young people had a summer job, and we gave them something to do with training. That's what I mean by big dreams and big visions.

It's not about standing on your vision with only 4,000 young people with jobs; you have to expand it to more of the community. If you're going to be a leader, you can't be the same old kind of leader that you just got rid of. You have to be drastically different with a diverse approach to your leadership. You want to affect more of the people who elected you. But as a young man, it was never my intention to get involved in politics; I was simply trying to survive in a segregated world, while fighting for what I thought was right.

So I made that promise with programs and whatever else was needed from the government to make sure that certain resources and opportunities were available to the people and small, minority-owned businesses, whether it was in education, health, jobs, or merely improving a person's quality of life. I was interested in building neighborhoods that could be functional rather than dysfunctional. That became extremely vital to me. And the only way you could do that was by raising the level of life of the people who lived there.

In the Eighth Ward of Washington, D.C. alone, 82 percent of the households are headed by females. It's tough enough to raise a child and family with two parents in the house, let alone one. These black women try to raise these kids, but many of them say: "It takes a man to teach a man." They try as hard as they can, but it's difficult; it's a disadvantage for a man to take a check from a woman. If a man can't hold his own, it becomes hard for him to function in that environment. A good job can mean the world to that man and to the stability of his family.

So people have to recognize the history of our blacks in this country and the things that have been taken away from us that make us whole. With so many of our neighborhoods and communities being jobless environments, where we don't own anything, it makes everything a more complex predicament to fix. So in those pockets of poverty, you want to build them up on a neighborhood level instead of throwing them away. Those neighborhoods are still a part of your city and community, and you have to remember that they elected you. So you have a job to do.

Most successful mayors and governors pick out five or six big dreams and visions that make an incredible difference in the eyes of the people. In Washington, D.C., over my sixteen years as mayor, as well as after my sixteen years, over 100,000 young people got jobs, and we put thousands of families in new housing. We put it in the budget and made it a priority for these youth and their families. We wanted to make sure we had more jobs and training for young people and adults and affordable housing for more people to live.

The biggest victory I had in office was with minority businesses, and making sure that the people in the community owned something. We had to make sure that the people could offer services and make products in the community that they could use. In other words, they needed opportunities to become self-sufficient. So the first thing I tried to do was strengthen the neighborhoods.

I tried to build up strong neighborhoods, and then I wanted to build a strong downtown; that way you have a strong city altogether. You can't have one without the other; you have to have both for your city to thrive. Then you'll have stronger people, who make a stronger downtown and the entire city strong. That's what I had a big vision to do when I first became the mayor.

In 1965, most people in Washington had no use for downtown. They had only one huge building on the north side of Pennsylvania Avenue, an FBI building. They had no business buildings and nothing of interest for the people. There were no high-rises; no fabulous architecture. But come to Washington, D.C. and look at it now. It's a fabulous downtown! And I was able to do a lot of things in the city because of my big vision, my ethics, my leadership and my hard work.

I quit graduate school at the University of Tennessee at Knoxville in 1964. I couldn't see my life moving forward, while fighting white folks for an education. So I joined the Civil Rights Movement and got involved in voter registration, fighting for the homeless, sit-ins, bus boycotts and integrating schools.

With the Civil Rights Movement, we had a big protest at the Democratic Convention in Atlantic City, New Jersey in 1964. At that time, we were trying to unseat an all-white Democratic Party delegation for the state of Mississippi, but we were unsuccessful.

There had been a lot of racial activity going on in the South with an assassination in Mississippi that year, and the Student Nonviolent Coordinating Committee (SNCC) went out and raised close to $1 million from direct mail, with bags of money sitting up in an office in New York. People sent cash, money orders, personal checks and anything they could afford.

So James Forman, who was the executive secretary of SNCC, told me to go to New York and get these bags filled with money out of these office rooms and deposit all of it in the bank. SNCC had a New York office with volunteers, and I was sent up there for about two months, gathering all of this money together to do as he had instructed. So I was used to efforts to raise money to benefit the people before I ever came to Washington.

After being in New York, I told James Forman I wanted to go back down South, to continue fighting white people for justice and equality. I didn't want to be up North in some office. I wanted to be where people were still active. Down South, people were still trying to vote and having sit-ins. People were still going to jail. People were still fighting against segregation and trying to get others to change their way of thinking. There was still a lot of work to do down South in the Civil Rights Movement.

So when James told me to go to Washington, I asked, "Why?"

I was imagining heading farther South than Washington. Outside of making speeches on the lawn, I didn't know of anything going on there.

James Forman replied, "Washington is a majority black town with a current white SNCC director, Jim Monsonis, running the offices. That's not right."

He wanted me to go there to become the director of Washington's SNCC office, lobby Congress and raise money for our efforts in the South. So I went to Washington, and once I got there, I discovered all kinds of problems. There was a 75 percent white police force. There were no recreational or structured activities for the community. Many blacks were living in the same old poverty as everywhere else.

It was the typical thing you would see back in the fifties, before the Black Power Movement emerged with Stokely Carmichael, who changed his name to Kwame Ture and later left the country for Africa. You also had Kwame Nkrumah, who was educated in America and went back home to Africa to fight for his people against British rule and became the President of Ghana. They called it the "Gold Coast" back then. So I fell right in line with the Black Power Movement and wanted to take a stronger position in politics to make a difference. We were all young leaders who were dedicated to seeing the global uprising of blacks.

At that time, D.C. didn't have any elected officials. The city was governed by three commissioners, who were appointed by the President. So we fought to get our first elected school board in 1968. Then we fought for our first elected city council and a Washington, D.C. mayor, Walter Washington, in 1974. He took office on January 2, 1975.

I was immediately moved and inspired by the many possibilities of the city. But with everything else that we had to fix, we had to make sure that downtown was ready. So we had to get involved in the big businesses, particularly the major construction companies that were all owned by white people. When I got in office, the black community received less than 3 percent of the contract business in the city, even though we made up the majority of the population. And with my minority programs, when I left office, we had increased from 3 percent of the major contract business to 47 percent of the total city.

That was the hardest thing to get black folks to see: the power of economics. That's what white folks really care about. They don't sit around talking about what we do or don't do, as long as it doesn't bother their money. So they'll let you protest. They don't care anything about that, as long as it doesn't affect their bottom line. But once you start messing with white people's money, or money that they were used to getting all of, that's when you start having problems.

A lot of whites inherit businesses, and some of them come up with genius ideas, like KFC, Google, and Facebook. But the biggest impediment of black folks developing the same type of businesses is the lack of capital. The banks purposely won't give most black businesses the money to start out because they don't really want us to succeed. Some of the banks realize that would only create more competition for whites. I felt a need to set up small business programs so blacks could get in and start something that they could own.

In the black community, we still manage to spend a total consumer amount that is greater than all but nine countries around the world. We spend something like $2 *billion* in the beauty and hair products business alone.

When you go from 3 percent to 47 percent of $2 billion in business in Washington, and that money's going from whites to blacks, that's what they care about. That's when some white people really start to pay attention to what you're doing. When you start giving black people real money, opportunities and a real sense of pride in themselves that was taken away from us, that's when outside people get mad.

That's what the sting at the Vista Hotel was all about. It was all planned out by the FBI, and it cost them at least $10 million. They went through my mail, my credit card accounts; everything they could get their hands on. That happened after I started giving opportunities to so many black folks to make real money. You had the local newspapers of Washington and the U.S. Attorney for the District talking all about corruption and so-called "friends of Mayor Marion Barry," but they couldn't find any. The drugs, alcohol and women; they don't really mind all that. They care, of course, but they get extra sensitive when you start hitting them in the pocket. That's what the truth is.

White folks may let you in their country clubs to play golf, invite you out to dinner, take you out to play tennis, but when it comes to dividing up the money, that's a whole 'nother story. They didn't want me creating all of these opportunities for black folks. So when the FBI set me up at the Vista, they were really trying to kill me. If they killed me, they wouldn't have to worry about me anymore.

That was the first time in history where they allowed someone to inhale a substance. Usually they would barge in before you inhaled. So they wanted me to overdose on some potent stuff. And they pushed it on me. You can see it on the tape.

They wanted to catch me up in the room with a crack pipe. Everyone in the community could see that, and they all recognized it was a set-up. I believe the FBI even told Rasheeda Moore that they would lock her up for five years for committing perjury in California if she didn't go through with it. But they couldn't lock her up without a trial or a court case. So once everything came out in the trial, I finally forgave her over time. Being a Christian, I forgave her. She was a pawn of the system too. I understood what they put her up to do. But it did make me think more about everybody I associated with.

I was embarrassed by the hotel sting. Sure I was. The federal government circulated the video to American embassies all around the world, and they sold them to discredit everything that I had done in the city. But I never stopped working. That's what they wanted me to do.

Even with the drug dealing and violence that hit D.C. and made us the so-called "murder capital," I never stopped working hard to make things better. The drug and crime epidemic was going on all over the country. There were drug wars, violence and people killing each other all over America; three and four hundred a year in D.C. Before that, New Orleans was the murder capital, where more poor blacks would kill each other, while trying to survive segregation and fighting one another over street money.

But when this drug thing hit the streets of Washington, the government didn't know how to deal with it. The law enforcement didn't know how to deal with it. And I didn't know how to deal with it.

It hit so fast, it crippled us, and it was so violent. We hadn't seen three and four hundred homicides like that in ten years. It also began to sway some of the young people that we had every year in our summer programs. Some of them didn't want to do our jobs anymore; it wasn't enough money. They started making a G a day on a phone. They weren't going to make that kind of money on our summer jobs. So what were you going to do?

These are all the things that people don't know about when I was the mayor in office. But I kept working for the people, and I never stopped working and fighting, no matter what they tried to do or said about me. That's why I keep teaching, you can't allow your future be determined by your past.

The big vision in writing this book is to enlighten, educate, motivate, empower, inspire and envision black people to use their various instruments and gifts to achieve success and greatness.

I would say I did an outstanding job to help develop the people in the Washington, D.C. community. It was incredible. I did extraordinary things. I did the impossible with my successes, overcoming the odds and was able to get back up after being knocked down. I got bigger than what Congress could control. They wanted to control the way that residents in Washington worked and had power over their quality of life. With this book, I simply want people to understand the truth.

One time, a white politician told me, "You can do all kinds of big things, but if nobody knows about it…you ain't done nothing."

That's politics; you're only as good as what you did for the people you represent. And I want the people to know that I did a lot, for all those who judge me but don't really know me. For the people who heard about me, but who don't know all about me. And for the people who never knew my record.

I always felt like I was two different people in politics; one as a personally religious man who was quiet with a lot of doubts and frustrations; and the other as the politician who had to be brave and courageous, while representing the desires of the people. I seemed to be brave enough to take on anything for the people. But deep down inside, I hurt like anybody else.

As you read this book, I don't want people to see this as just another memoir, but a book that gives hope, that's uplifting, and will help other politicians govern a major city and be aware of the many tricks that some in the media play.

CHAPTER 1
SON OF THE SOUTH

I remember overhearing conversations my mother had when I was young, where she talked about being tired of having babies with no money. She had smooth, brown skin—as brown as mine—and she was tall, like five feet eight, and she bragged about having big legs. She had a gentle spirit, but she was firm.

She said, "I'm tired of being poor and not being able to do what I want to do. This is not how I want to live." I can't remember who she said it to, probably a family member or a friend or somebody. But I do know this; my mother sent my oldest sister, Lillie, up to Chicago to live with our grandmother, then she left my father in Mississippi and took my baby sister and me to Arkansas.

I always think back to that as one of the strongest memories of my mother, because she packed us up and left. She wasn't just talking about it. We left Arkansas six months later for Memphis, Tennessee, on our way to Chicago.

Had my mother not done that or felt so strongly about what she wanted to do, I may still be in Mississippi to this day. I didn't really think about it much before, but I believe that's where I got my get-up-and-go spirit from; my mother gave it to me. I guess you can say she showed me the way to protest. You don't talk about making a change; you do something about it.

She was eighteen years old when she had me in Itta Bena, Mississippi. It was LeFlore County in 1936, during the era of the Great Depression and black people's migration north to the big city of Chicago. Thousands of black folks moved there from Mississippi, Arkansas and Tennessee. They had neighborhoods in Chicago where an entire town of Southern people had settled in the same area. A lot of black people from Texas migrated out to California.

My mother's plan was for us to take a bus to Chicago to join my sister and grandmother, but when my grandmother sent for us to come, my father took the money. I guess he opened my mother's mail and found it or something, and he wanted us to stay there on the farm with him. He didn't want us to leave Mississippi. He was already used to it there.

Sometimes people are so indoctrinated into a certain way of life that they don't know how to break it. That's how some people are; they get used to things being a certain way and that's all they know. A lot of people down South were that way. That's the way it was in segregation. There were no black politicians in Mississippi at that time, and the people there were trying to survive. They accepted segregation and poverty for what it was. Many of them didn't know anything different.

My father was forty-six when they had me. He was a very dark brown man from spending so many years out in the hot sun as a farmer. He was over six feet tall, about six-two, and robust. You had to be built like that with farming. I don't know if he had other children from a previous marriage or from other women. I don't know if he had even married my mother legally. A lot of people were married by common law in those days, especially in the Deep South.

In Mississippi, I was the oldest of three children in my family and the only boy. My two younger sisters were Lillie—named after my grandmother on my mother's side—and Elizabeth. My father's name was Marion Barry—where I got my name from—and my mother's name was Mattie from the Bland family.

I remember learning that Epps Bland was my great-great-grandfather, and that he and his four brothers were born into slavery before gaining their freedom. So I had Bland family members who had moved to various places at different times. Nobody kept family records back then, so I don't know where everyone moved to and when. I only knew they were in Chicago, Detroit, Cleveland, Gary, Memphis, Arkansas and Mississippi.

Before we moved from Mississippi, my mother had picked and chopped so much cotton that her hands were curled. She would chop and part the cotton fields with a hoe, and use a switchblade to cut crabgrass. That was what my sisters and I were born and raised into: picking, chopping and separating cotton as sharecroppers.

We lived in a segregated society on Mississippi farmland, where a white man would lease you the land and some cotton seed to harvest the cotton. You would pay him off by picking and selling your crops. They called it sharecropping, but you weren't sharing anything. It was a slick way of being slaves again. The white man owned the land and you worked it for him unless you could afford to buy some land of your own, or inherit the land.

But few of the sharecroppers ever made enough money to pay the land-owners off, unless you had a big enough family to pick all of the cotton you needed to sell to make a profit. That's why you had so many large families with five or six children on the farms. On top of that, the white men would always buy the cotton for less than what they sold it to you for. So they would make their money both ways, and you would be poor and in debt until you decided to leave.

We lived in what they called a shotgun house that went straight from the front door to the back door. The house had a tin roof that made a bunch of noise whenever it rained. We had an outhouse to use the bathroom, a pump for water and a kerosene lamp for light and for heat. We often went barefoot or had shoes that had holes in them. So we would strap cardboard on the inside to the bottoms. But on many days I went barefoot.

As the only boy, I wore mostly shorts and T-shirts or no shirt at all in the summertime. My father wore bib overalls for farming. My mother and sisters wore dresses made of cotton. It was nothing fancy, only the bare necessities. That's the kind of poverty my mother was talking about when she complained. She couldn't see herself and her family being that way for the rest of our lives. Sharecropping was a hard way to live.

On our farm, we had chickens, pigs and a mule for long-distance travel. We also used the mule to carry the cotton to the cotton shack and to take us to church or to the schoolhouse. We would strap a wagon to the back of the mule and climb in the wagon.

For food, we ate chicken and every part of the pig but the squeal. We ate pig feet, ham, pork chops, chitterlings, sausage, pig tail, pig knuckles; everything. I remember my mother and father would raise and kill the pigs by jabbing them in their sides with a sharp knife. And the pigs would go *eerrkk!*

From the time I was a young child, I remember my mother carrying and picking cotton with two sacks on her shoulders—one on her right and one on her left. The sacks hung over her shoulders on a strap, and she would pick cotton with both hands. With no babysitter during her field work, my mother and father would often drag me on the end of the cotton sacks. My mother said she would pick nearly 250 pounds of cotton a day. That's what she told me; I was too young to weigh it. I just know she was chopping and picking cotton from sunup to sundown.

I started picking cotton around five or six years old, and we would put three or four, forty- to fifty-pound sacks on the mule to take to the cotton market. We had a short sack and a long sack that held more cotton. The short sack was for me. I couldn't pick nearly as much cotton as they could. And we had crops of tall cotton and short cotton. For the tall cotton, you would walk over and pick it standing up, but for the short cotton, you would get on your knees to pick it. Sometimes we wore kneepads to prevent our knees from getting scuffed.

Outside of picking cotton all day, there wasn't much for kids to do. I remember walking for miles and going to church or to the convenience store with my mother to buy the groceries. Even our neighbors lived a mile or more away.

I remember playing out in the yard and going to the schoolhouse, where they had one big room for students, no matter what age you were. I liked going to the schoolhouse; it was something to do. I don't know if we learned anything in there, but I didn't think anything bad about it. And I liked the sweet Carnation milk they gave us at the schoolhouse.

I helped my mother to pick cotton until I was around seven or eight. That's when she started teaching me to chop the cotton. But that process was hard and it would hurt your hands. I didn't like that. So I told my mother, "I can't do this no more." That was a hell of a way for a young kid to spend his days. But that was Mississippi sharecropping for you.

All of that led to my mother wanting to leave Mississippi. That's when she sent my sister, Lillie, to Chicago to stay with our grandmother in anticipation of us going to join them later. The plan was for my grandmother to send my mother, Elizabeth and me some Greyhound bus fare. That's when my father found the money and took it to prevent us from leaving. You were raised in that system in 1936, and my father accepted it. But with my mother, she may have been poor financially, but she wasn't poor in spirit, and she'd had enough of poverty.

So she took Elizabeth and me on the ferry boat across the Mississippi River to stay with my uncle and his family in West Helena, Arkansas. My uncle had a job cutting timber to build houses, and when my mother took us over there, that was the last time I ever saw my father. There were reports about my father being dead before we left Mississippi, but I only told people that later on in high school to avoid the shame of not having my father in my life anymore. It was embarrassing for me, so I said he was dead when people asked me about him. I don't know if it was true or not. I never tried to find him. But my father had never abused me or anything, like some of the other kids' fathers. He tried to give me anything that I asked for. On weekends, my father ran a corn liquor operation.

When we arrived in Arkansas, black people were still segregated, but the schools were more structured and the families lived closer together. We were all able to play out in the streets and at the playgrounds and schoolyards. The schools in West Helena had everyone separated by their age groups instead of having us all in one big room at the schoolhouse, like they had us in Mississippi. So I was back with kids my own age.

My mother became a domestic in Arkansas, working in white women's kitchens. But she had a rule where she always insisted that she go in through the front door and not through the back. She told them to call her by her last name, Ms. Barry. She was a good worker and a good cook. She also babysat for families. But she wouldn't take anything from them as far as people trying to put her down. My mother earned her respect and showed me how to earn it.

Sometimes she took me to their houses with her, but I would never get too friendly or try to play with the white women's kids. I may have played with a boy a bit, but definitely not with a white girl. That was suicide. I recognized that early on. You didn't mess with white women; white girls or women. Nobody had to tell us that; we automatically knew what not to do in segregation. It was ingrained in us. That's how segregation was. And you didn't ask why.

I mean, I was curious. Sure. But that was it. You didn't go there, or at least not me.

We only stayed in Arkansas for about six months before we left for Memphis.

My mother had relatives from the Bland family who lived there. I was about eight years old and in the third grade.

When we moved to Memphis, we stayed with my Aunt Mattie in Hyde Park, North Memphis. We later moved to an area called Douglas on Sydney Street at 1492. How we got to Douglas, I don't remember.

I enrolled in Douglas Elementary and High School. The school went from kindergarten to the twelfth grade. The story was: the white politicians of Memphis did not want to name a school after Frederick Douglass, the abolitionist, so they insisted they name it Douglas with only one "s."

I remember I was still bothered by my name when I got there. I never liked the name Marion. I thought it sounded like a girl's name. Marion was too close to Mary and Mariam. I didn't like my mother calling me "Junior" either.

I told my mother, "I don't like you calling me that." I didn't want to be known as a junior. But she didn't stop saying it. I guess that was her way of respecting my father even though we had left him.

In my fourth-grade year, I met Richard Kirkland Bowden, who was in the fifth grade. I competed against his class in the spelling bee. I was representing the fourth grade and he was representing the fifth grade, and I won. Richard still talks about losing to me in that spelling bee to this day.

I had a reputation of being very smart in school. And after the spelling bee, Richard and I became good friends. He lived two blocks away. I remember we shot marbles and played football together around the neighborhood. Richard later became a Deputy U.S. Marshal for Washington, D.C.

Memphis, Tennessee was still segregated when I lived there, like it was in Mississippi and Arkansas, but the school system was a lot more organized, even more so than it was in West Helena. Everyone had their own rooms and was in their right grades. The teachers were better trained in Memphis, and they were mostly women. You had a few men teaching math, science, history and coaching sports teams, but not a lot.

We used to go to the meat packing company called Fineberg after school and for lunch to get hot dogs and buns to eat. We had guys who would walk two or three miles from the school and back to go to the meat company. They also had more of the sweet Carnation milk that I liked.

We moved to 1492 Sydney Street when my mother married Mr. Bacon, who became my first stepfather. We later moved from Sydney Street after the closing of the packing company, where my mother had worked as a meatpacker. He took me around town to a few places but not many. Sydney Street was his house, which did not have any gas. There were two stoves in the house—one for heating and one for cooking. The cooking stove had an oven that was fired by coal. Instead of a refrigerator, we had an ice box, where you had a fifty-pound block of ice on the top part of the box with a swinging door to open it.

I don't remember what happened with my mother and Mr. Bacon, but my mother later married Prince Jones, who had three daughters and a son from a previous marriage: Gwendolyn, Amy, Jacqueline and Sammie. So my mother, Elizabeth and I moved from the north side of Memphis to the south side, and into Prince Jones's house. I don't remember much about it, but I do know the house wasn't big enough for eight family members. My mother had two more daughters with Mr. Prince Jones: Gloria and Shirley, creating a household of ten people, where I was the oldest of only two boys. So I learned a lot about leadership and responsibility, even in our own household. And I was surrounded by young women.

As a kid, I was never punished much or abused or anything. Sometimes my mother used to discipline me for falling asleep in church, but that was about it. She'd pop me in a minute for not paying attention, but she was never abusive to me. Sometimes you deserve punishment.

So my mother would catch me dozing off in church, and *pop!*

"Boy, wake up and pay attention!"

I got a whupping one time for leaving my sister at the movies by herself in a community called Hollywood, close to Douglas. I didn't want to see the movie anymore and she did, so I left her. I got home and my mother asked me, "Where's your sister?"

I said, "I don't know."

My mother whipped me good, and I screamed every time she hit me, "Momma, it hurts!" But she kept going and she and I walked the three or four miles back downtown to the movies to get my sister.

Sometimes, my mother used to whip me with the ironing cord. She would say, "This hurts me more than it hurts you."

I would say, "Well, stop it then."

I wouldn't ever say we were a close family, though. My mother and stepfather were always doing separate jobs and things. One of them would cook for one night and not be home or around for the next. That's part of the reason—years later—that I wanted my own family to gather around at the table at night for dinner. I wanted to create a feeling of togetherness that I missed in my own upbringing. I liked for my family to be able to talk to one another about our day around the table. I think that's important in a family.

Thinking back, I didn't like how I looked when I was growing up in Memphis either. There was nothing in particular that I didn't like; it was my overall look. I didn't like my face. But when I got older, I began to like my looks and my name; no one else had it. I guess you can say I went through a natural evolution. God gave me my name, my face and my look. It was the only name and face I had so I had to live with it. I didn't complain too much and I worked hard for everything I got in life.

The biggest disappointment I had as a child was finding out there was no Santa Claus. I always wondered how he got himself and all those toys down the chimney. So when I finally found out that it wasn't true that Santa Claus left us toys, I was devastated. I felt like we had been lied to for all those years. But I got over it. I still enjoyed the pop guns and Christmas toys that they gave me, regardless of whether Santa Claus existed or not.

My mother worked as a domestic in Memphis. Sometimes I would cut the grass at the women's houses where she worked and tag along with her to help out when she asked me to. But I still didn't bother with the women's kids; Memphis was still segregated. We lived in an all-black part of South Memphis, but black people lived all over Memphis: East Memphis, North Memphis, South Memphis.

Memphis was run by a powerful white man named E.H. Crump. We called him "Boss Crump." He was the former mayor of the city, but from a political context he was the governor. We didn't know where his money came from—black people didn't ask questions like that—we only knew that he had a lot of power in the city. He ran all of the city's politics and was the czar of black people. He made sure whoever he wanted to be mayor got elected.

There were no black politicians in Memphis at the time, and everybody knew that Boss Crump ran the city. Nothing happened in Memphis without him being a part of it, no matter whom the mayor was or who was in office. We all found it fascinating that this man was able to run the city like that. I think it may have influenced me in some ways to make an impact on city policies when you're empowered to. I didn't want to be like Boss Crump, but I would rather have been a man who could have an influence than not. What's the point of being a leader if you have no influence?

Once my large family got settled in, we needed a larger place and moved again to Latham Street, where I graduated from the Florida Street Elementary School in the eighth grade. I went there in the seventh and eighth, and I remember the first girl who gave me a kiss.

She said, "Come here," and called me back into the cloak room, where we hung our coats. I walked back there with her and she kissed me on the lips. I almost fainted. I didn't have that much experience with girls. My heart was racing a mile a minute.

Around that time, in the early 1950s, Benjamin Hooks, A.W. Willis, Jr. and Russell Sugarmon, Jr. were the first black officials and lawyers to put the city of Memphis on the map with their activism. They were three black people who stuck out and began to fight against the practices of segregation in the city. We were all proud of them, and they went down as some of the first freedom fighters in the city of Memphis. They influenced me as well. They were all educated black men who used their education and popularity to do something with it for the benefit of the people. What wouldn't you admire about that? There are too many educated people who don't use their degrees for the benefit of the people, but to be a good leader, you have to use them. You have to use everything that you have to make a difference.

Benjamin Hooks later became the head of the NAACP, Russell Sugarmon became a high-ranking judge and A.W. Willis became the first black elected official to the Tennessee General Assembly since the Civil War era in the 1880s. They were an inspiration to us all.

After graduating from Florida Street Elementary School, I went to Booker T. Washington High School. Booker T. was another segregated school in Memphis, but I was happy to go there. We won Tennessee state titles in everything we played: football, basketball, track and band. Our colors were green and gold and our school name was the Warriors. It seemed like we went to the state finals nearly every year. So I learned how to be a part of a winning tradition, even if I couldn't play on the teams.

I was proud to go to Booker T., and the athletes got a whole lot of attention there from the girls. The girls liked jocks and the athletes were the most popular guys in school. So it was a perfect match. But in my freshman and sophomore years, I was too small to play any sports. I didn't have the size to play football and I wasn't tall enough for basketball. I hadn't played that many sports before high school, so I wasn't any good at them. But I wanted to be popular for something, so I focused on academics.

The first time I brought my report card home in the ninth grade, I had done so well in school that my mother broke down and cried. She couldn't believe it. That made me feel that getting good grades was definitely something that I could do to be popular. So I kept at it, knowing that academics could take me places and give me something to toss my hat in.

I still wanted to be involved in sports and other things at school, though. So I took up boxing and band. In boxing, I used to go down to this gym in Memphis without my mother's knowledge. I got a little bit of attention from the girls with my boxing. I even won a few fights. I had about fourteen or fifteen fights, but I stopped after my last two. I had moved up from the 112 weight division to 118, and I got punched in the face so hard I saw stars. I didn't go down, but it felt like I was out on my feet. My head was aching and spinning like a top. I was saved by the bell that night. Then I had my next fight and I finally got knocked down.

I said, "Yup, that's the end of me boxing." I told my coach that it wasn't for me. I guess I didn't have boxing in my blood. I didn't want to keep getting knocked down with my head hurting. But I understood the courage and the preparation that it took to go into a good fight. My experience in boxing helped me to view everything as an opponent. It was you against them in a big ring and everybody was watching. I always wanted to do well in a fight.

When I went out for the school band, I tried to play the trumpet. The music director let me take a trumpet home with me to practice. You couldn't be in the band if you couldn't play an instrument. You had to know how to play. Then they told me I would have to buy my own instrument, so I quit.

We couldn't afford it and they didn't have instruments to allow you to rent, so I had to quit.

I had a lot of fun in high school. We had some good teachers at Booker T. Washington who really cared about us. I was pretty popular and hung out with all of the athletes, but I didn't get my growth spurt until later on. I grew about three more inches in college. But in high school, I hung out with all the popular guys who played sports.

One time I had to set a few football players straight in my English class. These guys were shooting rubber bands around the classroom with their fingers, goofing around and being disruptive in the back of the room. The teacher turned and asked me, "Mr. Barry, are you shooting these rubber bands?"

I said, "No, I'm not shooting any rubber bands. I don't know what you're talking about."

He was thinking that I was doing it because some of these football players were shooting these rubber bands right around me. So after around two or three weeks of this rubber band shooting, I got tired of it and after class, I told them, "Y'all gotta cut that shit out."

I was all right with the football guys and the other athletes, but I took school seriously and I didn't want them to jeopardize what I had going academically. I wouldn't shoot off rubber bands or try to mess up their football or basketball games, so I didn't want them doing that in my classes. Sometimes you have to speak up as a leader, even when it involves people that you know and like. They knew it was the right thing to do so they didn't really argue or complain about me saying anything about it. All the guys already knew that I was into my schoolwork.

On my weekends in high school, we would sometimes go to a party in North Memphis, and you would have your typical neighborhood fights with guys from the other side.

They would start complaining, "Hey, man, leave our girls alone."

We would always end up in a fight, but after the fights were over, I would keep dancing. We had a lot of fights in Memphis, but the fights never stopped me from having fun. I never allowed any circumstances to stop me from doing what I wanted to do or achieving my goals. Even as a teenager, I noticed how some people would have a bunch of excuses in life, but I didn't. I never made those excuses; I would simply find a way to push forward. I was always able to focus through chaos.

I remember we would have Friday night football games against Manassas—an all-black high school on the North side—and after the games, we would have fights with the school's fans. So the school system moved the Friday night games to two o'clock in the afternoon to avoid any fights. So you would only have the home team fans at the games since we couldn't get to the other school in time to see them.

On the weekends and during the summertime, we would go downtown to Beale Street to the Old Daisy and New Daisy movie theaters. They were the theaters that black people frequented. We went to the Hippodrome—a skating rink and ballroom on Beale Street—where they had events, parties and shows. We would ride on the Main Street trolley and have a ball, pulling the strings to stop the car.

With the shops downtown and around Memphis, I would always look at the price before I would buy anything. That's what poor people often learn to do with clothes and groceries. We couldn't focus on brand names or quality. We focused on the price. But I figured when I got some money, I would look at the quality first.

We even had doo-wop groups in high school, listening to Sam Cooke's "You Send Me" and other songs that we liked, including songs from The Clovers and The Midnighters.

We had this one song from The Midnighters, where we sang, "Annie had a baby / can't work no more..."

I had a bunch of good times in high school. I had a sweetheart named Vernell and I kept my good grades in school. I even took up speaking and going to poetry events back then. I wanted to learn "House by the Side of the Road" by Sam Walter Foss and make my own version of it. I would hear other people recite it, and I told myself, "I'm gonna learn this poem myself."

I liked this poem because of the message about life when you live in a house by the side of the road. But it wasn't the only poem I liked.

I listened to Harold Sims, a church member who performed "The Creation," a poem by James Weldon Johnson. This poem, written by a black man, discussed the creation of this world and God's role in it, and I wanted to learn this great, long poem to enhance my speaking as an orator. And Harold Sims became the acting head of the National Urban League right after Whitney M. Young in 1971.

I had an older colleague from church, William J. Hawkins, who was in school at LeMoyne-Owen College around that time. He would take me around to some of these poetry events on campus, and he was a member of Alpha Phi Alpha Fraternity. Going to these poetry events on campus made me want to go to college and pledge for Alpha myself. Reciting poetry also helped me with my public speaking and confidence. So I've always had a strong affection for poetry and how using different words and sayings could fire up and inspire an audience.

Looking back at it all, I realize how many of my early experiences helped to prepare me for the big stages of my later career. Sometimes, when you look back at a person's life and experiences early on, you can see the traits of what kind of a person they will become. And my very humble and determined beginnings definitely helped to make me the leader that I would become. So if you really want to understand who I am now and what made me do the things I did to become the leader that I wanted to be, you have to first understand the people and the places where I was raised and how I adapted to those environments to survive and to make progress—like how I used to always find odd jobs to make money when I was young. Coming from the cotton fields of Mississippi, I was used to hard work. It didn't bother me.

I used to do all kinds of odd jobs growing up in Memphis. One of my main jobs was a newspaper carrier. The man who was the director of the newspaper distribution for *The Commercial Appeal* for that part of South Memphis, said that they had openings for paper carriers. So I asked them for a job carrying newspapers. In Memphis, like in most cities, you had a certain geographical area where you would deliver your papers. We would go to pick up the papers early in the morning and we would fold them up in fours and put rubber bands on them. Then I would put them in two bags and deliver them on a bicycle. We liked to fold them inside of an early breakfast restaurant, but the black carriers couldn't eat inside there, so sometimes we would order something to go.

I had about a fifty-fifty split of white and black customers that I would deliver newspapers to. Most people paid me on time. However, there were some people who didn't pay me. Newspaper carriers had to submit subscriber payments every Saturday. Sometimes, my mother lent me the money for the nonpaying customers out of her meager earnings until I could collect the money.

I had fun doing it, though. I was still making some money, but some subscribers would tell us, "Come back tomorrow," when it was time for them to pay.

At that time, if you got a certain number of new subscribers, say fifteen or more, then they would send the white kids to New Orleans as a bonus. We found out about that, and we could see the money that everyone was getting from the things they were buying with it. It just so happened, I had a cousin who was delivering papers on the North side of Memphis, who was going through the same thing with inequality. Since we were networking around Memphis, we decided to stop delivering the papers. There were no computers back then, only notebooks to keep track of everything.

So a few other black carriers and I decided not to deliver our newspapers for three or four days. We saw these white newspaper carriers getting sent to New Orleans and black carriers only getting new bicycles, and we didn't think that was fair. We were delivering these papers just like they were. This inequality in relation to newspaper distribution was an extension of the segregation we had in our own schools, barbershops, churches, beauty shops and funeral homes.

Our elders were not used to asking white people for fairness or fighting back. But here you had a group of young fifteen- and sixteen-year-old boys mixed into segregation and we were striking against inequality and fighting back for our rights. That was a little different for our parents and for older people in our community to accept. Most black people in Memphis didn't do that. The deepest custom of segregation was that those who were colonialized would take on the habits that the colonizers wanted them to take on. But we knew, as young people, that it was something wrong with segregation and how we were treated as opposed to how they all treated white people. We wanted to be treated the same way the white boys were treated for carrying the same papers. But that kind of mistreatment with segregation was so customary in the South that people thought it was the right thing to do.

We withheld our lists of subscribers from everyone and we decided that we weren't going to deliver any papers. It lasted for about three days. *The Commercial Appeal* then gave in and provided us the same bonuses as the white carriers and sent us to St. Louis, which was better for us anyway.

That was one of the first times I stood up to segregation, but it definitely wasn't the last. I realized that if you didn't fight back in Memphis, and if you weren't willing to get your behind beat, then you wouldn't get anything. People wouldn't just give you what you wanted. You had to organize yourself with plans to take it. I realized that early in my life. If you want change, you have to make change happen for yourself.

To tell you the truth, I don't know where I got my militancy from, but I got it. I can't attribute it all to my mother either. She was surprised herself by some of the things I did. Sometimes I even tried a sip of the cold "white" water from the segregated water fountains. I remember when my mother saw me drinking from a fountain. She snatched me from the fountain and said, "You better watch yourself, boy. You'll get locked up." I had decided that I wanted to drink some "white" water.

Blacks were only allowed to go to the Memphis Zoo on Thursdays. One time a group of five of my friends managed to walk into a segregated state fair in Memphis without being stopped. But after about ten or fifteen minutes, the Memphis police offers arrived and put us out. I didn't consider it right that only white people got to go. Blacks lived in the state of Tennessee, too. How come we couldn't go to the state fair?

I figured I had to get some of my defiance from my mother, and from being young and not knowing any better. But with most of the older black people in the South, they accepted things for what they were. We didn't call it racism back then; we called it segregation. I didn't have enough contact with white people to call it racist.

I remember we used to have this game we played with some of the white paper carriers called "The Blood Bowl." We would play football in this vacant lot on Third Street, black against white. They knew that some of us went to Booker T. Washington High School, and they wanted to see if they could beat us in football. That's how popular my high school was for sports and winning.

We called this football game "The Blood Bowl" because we played with no pads, helmets, nothing. We were really trying to draw blood out there. It was a tough game, where we went hard to battle and beat each other. The first time we played it, though, the police caught us and tried to break it up, but the white boys wouldn't let them do it. They wanted to play us to prove they could beat us so bad that they didn't let the cops stop it. Then we started mixing up the teams with black and white. That was the only way we could get around the cops trying to break up our playing. That was something else. Sports have always had a way of evening out the playing field between the races. Either you can play or you can't. And either you win or you lose. There's no politics in that.

Willie Herenton, another paper route carrier who was four years behind me, became the first black mayor of Memphis. We had been childhood friends for years. He often ate at my house, and I ate at his. We talked all about distributing newspapers in the old segregated Memphis.

I spent four or five years in a segregated Boy Scouts unit to become an Eagle Scout. We had all-black and all-white units back then. So whenever we did big events with the other Boy Scouts, we would have meetings with our black scout masters to talk to us about what to do and how to act. My friends didn't want to finish or go on as long as I did, but I wanted to be an Eagle Scout, so that's what I did. I always worked to be the best, and an Eagle Scout was considered the best. I don't remember being the first black Eagle Scout of all of Memphis, but I was the first amongst my friends in my unit. I was determined to finish what I had started.

But segregation was like that. You had to be determined to fight it because it ran through every part of society. That's why it was going to take the kids and young people to be able to break it. We even had a bus line back then, where you would ride through a black neighborhood, and the passengers would be mostly black. The same bus would cross into a white neighborhood, and it would be the reverse, with all white folks. The few blacks that were on the bus had to move from the front to the back. In fact, in New Orleans and other places, there were signs on the buses separating the seating. So when the bus would ride down Fourth Street, with a significant amount of white folks on it with the windows open, we used to throw water on the white people.

We didn't know what we were doing back then; we felt something was wrong about how they treated us and we were angry about it. I'm not saying that it was right, but animosity directed toward you can make you show the same animosity toward someone else. This was before I learned anything about nonviolent resistance. We didn't know anything about that. All we knew was how to fight.

The Memphis City Schools system even had a Central High School in Memphis, with all white students who called themselves the Warriors with the same green and gold colors. But they weren't state champions or anything like we were. So years later, after Brown v. Board of Education, we had a dispute to see who was going to change their school name and colors, and it wasn't going to be us. We had established ourselves in the state and they had not. So eventually, Central High School changed its mascot name to something else.

The segregation of Memphis never stopped our fun in high school, nor did it stop me from finding jobs and trying to make some money. In my junior and senior years, I could work after school, so some of my high school friends and I took jobs plastering houses and church buildings that were new or being remodeled. I had taken plastering in high school and we were allowed to work part-time. This was long before drywall. I went to a Baptist church with my mother and family, but there were Episcopal churches that would hire us for the plastering jobs.

I took a job as a waiter and a busboy at the American Legion in my late years of high school, but it only lasted for two weeks. The American Legion was an all-white veteran club in Memphis, where they served liquor in bottles with the American Legion name on them. In Memphis, you couldn't buy liquor by the drink, so they had you buy these blue tickets in order to get a drink. And if you wanted five drinks, you would buy five blue tickets. You had to have several tickets for a drink.

While waiting tables there one day, this one white man said, "Hey, boy! Nigger!"

He was very loud and disrespectful to me, so I said, "That's not my name." I was mad and embarrassed by it, so I told the management that they needed to get him out of there before I punched him in his mouth.

They made the disrespectful patrons leave, and the same thing happened a few days later, so a couple days after that, I quit. I had a natural fight in my spirit that wouldn't allow me to accept that kind of disrespect from white customers, where other black kids would. They could never understand that from me, my fight for respect. But I waited tables at white establishments throughout my college career at different places where I made sure that the customers respected me and didn't call me out my name. I never allowed that one incident or anything else to stop me from doing what I wanted to do. That was a common trait throughout my life. If I have it in my mind that I want to do something, I'm not going to allow anyone to stop me.

I remember the Peabody Hotel downtown was segregated back then, too, and they had a Peabody Duck March. The ducks had their own penthouse at the top of the hotel and everything. They treated those ducks better than they treated us. Of course, they let blacks work there, cleaning up rooms and taking out the trash, but we couldn't go in certain parts of the hotel that the ducks could go in. We used to see the ducks waddle around in the hotel and couldn't believe it. Then the Peabody closed down for a long time. But when it reopened years later, when I became the Mayor of Washington, I went back for a visit to Memphis and I ordered the biggest penthouse suite in the hotel. It was my way of making a statement and showing that I had risen up past all of their segregation, had overcome all that I had been subjected to and returned home as a black man in power.

Before I graduated from high school, at age eighteen, I registered for the United States Draft, which at that time, was required of all young men. I also joined the Naval Air Reserve at seventeen as a high school junior. I became one of the first black Naval Air Reservists in Memphis. In fact, I may have been the first in the entire state of Tennessee. I joined the Reserve because I was on a tour of a naval air base at Millington, Tennessee, right outside of Memphis, when I noticed there were no black reservists on the base.

I asked the white commander of the base, why there were no black Reservists and he said, "Why don't you join?"

So James Truly, another black student who was interested, and I joined the Naval Air Reserve. I became an aerial photographer with duties of one weekend out of every month, and ninety days during the summer. We also were paid, which made it easier for me to want to join. My fondest memories of that time were when we went to Treasure Island, right near San Francisco, over the summer after my graduation from high school.

I graduated from the first class of Booker T. Washington that had a brand-new gymnasium in 1954. I was also inducted into the National Honor Society while in high school at Booker T. It was our shining moment to graduate from a proud high school of winners. However, a lot of my high school friends didn't go to college. Most of them finished high school and went looking for jobs or entered the military. We didn't have all of the scholarships for sports back then, or a lot of my athletic friends would have gone to college. We didn't have a lot of school counselors or anything to prepare us for college either, so most of my high school friends and classmates went right to work after high school, if they could find a good-paying job. A lot of them were unprepared and didn't know what to do. I didn't take the SATs and I had no idea how to go to college myself; I knew that I wanted to go, so I got in motion again to make it happen.

I can't remember everything about my early years in Mississippi and Arkansas, or everything about my upbringing and high school days in Memphis, but I feel like I want to say more about my family and the people that I grew up with. I feel like there are still so many gaps to fill in. You can't remember it all; nobody can. But from what I can remember, my foundation was already set for what I would need to do to evolve into the man and leader that I would become.

William J. Hawkins wasn't the only person I knew in college, but very few people in my neighborhood went. You have to understand that college was a very special privilege for black folks in those days. It was the early 1950s when black students still couldn't go to certain elementary and high schools, let alone attend major white colleges and universities. So I became the first one in my family to attend college, and many of my classmates were the first in their families to go.

In my junior year of high school, we had no one to counsel us on how to fill out a college application or any of that. Most blacks didn't know how to fill out applications either. Knowledge was very limited. Before my junior year of high school, I didn't even know what college was. It wasn't part of everyone's dream back then. I believe that was another byproduct of segregation. A lot of young blacks didn't think of college as a realistic option.

The white universities in the South were not inviting us to go to college back then, and we didn't have the money to go if they did. I didn't even know what schools I wanted to apply to. I only knew that I wanted to be able to have enough skills to do something with my life. A number of my friends from Booker T. Washington High School didn't have those same goals, so they didn't go to college. I'm not saying that they didn't have any goals, because for a lot of them, getting a factory job, a house, a wife and a car to start a family with were goals. Those basic life goals were not only for black folks back then, but for a lot of white folks at that time as well.

To prepare myself for college, I read the newspapers and picked out the names of some schools I thought I might want to attend: Fisk, Talladega, Tennessee State, Arkansas State, Dillard University and Morehouse. They were mostly black schools in the South and the Midwest. With black college students from Memphis, a lot of them went to Tennessee State or Fisk, or if they left the state, they went to colleges in Alabama or Arkansas.

Because of my good marks and activity in high school at Booker T. Washington, a number of four-year institutions accepted me to go to college, but the problem was they didn't give any financial aid. You had to pay tuition to go to college. You needed money for books, rent for a place to stay, and food money to eat. Those were things that only the middle or upper class could afford. I still had younger sisters and family at home that my mother and father had to provide for. They couldn't spend much money on me. I needed to look for a job even to go to college.

My first college choice was Morehouse. Even though Morehouse did not offer financial aid, they had a work/study program. As part of the work/study program, in the summer months, I was told that students would go to Connecticut to pick tobacco. Morehouse sent me a letter advising me that I should have a raincoat, a rain hat, an umbrella and other paraphernalia to work in the tobacco fields. However, I had been out in the hot sun, picking cotton and chopping cotton, and I was tired of that type of fieldwork. Therefore, I sent them a letter informing that I would not be attending.

In retrospect, I should have agreed to the summer work/study program and picking tobacco to attend and graduate from Morehouse College. I always wonder how my life would have changed had I made that decision.

LeMoyne-Owen College in Memphis offered me a partial academic scholarship for being a good student in high school. That was the only reason I went there. They made it possible for me to go. The National Council of Negro Women also gave me a scholarship to make up the difference and purchase my books. And I continued to wait tables and do other odd jobs throughout my years in college at LeMoyne to help pay for my education.

LeMoyne-Owen was a small, black commuter college, where we would commute to school, and most of the students there were older than me. The men were older because they had been to the Korean War and other places. There were less than a thousand students. A lot of them were veterans from the military. They had wives and families and were mostly in their mid-twenties. I was one of the few students there who had attended college right out of high school and I was there at my right age. Most of the students were studying to be teachers. And back in 1954-1958, a lot of the teachers and college students were still women. Young men were more concerned about going off to work and making a living.

James Hawes, my friend and classmate, used to pick me up to walk the two to three miles to school in rain, sleet or snow. James Hawes and I couldn't afford to ride the bus to LeMoyne-Owen, so we were busy walking and talking. James and I talked about school work, the ladies, dating, life aspirations and everything else. And with all of this walking to school, I was teaching myself about the hard work it took to meet your goals. It was never easy for me, but I knew all about the work. You did it and you didn't complain. I was still happy to be enrolled in college at all.

At first, I didn't know if I wanted to be a teacher, a social worker, preacher, pastor, undertaker, lawyer, a doctor, a dentist or what. These were the only professions for black people. There were a limited amount of vocations for black students. I also couldn't envision what I wanted to do. I definitely didn't want to be a laborer or anything like that. I was too poor to think of being a doctor, dentist, or a lawyer. So I decided I wanted to be a teacher and do research work as a scientist who could study space and orbits. Research and science allowed you to explore and see more of the world. I was interested in that.

Outside of William J. Hawkins, I had another older mentor at LeMoyne-Owen College named Kenneth O. Cole. Kenneth Cole was one of the first people who said I should become a science major. He was studying biology and taking a lot of similar courses that I would have to study. So I took up science in college and did very well in it. Once you know the basic principles and formulas, the science fields take a whole lot of memory and a lot of figuring things out with logic. I excelled at that. I also played basketball and ran track at LeMoyne.

By my second year, I formed my own friendships at school, with Kenneth O. Cole, Logan Westbrook and Allen Hammond. We were "The Big Four," including me, and we helped each other throughout college. During our down time, we shot pool in a local pool hall, where the loser paid for the next game. We pitched pennies up against the school walls, and we all played hoops, shooting the basketball. Those were the kind of things we did to have fun and still I maintained my good grades.

I became a lot more popular in college from being involved in a lot of different clubs, organizations and school activities. I also pledged Alpha Phi Alpha at LeMoyne-Owen to join William J. Hawkins, George Cox and several others. William Hawkins attended my church and he convinced me to pledge Alpha. Before that I knew nothing about fraternities. Kenneth Cole and I and eight other students were on the line together. As a sworn member of the fraternity, some of the secrets I can never reveal, but we all made it over line together.

As part of the pledging process, students who were on the line together were taken out to unfamiliar areas, particularly in the woods, and we were blindfolded and left alone to find our way back to the city. Well, first, we had to find our way out of the woods. We weren't supposed to lift the blindfolds, but we had to know where we were going, and my Boy Scout years helped me out in following the North Star. Then we had to find a pay phone to call someone. We had taken dimes with us to make phone calls and taped the dimes to our genitals so that the older brothers couldn't find them on us. But don't tell anyone I said that.

The Alphas had a saying; "All great men are Alphas and all Alphas are great men." I felt the saying described my work and career to a tee. We would find our ways to be great. I have been an active member of the Alpha Phi Alpha Fraternity for the past fifty-something years.

Outside of recreation and pledging, we were all very active in college activities with youth councils, the NAACP, social clubs and the fraternity. My friends and I really spread ourselves around and took several courses together. We were all good students, participating in our classroom discussions by raising our hands and taking over the classroom, especially in our philosophy class. We challenged each other so much and made such a ruckus in the classroom by going back and forth in our debates that we were nearly kicked out of the class one time for causing too many distractions. College had become that interesting for us.

We all did well in school and all of us wanted to be experts in something. Allen Hammond played on the basketball team with me, and we all used to spend time helping him out with his speaking. He hadn't recited any poetry to learn how to speak in front of crowds like I had. He still had a lot of work to do in that department, so we would correct him every time he spoke. He had problems speaking correctly in general conversations. He had problems with splitting verbs, dangling modifiers and incomplete sentences. But he later turned out to be a good student and an excellent conversationalist.

Kenneth O. Cole was the expert in women. He would often tell us what to do and what not to do with certain girls, and he had a lot of confidence about it. He used to say that I was aiming too high with the kind of girls that I would go after. I often liked the fine women, who had something going on. I guess Kenneth wanted me to lower my standards, but I never did that. And Kenneth ended up becoming a great teacher and musician. He played the piano very well and was a member of a popular local band.

Logan Westbrook stayed connected with the restaurant jobs. He got us all positions at a restaurant called Tony's and at other restaurants when waiter jobs opened up. He was always getting in with the restaurant managers. So Logan kept money in our pockets. He moved to California and became a high-ranking executive at a record company, and later became a minister of an AME Zion church.

I was the one who was always reading something in the newspapers or from a book to stay sharp on current affairs, politics and the community. I was political and active in school and in the community, asking questions and fighting for what was right even before college, so it was nothing unusual or unexpected for me to be involved at LeMoyne-Owen. I even became the youth council president of our NAACP chapter in college. I was still younger than a lot of the other students at school, but my leadership positions never bothered anyone. I was prepared for it. And I would never call myself a nerd. I was more tough-minded about being knowledgeable.

My sophomore year, I took a few of the science courses that were needed for my major—biology, chemistry—and I took political science as an elective. With more courses than my friends and most of the other students, I had a lot on my plate. I even began to take advanced courses in Algebra II, advanced chemistry and calculus. I hadn't been introduced to a lot of these types of courses in high school, but I was always up for the challenge. And with all of that, I remained active in student government as an officer, helping to organize and stay involved with campus programs and events.

The activity load in college was nothing special to me. I had always participated in a lot of things. I liked being active as a student and as a person. I think I was born and raised as a multitasker before I ever knew what the word meant. I was always busy and I liked it that way. I didn't know how not to be busy. I would go from one activity to the next to stay involved with something to do, and my age never seemed to be a problem.

I was well respected by the older students, who enrolled at LeMoyne-Owen a year or two before me, including Carl Johnson, who later became a long-serving member of the Memphis School Board. We were all very fond of each other. It was like a college brotherhood. We all began to come up with nicknames and middle initials for ourselves. I studied up on Dmitri Shepilov, the Russian leader of propaganda, who was also a scientist with a great memory, and I began calling myself Marion "Shepilov" Barry. People caught on to that and kept using it, but it was only a fad at the time, and something we all were doing. I had picked out "Shepilov" as a middle name because it was the only one that I knew and liked. And the fad ended up lasting a lot longer than I thought it would.

I was also good friends with Willie Herenton, who later became the superintendent of the Memphis Public Schools, and rose to become the first black mayor of Memphis. He went to LeMoyne-Owen College and played on the basketball team like Allen Hammond, but Willie Herenton was four years younger than us.

Once I began to make a name for myself around campus, some of the younger students behind us began to look up to me. They all knew that I was one of the few young students who was going into the science fields. In Chemistry, I had memorized over 200 chemical equations, and made over 90 percent on every test. Around that time, I started writing with the school newspaper called *The Magician* in the spring semester of 1955. That's when about eight of us pledged Alpha Phi Alpha, including Kenneth Cole and Johnny Watson, who later became the president of LeMoyne-Owen College. We were all becoming successful. But it wasn't all smooth sailing for me.

In my freshman year of college, my draft classification from the U.S. Draft Board was a 1-A. A 1-A meant the Draft Board could draft you at any time. But since I had enrolled in college, with a major in science, I appealed my 1-A classification and asked the Draft Board to reclassify me as a 2-S. A 2-S meant you were a student who was exempt from immediate drafting. However, the U.S. Draft Board turned my request down.

At the time, a number of white students from Memphis, who were newspaper carriers with me in my high school days, and were also in college, were allowed to be classified as 2-S. So I appealed my earlier request for 2-S status and went down to the Draft Board. Three old white men sat on the board and were in power to accept or reject my appeal.

During this Draft Board session with these three old white men, the chairman of the Draft Board continued to refer to me as a boy, which was still an insult for a white man to address black men. So I immediately got up and walked out the room. I was not going to stand for the disrespect. And while studying at LeMoyne-Owen College, I was drafted five or six different times. Each time I appealed to the state's selective service directors, and each time my appeals were upheld, so I never had to leave school to serve. If I had been drafted, I would have registered as a conscientious objector, which would have allowed me to fight in the war.

The last time I was drafted was right before my graduation from LeMoyne-Owen. I had been accepted as a graduate student at Fisk University in Nashville for chemistry. I later found out that the induction for the U.S. Draft in Nashville would take place in October. Since I would become a student in Nashville that September, I personally went to see the selective service director. The director then cancelled my last draft notice. And that was the end of my continuous fight with the U.S. Draft Board.

I was a proud college student and looked forward to being the first one in my immediate family to get a higher education and to graduate with a degree. My older sister, Lillie, had only gotten a high-school diploma in Chicago. Even a lot of my college friends didn't graduate. They all went, but they didn't all finish the job. So graduating was big to me. And to graduate as a chemistry major was even bigger, because we didn't have a lot of science discipline majors in the black community. A lot of students didn't find chemistry and science all that interesting.

Throughout my years of school, work and activities at LeMoyne-Owen, I still managed to have a girlfriend. Sure I did. There were eight or nine female students to one male at school. The women outnumbered the men significantly, and I made a point to go after the girls who had a lot to offer in terms of their intelligence, their beauty, or their activism. I wanted to be involved with people who had high goals for themselves like I had. I wanted women who were go-getters and who presented a challenge to me. My friends felt that some of the women I went after or was interested in were out of my range, but I didn't think so. You have to have goals for what you want in life and that includes the people you get involved with.

But my main focus was to get my education. Keeping up with my regular exams and all of the other college activities I was involved in didn't leave a lot of time for women whom I did date. So you basically had to be involved in what I was involved in to date me. I didn't have a lot time otherwise. Dating and figuring each other out was all a regular part of growing up and maturing into men and women.

Throughout my early life, I was already developing into the busy man that I was going to be as an adult, so dealing with me meant that you would have to be just as busy. I didn't like any lazy women, nor did I have time for women waiting around for me all day. At a commuter college like LeMoyne-Owen, a lot of the older students were already married anyway, so the pickings for single guys were slim, and the women all realized it.

None of my biological sisters, Gloria and Elizabeth, went to college, but they were proud of me for going. Lillie grew up in Chicago and graduated from high school there, Elizabeth went to high school behind me in Memphis, and my three younger sisters—the Jones girls—went to school in Memphis too, and Shirley passed while attempting to deliver her second child. Going to college wasn't something that was really pushed in our community at the time, especially in the segregated South. If you didn't make it your own mission to go, like I had, you pretty much went to work after high school and started a family.

But I almost got expelled before I could graduate from college. In my leadership role as the head of the NAACP Youth Council at LeMoyne-Owen, my friends were constantly telling me not to stir things up, but I didn't know how not to. So I wrote an editorial article during my senior year for the student newspaper, *The Magician*, where I addressed a letter to the president of the school about Walter Chandler, a white trustee and a lawyer for the city in the

Memphis bus desegregation case, who I felt needed to apologize for his statements about African Americans.

Walter Chandler had said something to the effect that African Americans should not complain about their treatment as second-class citizens in regards to their rights to ride public transit. He made it seem as if we should be respectful that whites let us ride the buses at all, and that we should be thankful of their guidance, as if we couldn't govern or run anything on our own. So I told the president that Chandler should apologize for his comments about black people or get off of the Board of Trustees at LeMoyne-Owen College.

Around that same time, Dr. Martin Luther King, Jr. was coming to Memphis to speak at a rally at the Masonic Temple in front of 4,000 to 5,000 people. I was asked to speak there by NAACP member Maxine Smith on behalf of the Memphis Youth Council.

My letter addressed to LeMoyne-Owen President Hollis Price was delivered to him that same week and was published in *The Magician* on that Thursday. On that Friday, *The Commercial Appeal*—the main Memphis city newspaper—got a copy of my letter to the school president about the apology demand to the trustee, and they published it on the front page of that Saturday morning's paper: "Barry Demands an Apology or Resignation."

Dr. King was to speak that Monday at a rally in Memphis about the transit bus boycotts, and in the mid-1950s, they were doing demonstrations and suing the bus companies all over the South. My letter and protest was perfect timing. Not that I had planned it that way; that's how it happened.

So I wrote out my speech for the Martin Luther King, Jr. rally and let my friends hear it before I would deliver it that Monday, and I was scared to death. But once I delivered it, Dr. King said he was very impressed with me, and my speech made the Memphis newspaper the next day on Tuesday morning.

After my initial published letter to the LeMoyne-Owen president, Hollis Price, the first black president of the college, he was so angry and embarrassed that he called me into his office. He said, "You've been a disgrace to the college," and this and that, and he threatened to expel me if I didn't apologize for calling out this white trustee for what he had said about black people. He wasn't impressed by my community activism at all; he was only trying to save face as the school's president, even though I was right.

This was about two months or so before my graduation in chemistry. So I and a few of the students who supported me threatened to close down the campus. With the new popularity I had from the newspaper articles and the Dr. King speech, I started telling people around campus that we would organize to shut it all down if they didn't allow me to graduate.

The president called me back into his office that next week and asked me, "Did you say that? You threatened to shut down the campus?"

I told him, "That's right. Sure, I said that."

I was not going to allow him to expel me. So that same day, I started organizing the students on campus, and the school president called me back in and said that I could go on and graduate. He didn't want me raising hell at the school a month before graduation. He thought it was better to get rid of me.

Of course, the bus systems were eventually desegregated, where we could ride anywhere we wanted to and not give up our seats to white passengers.

After I finished school as a chemistry major at LeMoyne-Owen in 1958, I wanted to get a master's degree. I applied to a number of college programs, including several white schools, but it was very difficult for black students to get accepted to those schools in the 1950s. A lot of those schools had to have court orders for you to go there. I even applied at MIT in the Northeast, which had a great chemistry program. But in terms of college, even after Brown v. Board of Education, most Southern colleges and universities were still segregated.

In Tennessee, we couldn't go to a lot of the large white schools in the state. I suspect that 90 percent of the schools in the South and in the Midwest were closed to black students and to people of color in general, particularly when you started trying to get a master's degree in something as important as chemistry. That's how difficult racism was to break, even in terms of getting an education.

Along with a bunch of other schools that I applied to, I filled out an application to Fisk University in Nashville, which had a pretty good reputation. I enrolled in Fisk in the fall of 1958 to get a master's degree in chemistry. Around that same time, Dr. Samuel Massie was the chairman of the Chemistry Department. Dr. Massie later became the first African American professor to teach at the Naval Academy in Annapolis, Maryland.

While at Fisk, earning my master's in chemistry in the fall of 1959, I participated in my first nonviolent demonstration and workshops with James "Jim"
Lawson at the Clarke Memorial United Methodist Church. We would meet
there every Tuesday night. Jim Lawson was one of the first African Americans
admitted to the School of Divinity at Vanderbilt to get his master's. We had
these workshops with him on Tuesday nights, where I first met the future
Georgia Congressman, John Lewis, and Diane Nash, who became a fearless
student spokeswoman and leader, and a bunch of other students, including
Bernard Lafayette and James Bevel, who all got involved in the Civil Rights
Movement. We had students from Fisk, Tennessee State, Meharry Medical
College and a few students from Vanderbilt all learning the principles of
nonviolent direct action. That's where some of us got a chance to study and
debate the different religions and philosophies of the world. We studied the
international struggles of India and South Africa, and Dr. Martin Luther
King, Jr. in Alabama.

We all became a circle of trust with young brothers and sisters in these
workshops and meetings, where we all committed to the upliftment of the
people. The other students all looked up to me at the time. They were aware
that I was a grad student who was taking care of business in chemistry. I was
also a lot more streetwise than they were at the time. I was from Memphis
whereas most of them were from much smaller Southern towns. And they
understood that with everything I had going on with my school studies, I still
found the time to stay involved in the black community. They didn't really
know me yet, so they considered my activism in the black community to be
unique, but I had always been active.

Not only did I become one of the first black Eagle Scouts in the city of
Memphis, I was always in leadership positions. People respected my organizational skills, my drive, my determination to be the best and my overall
confidence. I didn't just speak out; I organized people with plans of execution
for success. So every organization that I was ever in, I became the head of it.

A lot of black students in those days had very religious backgrounds and
our meetings at the church became a haven and an outlet for us. It also became
a training ground for some of the ideas that we would use later on in the
movement. Jim Lawson was a pacifist who had been forming these ideas

through what was going on around the world in the Korean War, with Mahatma Gandhi in India and with Martin Luther King, Jr. in America.

These workshops were where we first began to figure out what we could do to effect change with segregation and discrimination as young college students. We became a core group who formed a circle of trust and a band of young brothers and sisters. With me being from Memphis, a much bigger city than where some of the other students were from, I was a lot more aware of what was going on around us. They gravitated toward me to speak up and make sure everyone knew what was needed. That led to us organizing sit-ins at downtown restaurants and department stores that we were arrested for in Nashville that I'll talk about later.

Around that same time as these nonviolent workshops in the fall of 1959 at Fisk, Bradford Giddings talked to me about going to grad school for chemistry at the University of Kansas, where they could offer me a fellowship grant. Bradford was a year older than me and he was already out there. So I ended up going to the University of Kansas at Lawrence, Kansas under a teaching fellowship grant in the fall of 1960 and the winter of 1961. Studying at Kansas was very hard. They had co-ops where eight or nine students would live together in a building near campus and take turns cooking and taking care of one another. They were all curious about me and how I would do out there. The Kansas chemistry department had been known as one of the best, and the tests were very difficult to pass.

For the most part, I was one of the best students in chemistry, but as I continued to study and pass all of my tests, memorizing all of the formulas and such, the isolated experience of campus life out there was very difficult for me. There were only three or four other black graduate students in the chemistry program and not much for blacks to do. I remember some of the white guys being invited to a bunch of beer parties with girls, but I wasn't interested in that.

I was used to being around hundreds and thousands of black students, where I would be invited to activities, events, social clubs and so on. I always felt a part of something, but not at Kansas. While studying chemistry at the doctorate level, I was in rare air.

I didn't have a car to get around in, so I would ride with a few of the black students out to Kansas City, Missouri, about forty-five minutes away, for a basic social life. They had more black students out in Kansas City, where we could go to parties and find more to do, with parties, restaurants, social clubs and so on. We would head out to Kansas City on a Friday afternoon after class and hang out there all night before driving back to Lawrence in the morning. So I spent most of my time studying and trying to master my techniques. I was studying quantitative and qualitative organic compounds in chemistry, and I was supervising the lab research work of the undergrad students, all of whom were white students. I wanted to be a research scientist even as an undergrad. That was my goal. But in my first year at Kansas, there were a couple of racist incidents that distracted me from learning.

I remember basketball player Wilt Chamberlain had just graduated from Kansas in the spring of 1960 before I arrived there in the fall. He was in a special place as a celebrated athlete with his basketball talent. I doubt he was treated like the rest of the black students. So a lot of the open attitudes that white students and teachers had against black people being there in Kansas made it very challenging for us.

I specifically loved the lab classes we had in chemistry, where twenty-five or so undergrad students would be supervised by a graduate or doctorate student. I once overheard parents of some of the white students say, "I don't want that nigger teaching my sons and daughters."

I had been tutoring some of the white undergrad students in chemistry lab, and the other grad students didn't like me doing that. So I got tired of some white people's attitudes out at Kansas and transferred to Knoxville, Tennessee to finish my chemistry doctorate in the fall of 1961. During my second year there, I married Blanche Evans, but it was annulled.

At the University of Tennessee at Knoxville, I accepted a research grant of $200 per month, while completing my doctorate work. I didn't have to teach or supervise the lab work at Tennessee, but segregation was still all around me. There was still not enough integration in academics. There were at least 3,000 grad school and doctorate students, but again, I was one of the only blacks. The only two blacks in the Tennessee law school were there because of a court order by the federal court. And they were flunked out in the first year by the faculty.

While completing my course work at Knoxville, I applied for law school and started a human rights activism group. I was still involved in civil rights the whole time and remained active during the daytime, while doing my chemistry research work at night. I usually traveled during my summer breaks.

Understanding that the evils of racism and inequality were all around me, I never stopped working for the benefit of the people. And with my goals of higher education, I couldn't escape it anymore. Everywhere I turned, there were roadblocks. So I had no choice but to get involved in fighting for equal treatment for blacks and breaking down the barriers of segregation.

I spent one year at Kansas and three years at Tennessee at Knoxville, working on my doctorate in chemistry, and it was very difficult in the early 1960s. For my dissertation, I wanted to be able to incorporate research work from German scientists, so I studied a course in German. I learned more about English studying a German course than I did in English.

I was required to take a reading course in French and German to be able to read and incorporate research work by French scientists that was a necessary component for my dissertation. For my master's degree from Fisk, I had explained the impact of ultraviolet light on molecular composition.

These were heavyweight subjects that I was studying, but in the fall of 1961 at Knoxville, I began to think as much about applying to law school as I did about my studies in chemistry. I remained active in civil rights, and my desire to fight for my people was growing even stronger.

I completed all of my coursework at Knoxville for a doctorate's degree in chemistry by 1964 and had everything done but my dissertation. I call it an ABD (all but dissertation). I even took a chemistry teaching position at Knoxville College, a small black school, in the fall of 1962. I was teaching qualitative organic chemistry to a class of seniors who hadn't gotten the preparation that they needed in high school. A lot of segregated high schools didn't really focus on chemistry and natural sciences, so by the time they got to college, they were basically starting all over with the basics.

Well, these college seniors thought that I was being extra hard on them, so I had a few of them to come over and sit in on classes that white sophomores were taking at Tennessee. It was the exact same class that Knoxville College seniors were taking. The white students at Tennessee couldn't believe that black students weren't learning certain things in chemistry until they were seniors. I couldn't believe that blacks at Knoxville weren't learning certain things that white students were.

They asked me, "They're just taking that? They haven't had it already?"

I even had to ask the president of Knoxville College and officials to open up the lab room longer and over the weekends. The students there were not getting enough experience in the chemistry lab work that they needed. The lab closed at 6 p.m.

These were just a few of the many injustices of segregation and inequality that convinced me that I needed to fight for the people and civil rights full time. I couldn't ignore it in education. Blacks were behind in education because they were so behind in life. They were not getting a fair chance to compete in anything, and I wanted to do something to change that.

I was angry and disappointed that black students I was teaching hadn't been prepared in sciences at segregated black schools. Black students were doing so poorly I waited until the drop period to give them all D's and F's as a way to stimulate them to do better. They all eventually passed the course. Many of these students went on to have successful careers.

CHAPTER 3
CIVIL RIGHTS MOVEMENT

Like I said, I had no choice but to join the fight for civil rights. The injustice of segregation was all around me. Serving in the NAACP Youth Council had helped me to understand what the fight for civil rights and equal opportunity was all about. So I was pretty fired up about the movement early on and I remained that way. I had been the same determined young student, fighting for black people and fairness in my high school days, while delivering newspapers for the paper routes, while waiting tables at the local restaurants of Memphis, and throughout my years in college. Fighting for what's right was already in my system.

In February 1960, before we heard anything about the sit-ins in Greensboro, North Carolina, by North Carolina A&T students, we had already been discussing our own sit-in movement at the segregated stores and restaurants in downtown Nashville. So once it got started in Greensboro, we were quick to organize a much bigger sit-in of about 300 students from Fisk, Tennessee State, Meharry, and the American Baptist Theological Seminary to demonstrate at the segregated bus stations, restaurants and stores in downtown Nashville that following weekend. Diane Nash and I were a part of those sit-ins as leaders at Fisk. John Lewis, Bernard Lafayette and James Bevel were leaders at the American Baptist Theological Seminary. We even had some of the white students from Fisk involved in the Nashville sit-in to make it more multicultural.

We were arrested for our demonstrations and taken to jail that weekend on a Saturday, and we decided to stay there until that following Monday. They gave us sandwiches and drinks. At the time, I was finishing up my second year of graduate school at Fisk in chemistry.

Our student leadership groups had decided to put Jim Lawson's ideas of nonviolent resistance to the test and teach other groups of students to get involved using these tactics to impact the culture of segregation. The idea of sit-ins caught on, not only in Nashville and Greensboro, but all across the country at restaurants, swimming pools, churches, schools and everywhere else.

But when I called my mother from jail in Nashville to tell her what was going on, she said, "Boy, what are you doing in jail?"

You have to realize that for a lot of black students at that time, it was a major sacrifice for us to get involved in the Civil Rights Movement as many of us represented the hopes and dreams of our families. But that's what made us so determined to stand up. We understood that if we didn't take those opportunities to push the people forward, then who would? We figured it had to be us. We had the most to gain from it. What use was getting an education if you couldn't get a job, or vote, teach where you wanted to teach, or live where you wanted to live?

After all of these sit-ins started in February 1960, Dr. Martin Luther King, Jr. called a meeting of several hundred student leaders to come to Shaw University in Raleigh, North Carolina. We started having meetings on a Friday night, and they lasted until Sunday, talking about our strategies, needs and struggles. There were students from black schools throughout the South. The only state missing was Mississippi.

Having all of these young, brave, intelligent and politically active college students, who were willing to lay down their books and fight for the rights of the common people, was really something to see. Who else would you want to lead the movement but students from the next generation, who would become the new black professionals? We all understood that we wanted to change the world and the workplace that we would graduate and enter into.

At the time of these meetings in Raleigh, the Nashville group that I was a part of was the most organized and experienced. With all of the things that we had already been exposed to in Nashville, we were more prepared for what we wanted to do and how to do it. We had several days and many hours to talk about what we were doing, and we decided that we should have a chairmanship. We wanted to elect a chair from one of our group leaders, and it became only natural when they elected me as the leader. Diane Nash was supposed to be the chair, but for whatever reason, she wasn't present and I was next in line.

The experience and know-how of the Nashville group was what carried me, and I was older than most of the other students with some leadership skills already. Then we got the news out to all of the members who were a part of the initial formation of SNCC. The student committee confirmed me as the first chairman that spring semester in April. They chose me as the speaker of the leadership team to address our concerns to the more established and older civil rights activists and organizations, but we had capable student leaders all over the South, including Bernard Lee, who became a fiery leader at Alabama State. There were different leaders on every campus; we only wanted to organize them all with more of strategy and cohesion.

We decided to name it the Student Nonviolent Coordinating Committee because it fit. First of all, we were all students, and we believed in the tactics and strategy of nonviolence, and we were a coordinating committee to fight the injustices that America continued toward our people nationwide.

We also wanted to lead other young people in the fight against segregation and discrimination in public facilities. Our ideas of youth and urgency led us to a heated discussion of not joining in with the older establishments of the Southern Christian Leadership Conference (SCLC) or the NAACP, because we wanted to be more active than they were. We didn't want to put ourselves in a situation where we would be arguing back and forth with our elders about our strategies and tactics.

So on the way back to Nashville, I was the interim chair of our new college-student organization. Initially, we wanted to be active in the Southern cities and states where our members were represented: Tennessee, Alabama, Mississippi, Georgia, Arkansas, and the Carolinas. We wanted to continue agitating throughout the entire South—desegregating lunch counters and public facilities through direct action and organizing voter registration within the cities that we knew.

My responsibilities included traveling to the cities and towns up North and around the South to establish our name and visibility. We wanted to educate more young people in the community about who we were and what we thought was important. We wanted them to be aware of what we were all fighting for, and we wanted more young people to join us. We also needed to raise more money and support.

Dr. King then invited us again to officially join the SCLC based in Atlanta, but we didn't want to do that. We wanted to stick it out with our own organization. SNCC was organized by a bunch of young people and college students, and we wanted to keep it young. We believed that the young would demand the most change, and that they would be affected by it the most in the future.

We had this second meeting in Atlanta that same year of 1960 in May at one of the offices of Dr. King on Auburn Avenue. Ms. Ella Baker, a longtime Civil Rights activist who was a director with SCLC, helped facilitate us getting our first office in Atlanta. She told us that we could continue to use one of Dr. King's offices on Auburn Avenue. She was very important, particularly in guiding us on what we needed to do to form our own organization. Ella Baker had organizational skills from her work with Dr. King and SCLC, and other Civil Rights organizations. But we knew that we didn't want anything as long-term or as a rigid as the Southern Christian Leadership Conference. We wanted to do something where we could create immediate change for young people and move on.

I acted as an interim chairman while I was still at Fisk University in Nashville that first year of 1960. I graduated with a master's degree in chemistry that year and then went on for my doctorate at Kansas that fall, so I couldn't really fulfill a full-time chair position. We later decided to have annual elections, where Charles McDew from South Carolina State became the organization's second chairman, and John Lewis became the third chairman as I began to work as a field secretary during the summers in 1961, 1962 and 1963. I wanted to join other students and continue to fight for civil rights.

After I left Kansas to finish my doctorate degree at the University of Tennessee at Knoxville, starting in the fall semester of 1961, I even decided to study law. I was still working on my doctorate in chemistry, and the Tennessee law school was right across the street from the chemistry research building. I figured it was an ideal goal, and I felt we needed more lawyers to help us to fight and keep more of our people out of jail, who were being arrested for their involvement in the movement.

Of course, I had already been involved with influential lawyers in Memphis back in high school, and in my early years of speaking out like I did. But when I was growing up, I was too poor to even think about law school or any other professional school. However, I was always around lawyers in the Civil Rights Movement. They advised us on what we could and couldn't do legally, and I respected them and was inspired by them. The most influential black men in Memphis were lawyers: Benjamin Hooks, A.W. Willis and Russell Sugarmon.

Well, the dean of the Tennessee law school, whose name I don't remember, told me, "We don't want you coming over here if you want to raise hell." He added, "You're not really interested in law school for the law; you're interested in it to raise hell."

He knew that I was a fiery student, and he figured that I wouldn't stop my Civil Rights activities on campus simply because I was in law school. I already had a reputation for bucking the system, and they saw my going to law school as another way for me to cause them problems.

The dean asked me to write a paper on why I wanted to become a lawyer. I would love to have that paper right now to read the spirit of what I wrote. It was a wonderful paper. I wrote most of it about how the character and courage of various activities were invaluable to the Civil Rights Movement of the 1950s, and how I felt about it personally. I had been able to provide direction and leadership to the people at a very young age, so I understood what was needed. Even as a young college student, my mind was already designed for leadership.

I followed up my entrance essay by taking the LSATs. I took the test and I did very well on it. I didn't do Harvard scores on it, but I did well enough for Tennessee. So they took my LSAT scores, my essay and some other things into consideration for them to make a decision to accept me to law school.

The dean called me up in Memphis on Christmas Eve with an answer, while I was back home with my family on break.

The dean said, "I got good news for you, Mr. Barry. You've been admitted to the law school."

They needed me to come back to school two or three days early to get integrated into the system before the new quarter would start. So I traveled back to Knoxville to see the dean, and he had three or four people sitting there to meet with me. He knew that I was going to be very observant of what was said or wasn't said. Then he went through the particulars of law school and a bunch of other small talk. The dean was trying to get at something with all of his small talk, so I waited for him to lower the boom on me. I sensed it was coming. The meeting was going too good without having a downside.

Then the dean hit me with it. Even though they had accepted me into law school, they told me, "Unfortunately, we've already spent the money that we have allocated for the quarter, but we would surely be able to offer you some money for the next quarter."

I said, "I can't do that. I need some money to go." I needed the same amount of money for law school as I needed for chemistry.

I planned on doing double duty if I could; chemistry and law school. That's how driven and ambitious I was. And I needed to have the money to do it. I didn't need a lot of money. I figured the $200 a month that I received for chemistry research was enough. I had gotten used to living off of that research money. I was able to live off of that back then. But the chemistry department couldn't continue to give me money for research if I was going to be studying at the law school.

We spent another hour in the dean's office talking about how I could afford to pay for law school while still doing my graduate work in chemistry. And I didn't think I could do all of that without some extra money coming in from the school.

The dean said, "Well, Mr. Barry, if you could stretch it for the next quarter or two, then I'll guarantee you that—by the summer, since you would be here anyway—we could catch up and give you some money for the summer and going forward."

I can't say that he wasn't trying to work with me, but I didn't have the money to do that. So I said, "I can't make it that long." Then I told them, "Forget about it. I can't afford to not have income." I didn't want to go to law school anymore. I wondered what would have happened if I had gone to law school. I probably wouldn't have made it to Washington.

I went back across the street to continue my work in chemistry. But as I look back on it, I'm sure I could have probably found a job somewhere to make up $200 I would have needed to go to law school. I could have stayed on campus housing and continued working to make ends meet. However, that still would have been a lot of work, so I moved on.

Ultimately, I decided that I didn't want to be a lawyer. All of the long hours, the desk work, the court cases and the things that you have to do, I felt would have taken me away from the organizing and fighting that I wanted to be involved in with the movement. So it was a blessing for me not to go to law school. I think I had gotten to a point in my life where I realized what I was meant to do. It was time for me to move on to something that would be challenging and purposeful for me. I needed a bigger drive in my life; a bigger vision and goal than just chemistry. So I changed my mind about law school and continued to do my work with the Civil Rights Movement with SNCC until I decided to work full time in Civil Rights in 1964. I had been a longtime freedom fighter anyway, so it made sense for me to choose to join the movement full time.

I even started my own paper in Tennessee called *The Knoxville Crusader* when I was still a grad student at UT Knoxville. I put the newspaper out with my own money and solicited for advertising. I had volunteers who helped to write the articles and pull it all together with the typing, printing and delivery in the Knoxville community. We didn't have any black papers in Nashville, so I put one out to report the local black news. I remember when President John F. Kennedy was shot in the fall of 1963, I was at the printer when the news broke. *The Crusader* was the only paper to have it on the front page. And of course, we sold out that issue.

Our main two tactics in SNCC from 1961 to 1963 were "direct action" through sit-ins, protests, demonstrations, boycotts, marches and going to jail; and "voter registration," which involved getting more of our people out and registered to vote, while giving them more information about their options in politics. A lot of older and younger people in the black communities were unaware of what was going on or what they could do about it. So we had a lot of work to do to inform everyone.

At that time in our fight for civil rights, many black women were at the forefront of the movement. I want to say that because it was true. Black women really held it together. They understood how important it was to sacrifice their time and effort to push our people forward; Ella Baker, Diane Nash,

Fannie Lou Hamer, Gloria Richardson, and many other black women were right there fighting and organizing with us. Gloria Richardson led an anti-discrimination movement in Maryland in the early 1960s, and Fannie Lou Hamer later became involved in politics and was named the Vice-Chair of the Mississippi Freedom Democratic Party that was formed.

Black women have always been the strongest women of revolution, and I knew that it benefitted all of us for them to be so courageous and giving. They were a strong part of keeping the leadership and the movement going. And when the men became tired, the women were right there to pick us up and keep us going.

I remember nice black women asking us in different towns and cities, "Do you need something to eat; a good home-cooked meal? Come on inside and get something to eat. You need anything to drink; some sweet tea, lemonade, water?"

Sometimes they asked us, "You need somewhere to rest for a minute? You all look tired."

They were offering us whatever they had to give. We stayed at a lot of people's homes on the road, where supportive families fed us and helped us out in any way that they could. They understood what we were doing and it was really emotional for a lot of people. But our early work in Mississippi is why it became one of the most active political states for black people in America. And it's still one of the most politically active states today because of the work we did back then. We really put the state of Mississippi on the map.

Robert "Bob" Moses was the architect of the Summer Project of 1964, which had a thousand students who were mostly white and from the North. He was a highly educated Northerner, who came to Mississippi and worked with us in the SNCC movement, and put in place a lot of the voter registration infrastructure that we used. He started off as a field secretary, but his know-how in working the system and his courage made him far more important to us. So we named him as a project director to help SNCC organize our first voter registrations in the state with other field secretaries working under him. He was a tremendously brave man; Mississippi was rough. Every time you saw an old pickup truck with a bunch of white boys in it, your heart would jump in your throat because you never knew what they were about to do. It was common in Mississippi for white guys to ride around in pickup trucks with shotguns in the windows, looking for anyone who was causing them race problems or trying to stir people away from what they were used to.

I remember I got arrested one time while catching the bus back and forth on my way to New York from McComb, Mississippi because I refused to move to the back of the bus. Usually SNCC people didn't travel alone. However, the two people who were supposed to come that day didn't make it. Between McComb and Jackson, Mississippi, the police locked me in a jail, where there was a low fence that people could climb over and get in from the outside to do whatever they wanted to do to you. At that time, they considered anyone involved in voter registration and the Civil Rights Movement as invading; black or white. So you know they didn't care anything about me. I used to wear this white straw hat back then, sticking out like a fly in the buttermilk. That was really crazy, but that's what I wore. I always had a flair for my own look.

Let me tell you, I was scared to death in that jail, thinking the Klu Klux Klan would come and get me before they would let me out. So when the local official spoke to me the next morning, he said, "Mr. Barry, I'm gonna cut you a deal. If you promise never to come back here again, I'll let you go."

I looked at him and said, "I'm never coming back."

He didn't get an argument out of me. That's what we were dealing with in Mississippi. It was a very risky operation, where you made one false move and your life could be over with. SNCC workers would even drive at night with our tail lights out so they couldn't follow us in their trucks. It was so bad there, that you had counties and towns where 80 percent of the people were black, yet they had not one representative in the county or state government. That's why Bob Moses had chosen it. Black people made up more than 40 percent of the population, but only 3 percent were registered. Mississippi was our new base to show people exactly how bad segregation was. It was hands down the most oppressive state in the country. You had a place of 450,000 possible voters and yet only 60,000 were registered to vote, and anything that went against their closed society was very dangerous.

To help finance the SNCC field officers who would travel from city to town to county on behalf of the Civil Rights Movement, we began to ask for financial support through direct mail and the Friends of SNCC. They were mostly white people and some black movie stars and performers who could afford to help us. As a field secretary, I traveled as far west as Oregon, Washington and California, and as far east as Philadelphia, Washington, D.C., New Jersey and New York to get other delegates who would be attending the Democratic National Convention to unseat the all-white Mississippi Democratic Party delegates. I tried to get support for what we were doing and sometimes to get national Democratic delegates to vote for our causes. We even talked to the Black Elks of Alabama and different black Masonic groups and we had a lot of meetings at the Masonic lodges.

Most of our field secretaries were still college students, who needed strategies and financial help. We had a lot of students from the Alabama campuses and all across the Bible Belt. We also raised a lot of money through free concerts with celebrity involvement at places like Carnegie Hall in New York with Harry Belafonte, Diahann Carroll, the music group, Peter, Paul and Mary, and more. We had fundraising events all around the country during the Civil Rights Movement to raise monies, including support from actors, singers and entertainers like Nina Simone, Lorraine Hansberry, Sidney Poitier and Marlon Brando.

I traveled to the March on Washington from Knoxville in 1963 with SNCC organizing committee member Avon Rollins. We were taking turns driving. We had a great time in Washington, too, visiting the historical buildings and the Lincoln Memorial. And there were still segregated trains riding up North to the event back then, where you would switch your seat from the back of the train to the front once you crossed a certain point in Washington. Washington, D.C. was the cutting point from a front or back seat on the train.

There were a lot of organizations involved in the March on Washington, including A. Philip Randolph, the Urban League, Dorothy Height and the National Council of Negro Women, Martin Luther King, Jr. and the SCLC, the NAACP; and they were all preparing to speak at the Lincoln Memorial. They had headline speakers and minor speakers, and a meeting to discuss it all afterward. But with our younger leadership at SNCC, and John Lewis as then chairman, they didn't want us to speak. Some of the organizers didn't want John Lewis to speak. They knew we were going to be more militant and radical. The older organizations didn't want us to say too much out the way of what they had in mind. The March on Washington was a major event with a lot of different people involved.

Our SNCC Chairman John Lewis got to speak anyway, and he told them that the Civil Rights Bill was too little and too late That was the kind of fired-up speech that they didn't want from us, but they still got it. However, the speeches kept on going, so the speech didn't have the impact that the older organizers thought it would have. It fired up the younger people though, and we were satisfied with that.

That next summer of 1964, Bob Moses convinced us that we should have a major program, where SNCC would invite one thousand young people from the North to come down to Mississippi in the summer and experience, firsthand, what the Civil Rights Movement and destroying the culture of segregation was all about. Most of these young students would be white—99 percent—who were sons and daughters of political leaders, church leaders and others and they began to expose Mississippi. There was a student network that was developed that we called the "Friends of SNCC" to help in our efforts to support the program. We called it the Mississippi Freedom Summer. We all realized that Mississippi was one of the worst off of the Southern states. Our hope was that some of these students and youth in the program would want to get involved in politics themselves and want to do what was right for the benefit of all people and not only white people.

The idea was to have these young people to experience how much needed to be done to gain equality for black people in the South, and we wanted them to experience that segregation in the belly of the beast. The program ended up getting major coverage from *Time* magazine and other national newspapers and publications that really helped to open up the problems that we were having in Mississippi. We were putting our lives on the line for our rights and for a better life, and the people took notice.

That led to the organization of several alternative political parties in Mississippi. The biggest one was the Mississippi Freedom Democratic Party. They even had Congressional mock elections, and they traveled around the state to gain recognition. And because of all our brave efforts at SNCC and other Civil Rights organizations to mobilize the people there, Mississippi now has the largest number of elected black officials in the United States today.

Direct action and voter registration were our main ideas with SNCC before

1964, and we were still primarily in the South. But in the 1964 Atlanta meetings, we decided to continue to expand our reach outside of the South and to include more groups and other organizations of student leaders. These meetings were very successful, and comedian Dick Gregory even participated and joined us in certain Civil Rights activities. We had other meetings in Nashville.

We increased the amount of SNCC members significantly from 1960 to 1964, with offices primarily in Mississippi, Alabama, Georgia and Louisiana. Ella Baker and other activists helped us to expand our reach with their contacts with SCLC, the NAACP and other active groups around the country. I met a lot of active folks in those years, including entertainers.

In 1964, I wasn't the chairman anymore, but I was working with the Civil Rights Movement full time and was willing to offer all of my effort and services however they needed me. I was getting tired of chemistry anyway. I know that I could have been very successful in chemistry, but I didn't feel guilty about leaving graduate school. I had no regrets about joining the fight for civil rights at all. Life is a series of various things that go well and some things that don't. Some expectations turn out, and some don't turn out. Sometimes things that happen are for the best. I feel that way about my work in the movement; it was some of my best work before coming to Washington.

I remember trying to raise voter registration in McComb in 1961, only two weeks before the trial of E. H. Hurst, a white man accused of shooting Herbert Lee, a black man who had tried to register to vote. Hurst was acquitted by an all-white jury in Amite County. When I got to McComb in Pike County, we were organizing sit-ins and demonstrations, but it was very difficult in Mississippi. We could have gotten everybody killed. There were several assassinations carried out against any kind of agitation in Mississippi, including the murder of Medgar Evers in 1963. Medgar Evers' death was the first time I had been that close to feeling the terrorizing effects of political assassination. When he was killed like that, his death hit me hard. I was shocked and angered by it, but I realized it wasn't anything I could do but keep fighting. I couldn't go into Mississippi and kill a bunch of white men. That would have been suicide.

Mississippi had terrorism like you wouldn't believe, right here in the United States. Black folks were scared to death for their lives, and the economy there for black people was very unstable. Sharecropping and basic tactics of intimidation and worker inequality held a chokehold on any kind of voter registration movement in Mississippi. You're talking about a large amount of people who were still tied to big farms that imported people to work, and small farms that were still sharecropping, with land ownership all by white people. So we wanted these thousand young people in the Freedom Summer to help expose racism, raise awareness around the country and to help galvanize the state of Mississippi toward black voter rights and registration.

We had two white men, Andrew Goodman and Michael Schwerner, and one black man, James Chaney, to help us to organize it. We all knew how tough Mississippi was going to be. They still had active members of the Klu Klux Klan in the state, and the police departments, the sheriffs' offices and the local and state officials didn't want to see any changes. So we all knew that getting the people the right to vote there was going to be very difficult. Goodman, Schwerner, and Chaney were killed together execution style in 1964 for their actions. It took many years to bring their killers to justice.

The fear of backlash from segregation was so extreme in Mississippi that when Curtis Hayes, a high school student, decided to walk out of the classroom to protest, the other black students hollered, "What are you doing? You can't leave! You better come back."

The kids really believed that there was no way out, and we had to change that. We had to change the culture there. Even black folks considered something wrong with you for trying to break the cycle. That's how ingrained the practices and beliefs of segregation were in Mississippi. That's why some people still refuse to change in Mississippi today. The feelings and beliefs of segregation and white privilege have been passed down through generations. But Curtis Hayes later became one of the leaders of SNCC in Mississippi.

During the Freedom Summer of 1964, I was traveling to various Northern states. I spent a summer down in Mississippi for six to eight weeks and watched all of these things firsthand, and I was conflicted, while trying to organize the people there in my home state. Those were all the reasons why Mississippi became our focal point.

Protecting ourselves as field secretaries became another big issue in SNCC. By the time Stokely Carmichael got involved as chairman after 1964, the organization got into another big debate when he began to advocate that the field secretaries be able to keep firearms in our Freedom Houses to defend ourselves. The breakdown stemmed from whether we should or shouldn't keep firearms at the Freedom Houses because of all the dangers of traveling across the country. Some of the group thought of it as a security measure, but we were still a nonviolent organization.

Mississippi was in such bad shape, that in 1964 we planned to take a trip to the Democratic National Convention in Atlantic City, New Jersey, where they had an all-white delegation to represent the state. We demanded that African Americans, who made up 40 percent of Mississippi's population, be allowed to register and vote without fear and intimidation. Only 3 percent of black people were registered to vote. We wanted black people to be properly represented in the state, but Hubert Humphrey—the vice president under Lyndon B. Johnson—and the Democrats only offered us two seats. We wanted all of the seats. So we rejected their offer and organized to boycott the all-white Mississippi representation at the DNC in Atlantic City. By that time, we had about 150 field secretaries spread throughout the country, including me, full time.

Even though our demands were rejected by the Democrats, no one thought much about joining the Republican Party. The Democrats made more sense, and black folks had made that decision themselves. Franklin D. Roosevelt was a Democratic president who had done a lot for black people with The New Deal, when more black government officials were elected into office. And over time, the Democrats became a lot more active and forceful for civil rights.

But after our failure to acquire more black seats for the state of Mississippi at the Atlantic City Democratic National Committee, James Forman, who became SNCC's first executive director, asked me to go to New York to help organize our New York office on Fifth Avenue. Along with Hubert Lee, there had been a few more assassinations that had occurred in Mississippi that were a result of the fight for voter registration. We started taking charity from black people who wanted to help us in the fight to make a change. People were sending money through direct mail to our New York office for us to organize and deposit into the bank.

We made an assembly line where one person would open the letters and the next person would take out the cash, checks and money orders. The next person would write down the person's name and address from the letter, then we would send them a prepared thank-you note from our organization.

I worked in the New York office for about three months. But I didn't want to be up in New York. I wanted to go back down South where the action was. So James Forman told me to go to Washington, D.C., where we had a SNCC office on Rhode Island Avenue, Northwest. He told me it was a majority black town that needed help in organizing and lobbying the government. But once I got there, after about a month, I knew I wasn't leaving. I wanted to do much more than lobby the government; the promise in D.C. was too great to pass up. I saw great promise in the city. It was like a calling, and I was ready to answer the call.

CHAPTER 4
WASHINGTON, D.C.

When I first got to Washington to lead the SNCC office in 1965, I saw how much was needed and what all could be done there, so I told James Forman that I wasn't coming back to Atlanta. Washington had the same problems that we had in Atlanta and other cities. The city had over 600,000 people, and 66 percent of them were black. A lot of them were unemployed; children without fathers in the home and young men without working skills. The government agencies and police force continued to practice blatant discrimination and brutality. Even the fire department, in a city of mostly black residents, only had a handful of black men trained and employed as firemen. I believed that the public safety employees should reflect the community.

I saw a lot that I could do in Washington, but I had to keep explaining to the SNCC leaders in Atlanta what I was doing. It didn't make sense for me simply to lobby Congress. The promise was too great. They weren't used to our tactics of resistance and agitation in the District. So I saw the opportunity to do something big and I ran with it.

James Forman wanted me to relocate again down South, but I told him, "I can't just get up and go to Georgia and Mississippi. I need to stay right here."

I remember they gave me a lot of flack for it, but I wasn't leaving. I liked where I was already. That first year in Washington, we had a SNCC office on Seaton Place, right off of 107 Rhode Island Avenue, Northwest. We decided to have a block party as our first activity for young people, and we had a good time with music, hot dogs and dancing. We had a deejay playing records mostly from Motown: the Temptations, the Four Tops, the Supremes, and all of those Berry Gordy songs. I was trying to get familiar with D.C. and give the young people something fun to do to enjoy themselves. The cops came to break it up almost from the beginning.

They said, "It's time to break up the block party."

I said, "You can't break it up. This is our neighborhood and we all agreed to do it."

Nobody was complaining. The neighbors all approved it, and we were all having a good time out there; people of all ages.

So I said, "What's wrong? We're not trying to start a ruckus around here."

At some point, somebody threw a bottle over where we were standing. I think it was the police who threw it. They were trying to give themselves an excuse to break it up.

These cops, who were mostly white men, and about ten of them, said, "If you don't break it up, we're gonna arrest you. Now let's break this party up!"

I couldn't understand it, because everybody was having a good time. It was something good for the community to bond. It was a nice clean Saturday, but these cops were not going to allow us to do it, and they were ready to arrest me. The cops finally broke up the party.

Then that Monday morning, I went to City Hall to report the incident, and I was told we needed a permit to have a block party with at least two weeks' notice.

I said, "Two weeks? That's too long."

I was ready to shake things up in the city already. I didn't see the point in having to wait fourteen days to get a permit if your block had agreed to a party. That was another way of controlling whatever black people decided to do. And with Washington having so many black residents, and a 75 percent white police force, it looked like your typical slave state when I first arrived.

They even printed an article about it by Leon Dash on the front page of *The Washington Post:* "Barry Leads Block Party," or something like that. I can't remember the exact heading. That was the beginning of a long relationship with *The Washington Post* newspaper reporting everything I ever did; negative or positive. I think my first article in *The Washington Post* may have been when I came there to replace the director of the SNCC office and to lobby Congress. It was like they already expected me and was informing me that they knew why I was there. And they were right; I had come to change the status quo.

That next year in January 1966, our SNCC offices organized a bus boycott in Washington. The nation's capital was still dealing with a lot of segregation, like the rest of the South, and the people of D.C. were not in control of their lives or their own government. They couldn't even ride the buses for a fair price or be hired by the city fairly. They had the white police officers and the federal government controlling everything. So when the transit authority sought a five-cent hike in the bus fare that the people didn't like and couldn't afford to lose every day, we reacted to it.

O. Roy Chalk was the owner of DC Transit, which was a privately owned bus company at the time. His company attempted to raise the bus fare by five cents, which we felt would affect more of the black passengers, particularly in the Northeast. We addressed the Board of Trade, which was an all-white group, about the discriminatory bus practices and the recent proposal to increase the bus fare, and we knew we had our work cut out for us. We had a lot of fights that we wanted to pick in D.C. to get the city back on track to where we thought it should be.

So we had Sam Abbott, a white design artist, create a poster of O. Roy Chalk as a "Boss Tweed" character, controlling the citywide buses. "Boss Tweed" was the name used for politician and landowner William Marcy Tweed in New York. We also had Abbott design our Free DC logo of a black man breaking from his chains.

Well, when we couldn't get what we wanted with the bus fares, we started the bus boycott with a very elaborate system of walkie-talkies, starting early in the morning and patrolling the streets with eight- and nine-hour shifts. We even organized street maps of the boycott.

Our bus boycott was so organized and successful, that next morning at ten o'clock, we won our argument to toss out a five-cent fare increase that we didn't want to pay. Five cents may not sound like a lot of money today, but in the 1960s, with black people working in a lot of small-time labor and service jobs, spending an extra nickel to get to work and back every day was big. Imagine getting an extra few thousand nickels every day from poor and defenseless black folks. It's not always about a big lump payment; it's about thousands of little payments adding up, and we weren't going to allow that anymore.

It ended up being a one-day boycott, or a half day. We later found out that it was a government agency that made the decisions about the fares. It wasn't the bus company itself. The bus company would only list the new charges.

People involved in the Civil Rights Movement already knew who I was when I first got to Washington. I was known in Tennessee, Arkansas, Mississippi, Missouri, Louisiana, Alabama, New York, New Jersey, the Carolinas, Chicago, Atlanta, Detroit; all over! I had been traveling all across the country to gather support for SNCC, making new friends, allies and sometimes enemies. But once we became successful with the bus boycott in D.C., a lot more people in Washington knew about me, and *The Washington Post* continued to report everything.

We called together a lot of the local black news media guys and TV anchors, including Jim Vance and Max Robinson. We wanted them to report and cover our concerns with the bus organization and the Free DC Movement to get the word out.

When I first started the Free DC Movement, we were very militant. I was young and more idealistic in those years and had a lot of energy for the politics of protest, where you had to make noise to be heard. We scouted the neighborhoods on Fourteenth Street and Seventh Street in the Northwest, and the H Street business corridor in the Northeast, and made a network of businesses to help in our efforts. We had these orange and black stickers with our cause and the Free DC logo to put in their front windows to support the movement.

There were news reports saying that we were strong-arming white and foreign business owners and blackmailing them, but these businesses had agreed to support our movement because their enterprises were mainly supported by black people. In my opinion, they had no choice but to support the people who kept them in business. If they didn't, they would hear more about it from us.

So I called some of them money lords until their businesses agreed to put a sticker in their window to show their support. We did that for some time. As far as I'm concerned, that's the American way of protest; you talk about what you want and need until you get it. And that forced some of these neighborhood businesses to put the stickers in their windows for our cause.

But the Washington Board of Trade continued to resist our efforts. The board represented big white businesses, and they would not support our fight for Home Rule, which was the goal of our Free DC Movement. So we went as far as to break up a Cherry Blossom event, which was sponsored by the Board of Trade at the all-white Omni Shoreham Hotel on Connecticut Avenue. We were that committed to get support for what we were doing. And they may have been loud and disruptive back then, but I knew that if we could get the people aroused, we could get the power.

This was all at the right time in the mid and late 1960s. There were plenty of poverty organizations popping up, and President Lyndon B. Johnson had signed bills for a lot of inner-city programs for the "War on Poverty."

In 1967, after all of our agitation around the city, President Johnson appointed Walter Washington to be the first mayor-commissioner of Washington, D.C. For more than a hundred years, D.C. had been governed by a federally appointed three-person commission.

The schools were still segregated when I got to Washington in 1965. They had just begun to desegregate in the early 1960s, but the city resisted it. You only had about three public high schools in a city where you had a 66 percent black population, at least.

A lot of black people who lived in Washington in 1965 were being pushed out of the Southwest and over to Ward 8 in the Southeast. They also pushed blacks out of the Shaw area in the Northwest. They were trying to push as many poor black people as they could over the Anacostia River. Before I even arrived in Washington, I was told they had pushed blacks out of the Georgetown and Foggy Bottom areas of Northwest for lower-income housing in the Southeast.

What typically happened was, black residents would not have enough money to renew their leases, due to increasing property rates, and the landlords and banks would not allow them to remain at the property, while offering them public housing across the Anacostia River. As a result, Ward 8 in the Southeast had the highest poverty rate in the city. In addition, their poverty caused the highest health disparities, the lowest test scores, and 75 percent of them were renters who did not own their own homes. These deficiencies increased the stress rates of the people, where joblessness and despair caused the highest crime wave in the city. And with the segregated bus companies, police brutality and unfair hiring practices, Washington was not a progressive town to live in.

Of course, a lot of the original Washingtonians would not want you to say that, particularly in the well-to-do communities, but that's what it was like when I arrived here. In 1964, if you were heading down South from New York and sitting in the front section of the train, you would get up and move to the back section once you reached Washington. But if you were coming from the South and headed North, you would start out in the back section of the train and move to the front once you got to Washington.

It was a time when black people couldn't sit in certain parts of buses, trains, or planes and that included Washington, D.C. as part of the more segregated towns. Washington may not have been as bad as the Deep South, where you couldn't drink at certain water fountains, but it was a town where, before I got here in '65, black people could only recently go to the National Zoo.

On Easter, you had so many black people still working as maids, butlers, servants and in those kinds of positions, and taking care of white people during the week and the weekends, that they gave us Easter Monday off. That's when they allowed black families to go to the National Zoo for an Easter Egg Hunt, because they wouldn't let them on the White House lawn with the white kids on Easter.

That's what I mean when I say that Washington, D.C. was still segregated when I arrived here. In 1965, you still had segregation in the social structure, education, business, housing, certain Washington neighborhoods, the police force, the fire department, sanitation contracts; everything. That's why we needed the Civil Rights Bills and all of the programs that were backed by President Lyndon B. Johnson. He put a lot of new laws and measures in place because they were needed. He didn't do it for the hell of it!

We were just starting to move into desegregation with the Social Services Department, education, the workers unions, the Civil Rights Bill, and anti-discrimination laws. We even had to have new laws for public accommodations and the free libraries. President Johnson had to sign the bills for a lot of desegregation and antidiscrimination laws at that time. He signed the Civil Rights Bill in 1964 and then the Voting Rights Act in 1965.

In 1964, the new laws and measures were only on paper. But you had to make sure the local and state governments enforced it, and that didn't really start to happen until 1965. We had to do a lot more than provide for the social accommodations. We had to figure out how to provide jobs and employment.

Like the South, segregation became a way of life in D.C. So when I got there, I created activities to get people thinking about the lack of fairness and government regulations for a majority black town.

D.C. still had the NAACP, the Urban League and black pastors and things in Washington, but I didn't consider them to have any strong organized efforts to make any big changes. D.C. residents had only been able to vote for the president in 1964. It was not until 1973 that D.C. was able to elect a mayor and city council—largely through the leadership of Walter Fauntroy and Congressman Charles Diggs. In the past, D.C. was governed by three commissioners nominated by the president and confirmed by the Senate. They were conservative white men.

President Johnson nominated seven council members to the District and they were confirmed by the Senate. Prior to that, the House District Committee would have a member from their various states to run the District, and at that time, it was run by John "Johnny" McMillan, the congressman out of South Carolina. A year after that, in 1968, we got the right to vote for our own school board. Because of the heroic and strategic work of Charles Diggs and Walter Fauntroy, who unseated McMillan, D.C. later was able to get Home Rule passed.

I remember Johnny McMillan went back down to South Carolina with a few other people to register folks to vote. He was trying to run for reelection in Congress and keep his position in District policies, but Walter Fauntroy told the people, "Johnny Mac ain't coming back. It's time to hit the road."

By that time, we had enough black folks who were fired up and aware of the political process in Washington, and the need for black people to have some power. It was time for black people to govern themselves and get away from all of these old white men running the District. So we didn't want Johnny McMillan back. And Fauntroy was right. He didn't get reelected to Congress, which knocked him out of his District position.

I presumed that Johnny McMillan would most likely want to remain down in old Dixie anyway, once black people took over the District. Johnny wouldn't want to come back, because he could no longer have his way. It was a new era marching in with black power. So he lost his seat and never came back to Washington, or at least not to run the D.C. government. We made sure of that.

The Free DC movement had gotten so big and strong with momentum that I had broken off from SNCC and gone my own way. This was after Stokely Carmichael had taken over the organization. At that time, a big argument broke out about whether or not field secretaries should be allowed to keep firearms in the Freedom Houses where SNCC members lived. SNCC continued to be a nonviolent organization, so having guns and talking about using force to combat force and fire with fire represented a major shift in the SNCC philosophy. I was conflicted by the argument. You had to be able to protect yourself to a certain degree, but I wouldn't go overboard with it. There was a fine line that you had to draw between self-preservation and complete nonviolence. But by that time, I had already moved on.

I understood that you can't stay in one place with one group of people and one philosophy and expect to make a difference for too long. I figured you always had to move into a new space and expand your abilities to help. So I was ready to take on more responsibilities to affect the lives of more young people in Washington. I don't see anything wrong with being active and participating in the process of human advancement. You have to be flexible enough to work with different people.

Mary Treadwell, whom I later married in 1972, was part of the Free DC Movement and the Pride Inc. organization that we had started. She also graduated from Fisk University in Nashville, but I didn't know her at that time. She was an undergraduate when I was in grad school. I had so much going on in my grad school days that it was impossible for me to know or remember everybody. So Mary and I talked about Fisk and going to school in Nashville, and it was part of the reason I felt so comfortable with her.

Mary started out by volunteering at the SNCC offices helping to organize block parties and galvanize support for the Free DC Movement. At the time, she was married to a naval officer named David Treadwell, but they were separated. She didn't seem to be bothered by it. She was more interested in spending the majority of her time involved with the people. She had been born and raised in Columbus, Ohio, but she had a passion for helping young people and the low-income residents of Washington.

When Mary first came to work at the SNCC office as a volunteer, I actually didn't ask her anything about Fisk. I was happy to have her to work with us, and our alma mater came up later in general conversations. And she became very instrumental, along with Carroll Harvey, in later establishing Pride Inc.

With so much promise that I saw early on in D.C., my first priority was to start a movement here and become a part of the community. I wanted to do things first and foremost to benefit the people of Washington, and Mary shared those same goals. Everything I did was for the people, and my track record will show that. So I naturally married a woman who felt the same way and who had spent a lot of time with me, organizing. That led to us forming Pride Incorporated, or Pride Inc. in 1967, which was funded by the Department of Labor to employ about a thousand young people, who were in school, and 300 adults who were out of school.

The year we organized Pride Inc., there was a shooting in the parking lot of a Giant supermarket off of Benning Road in the Northeast. A young black boy named Clarence "Bug" Booker had been shot and killed by a police officer over a bag of chocolate cookies, and I wanted to meet with his friend, Rufus "Catfish" Mayfield, to get more information about it. The story was that Clarence had stolen the bag of chocolate cookies from the supermarket, and when he ran out in the parking lot to avoid the police, they became entangled in a struggle before the young man ended up being shot in the back. I had read about it in the newspapers and I wanted to meet up with his friend Rufus to talk about it.

I found where Rufus lived in the Southwest and met him. We talked to him about not only what had happened to him and his friend, but about his life in general. It struck me that the young kids and teenagers of Washington really needed something to do and a way of feeling some sort of accomplishment. They also could use some money and early job training. I felt the same way about the youth of D.C. that I did about the young black chemistry students I had taught at Knoxville; they needed more guidance and preparation to compete for their future. So we founded this new organization called Pride Inc.

I wanted to get involved in a program to help teach young people how to learn some constructive working skills to make money and to establish a living for themselves. I wanted to influence young people's lives in that way. With Pride Inc., we went about trying to help the youth in what I hoped would give them not only a job, but some active skills that would inspire them to keep their heads up and to keep striving. That's why we called it Pride. We wanted to instill a sense of accomplishment.

At that time, I was working with the UPO (United Planning Organization), an anti-poverty group. UPO was trying to do exactly what I wanted to do with Pride; connect with young people to find ways of getting them employment and organized work. Of course, I had my own ways about how we should do it, which was a lot more radical than the UPO's ideas.

But when this shooting happened in the Northeast, I immediately connected the incident to our need to find employment for young people. So we gathered about 300 people to show up and protest outside the front of the supermarket, but our typical protest didn't work this time. People still wanted to buy their groceries, and a lot of folks in the community didn't see how the grocery store was at fault over a dispute about a stolen bag of cookies. We could blame the police for the shooting, but we couldn't blame the supermarket for the stolen cookies. That presented a philosophical problem for us.

That's when the U.S. Secretary of Labor W. Willard Wirtz first came to the community and asked us more about our youth programs. I believe it was at a Masonic Temple in Northwest Washington. A few of the other black leaders and I had already begun meeting to discuss summer job ideas and programs.

He asked, "You got some ideas about young people?"

I said, "Of course, I do. I have a lot of ideas."

"How many jobs do you have promised already?"

"I'm not at liberty to give you that kind of information," I said.

The truth was, we didn't have any jobs yet. We didn't have the money to create them.

Willard Wirtz then asked me to get him a proposal.

I couldn't turn this man down. He was the key to the money that we needed to start something big. He was an attorney who worked directly with President Johnson's labor programs for urban America.

So I said, "Sure, we can get you a proposal." That was the beginning of a long relationship with the D.C. government and summer jobs for kids. I started to meet with Willard Wirtz and the labor department often at his office on Constitution Avenue.

I didn't know enough about putting together a business proposal. So I asked a few business people to help us with it, and it took us about a week to pull it together.

Wirtz liked the proposal and awarded Pride a $300,000 grant to employ a thousand youths for the summer. Then we went back and got a second contract for another $2.2 million to run the programs for a year. By 1968, we became so successful that the labor department gave us a grant for $3.8 million to expand the program.

Our ultimate goal was to use the money and the opportunity to create more economic development and to keep the program going on our own. So we invested in running gas stations, bakeries, convenience stores, apartment buildings, and other business entities, where the young blacks could learn to work, and where we could teach them various skills. We wanted to teach them how to communicate with people and to learn a trade. About 90 percent of the 300 out-of-school workers were ex-offenders. So we were taking some real risks. They were some of the toughest guys in town, but I believed in second chances. Most of them turned out to be real good workers, who did not return to a life of crime. They appreciated the opportunity that we gave them to work and to learn different trades.

I became the director of operations, Mary Treadwell became the director of administration, and we made Rufus the cofounder and the first chairman at Pride Inc. Our first office was at a former convent on North Capitol Street, Northeast. Outside of economic development, Pride Inc. also provided youth leadership, and Rufus became our first youth leader.

I understood at the time that we would need to change our tactics, depending on where we were in our movements. It didn't make any sense to raise hell if you had the money to make change happen. So that's what we focused on at Pride—changing idle young people into good workers.

I had Rufus to speak out at rallies and events, because I wanted to teach him and young people about the power of speaking up. The younger kids had gotten used to hearing some of us older folks speak, but I understood again, from our SNCC movement, how important it was for each generation to have its own leaders to voice what was important for them. So we had Rufus "Catfish" Mayfield to do the speaking, and the young people really responded to him.

I was definitely ahead of the times in terms of the social programs that Mary and I were pushing and how to engage the youth. I also understood that society needed to have pressure in order to bring about change. So I used all of the tactics that I had learned in Memphis with the NAACP, and more so later on with SNCC. And I brought my experiences and know-how to the people of Washington.

Once we had our programs moving forward with Pride Inc., I told our organizers, "Meet me at the headquarters at North Capitol."

We got everybody together for a big celebration. Then we planned to utilize a thousand young people together in groups. We had uniforms, jeans, rakes, bags and everything to clean up the city. That would be our first job. We cleaned primarily in the black communities where it was needed, and where the young people lived. We even put down rat poisoning in some of the alleyways and commercial property areas.

The Army gave us about eight jeeps to use, and the city provided us with trash trucks to pick up the trash. We had thirty or forty sub-offices, which were meeting places for the young men who worked in the neighborhoods. We had a team leader for each group with professional experience to teach good work habits and to supervise the work. They would only work about ten hours a week during the school year, and forty hours a week during the summer. We had to make sure we did everything we were supposed to do and do it right.

We required them to open up their first bank accounts at the Industrial Bank of Washington at Eleventh and U streets, Northwest on their first pay day to teach them how to save money. We had a line of boys going out the door and wrapping around the corner for two or three blocks to deposit their first paychecks and open up a savings account. That was a very powerful statement to have all of those young black and Hispanic men lined up like that to put money in the bank. It wasn't much more than five, ten, twenty dollars, but it was something. It was more than a lot of them had saved. Of course, most of them didn't keep the money in there long. They would take it right back out, but at least we got them to open and start their first bank accounts. Most of them wouldn't have done so otherwise.

Then we started to hire 300 or so older guys, who were mostly in their twenties and early thirties, who earned a little bit more money. We had a nice program going on, where we even budgeted for entertainment, hiring groups to come and perform around town and inspire these young men. One time we had the Temptations, and they performed for a big enough crowd that we had to hold it in a building that could hold 300 or so. We had this big performance at our third headquarters at Sixteenth and U streets, Northwest. It was a big building of maybe 15,000 to 20,000 square feet with an upstairs, a downstairs and a basement that we used for meetings, classrooms and storage. Mary and I both had offices on the top floor, along with more classrooms. We had a big auditorium on the first floor with more classrooms along the side. It was a great place to teach, have meetings and big events, and everyone loved working there.

Whenever the city of Washington had any big-time performers in town, we would get them to stop by our headquarters and talk to the young men in our program. They were all impressed with it, and sometimes we would ask them to perform for the group, and they would.

One time, we got comedian Richard Pryor to stop by the headquarters and he cracked a few jokes that left us all in stitches. I later took him out to eat at the Florida Avenue Grill. The Pride Inc. program kept growing, and before we knew it, we were employing thousands of young people a year. Then I took the program and duplicated it years later as the mayor, because I knew that it worked and it did wonders for young people.

Our ultimate goal was economics. That's really what it was all about. Everything revolves around money in a capitalistic system. That became our most successful story; being able to provide jobs and employment training to the young people of Washington, D.C. We even leased and operated three Amoco gas stations around the District; one at Fourteenth and Euclid streets, another on South Capitol Street, and the third on New Hampshire Avenue. We also had three BP gas stations before BP bought Amoco. Our BP stations were on upper Sixteenth Street, at Fifteenth and U streets, and on Addison Road in Prince George's County, Maryland.

At one point, we were ready to start franchising. At first, we got the gasoline upfront and paid for it after pumping, like a consignment. But the gasoline companies stopped that after a while because our expenses were really high and we couldn't pay them on time. They were nervous about that and started the COD payments, which meant we had to pay upfront. Ultimately, we were not able to pump enough gas to cover expenses. Gas was about forty-three cents per gallon.

We dealt with a lot of rough guys and street dudes from Washington while running Pride Inc.; dropouts, some guys who had been in jail. You know, Washington was a tough city. So I had to learn the street language and how to survive out there. I even had to carry a pistol with me. Sure I did. We were around some tough young dudes every day, but we later banned the idea of carrying guns because we didn't want any ill-advised incidents of violence to pop up haphazardly.

We then formed several partnerships with the D.C. government and the labor department, and created a partnership with American University to advance more blacks in education. We discussed plans and ideas with American University to offer more opportunities through grant money and scholarships to enroll more African American students to receive a bachelor's degree. American University was unique in that you could attend without a high school diploma.

One Pride student was Gerald Bruce Lee, who later became the first African American federal judge in Northern Virginia, who came through our partnership program at American University. He was originally from Northern Virginia and was like our Rosa Parks figure. After his undergraduate studies, Gerald went on to American University's law school at the Washington College of Law. But he received his foundation at our Friday youth program, where we helped him to earn his high school diploma. We made sure that all of the kids in our program understood that you couldn't compete without education or skills.

Another was Ella McCall Haygan. She was homeless when she came to work for Pride. She graduated from AU and later received her master's in social work from Catholic University. She attributed her success to my encouragement and support.

That's what our program at American University was all about—giving our inner-city youth an opportunity to compete at the college level, where it counted. I used that same program at American as a model and expanded the partnership to more universities and colleges in the D.C. area when I later became the mayor. Judge Lee and others who came through the program helped us to create the kind of success stories that could inspire the youth to want more and to do better for themselves. Pride saved hundreds of young men and women from a life of crime and despair and gave many ex-offenders a second chance for a different life—and all of them a sense of pride in themselves.

Like most Southern towns, blacks in the District still owned mom-and-pop stores, funeral homes, barbershops, beauty parlors, soul food restaurants and Industrial Bank, but there needed to be more training and higher education jobs available for the youth and college graduates as well. I never lost sight of that, because I started off in education. Whether people know it or not, had I not been into education and higher learning, I probably wouldn't have fought for half of the things that I fought for.

Educating the community was at the center of everything we did, including the formation of Pride Inc. We wanted to boost the self-esteem of our youth and to get them thinking about their future. And let me tell you, in those first couple of years of Pride Inc., we had some of the roughest D.C. youth in our programs that you could ever imagine. A lot of them were the products of female-driven households without a lot of structure at home, but we set out to help them when no one else would do it. We dealt with a lot of people who other folks wouldn't want to deal with, but these young guys all learned to respect what I stood for and what I was willing to do for them. We had gotten our hands on some money and we were willing to stick our necks out to employ and train them with it.

I have learned over my years in Washington that there's only three ways that you can get some money: you can inherit it, you can make it, or you can take it. That's why Pride Inc. was so important for us to do, because the successes could change people's lives. Somebody had to show these young guys how to earn legal money and keep it. We showed them how to open up a bank account, how to save and budget, and how to develop employment skills. Most of us don't have anything to inherit, so we have to get jobs and start businesses.

This was still during the years when Washington had a 75 percent white police force, with not much in the city for the young black people to do. Black people were the majority population in Washington, yet discrimination was everywhere. The police force was only the tip of the iceberg used to enforce it all. There was discrimination against black cops, firefighters, blacks in the water department, gas and transportation departments, and the federal government had appointed a bunch of whites to run the D.C. government.

But I remained fearless to confront all of the inequalities, disrespect and intimidation that black people had to go through in Washington. From my time spent with SNCC, we had dealt with all kinds of oppressive white people, so I took the police head-on and didn't back down from them, which led to two arrests when I was still at Pride Inc.: one for jaywalking across Thirteenth and U streets, Northwest, and another for ripping up a parking ticket.

I was out late one night after being at the Pride Inc. offices when I walked across U Street to Ben's Chili Bowl to get something to eat. A cop yelled out from the open window of a paddy wagon, "Hey, boy, where are you going? Boy, don't you hear me? Boy, I'm talking to you."

He wouldn't leave me alone until I responded.

I said, "First of all, I'm not a boy. You know my name."

These police officers knew who I was. I had been involved with a special project to sensitize Third District police officers. The program was funded by OEO, part of the poverty program.

That's when the cop got mad and climbed out of this paddy wagon. I guess he was itching to lock me up that night. He said, "Mr. Barry, I should arrest you for jaywalking."

And that's what he did. The officer took me by the arm and led me to the back of the paddy wagon. I wasn't that concerned because I knew I had not been jaywalking. So I didn't even resist him.

It was all a process of harassment. More cops showed up after I was placed in the back of the wagon to take me to the station. When we arrived, they tried to say that I had destroyed government property by kicking in the doors of the paddy wagon. Well, there must have been some damage to it from the last people they'd had in there, because I didn't do it. Their paddy wagon must have already been broken when they locked me in there.

Herbert O. Reid, an outstanding attorney and a Howard University law professor, defended me as my lawyer. After a short trial, the judge dismissed the two charges: jaywalking and destroying government property. By that time, I had a reputation as an activist and organizer around Washington, but no one ever knew me as being violent.

The other time I got arrested, in the same area, I had just parked my car to go into the Pride offices at Sixteenth and U streets, when someone said, "They're writing a ticket on your car."

I ran back to the car and said, "I just parked here; you can't do that."

The police officer said, "You parked your car in an illegal parking area."

Right down the street from where I had parked, they had these white Republican wives' cars that were illegally parked.

"How come those cars can park there?" I asked.

He said, "You don't have a sticker."

"Well, if they're allowed to park on this street wherever they want, then I can park here, too." I ripped the ticket up right there in front of him and threw it in the air.

The police officer jumped on me and arrested me. They weren't used to that kind of defiance in Washington. They gave me a hard time and I gave them a hard time back. We even had a saying about white men and segregation: "If he red, he scared."

That's all I saw were a bunch of white people telling black people what to do, and it was all about who controlled the revenue. In fact, in the past at the District Building downtown on Fourteenth Street, black people were not allowed above the second floor unless they were cleaning up the offices and the bathrooms. Blacks were never on the third, fourth or fifth floors when I first arrived in Washington. But with Pride, even though we were getting our funding money from the government, I was still outside the system. So in 1971, I decided to run for the board of education. Prior to my arrival at the District Building, blacks had to pay their bills on the first floor and weren't allowed above the second floor to do city business.

My plan was to make change inside and outside if I had to. So I continued to serve as director of Pride Inc. while running for the school board. We had a good seven- to eight-year run with Pride, but I saw where I needed to continue to adapt to what was needed in the community, and we needed more power to make bigger change.

During my years at the school board in the early 1970s, we got more change when Congressman Charles Diggs from Michigan—who was second in command and the first black chairman of the House District Committee— helped us to put into play what would eventually become "Home Rule." Walter Fauntroy, the former pastor and community organizer, ended up becoming the first Home Rule delegate to Congress. He couldn't vote, but he could introduce things. When I first arrived in Washington and started the Free DC Movement, you didn't have an organization here that was prepared for a stronger push for civil rights and desegregation.

The SNCC bus boycott and the Free DC Movement we had started, along with Pride Inc. and the new Civil Rights laws, put a lot of what would happen later in D.C. government into motion. The things that I had started in D.C. really got the wheels turning because the federal government was opposed to self-rule.

We had our first election for mayor and for city council in 1974. That's when I ran for an at-large council member seat and won. We had thirteen members on the council; four at-large and eight wards, with the chairman also elected at-large.

Mary and I had saved a lot of young black men from the streets, and given them a sense of themselves and a brighter future with Pride Inc. from about 1967 to 1974, but once I got elected and began to serve as an at-large council member in 1974, it was too much for me to do both. I needed to focus on my job as a council member.

I decided to go into politics to see if I could get more power in the District to make more big changes with big visions. There was a list of things I saw where I wanted to make an immediate impact and change, including an end to job discrimination, more employment for those who needed jobs, more community services, fair and affordable housing, homes and delivery services for the elderly, and of course, more job training for the youth and for adults. Those were only a few things that I wanted to change. But I had a much bigger list to come.

Now, you still had many blacks in Washington who owned their own homes with a little bit of money up on the "Gold Coast" along Sixteenth Street, Northwest, but we didn't have enough black homeownership.

Not when I first got to Washington. You had your educated crowd from

Howard University and all of that, but they didn't have a real impact on the majority of the city or where the poor black people lived. The black middle class didn't really impact Ward 8 in the Southeast or Ward 7 in the far Northeast. Washington had well-to-do blacks who lived all over the city at one time, including Shaw, Capitol Hill, Georgetown, Southwest, and Foggy Bottom. But you had to fight the forces of segregation to stay there.

When whites wanted the properties, they decided to push blacks out, and they were usually able to do it because they owned the buildings. In most instances, the occupiers were renters. So when black folks lost a lot of their old service jobs, and the cost of living increased in those areas, the banks would help young employed whites by providing them with the housing loans that they needed and wouldn't give the same loans to black people. That's how they pushed a lot of blacks across the Anacostia River to Wards 7 and 8.

Anacostia High School was mostly filled with white kids when I first arrived in Washington. Then the whites all left the area. Desegregation of the D.C. public schools was just starting, and black students were beginning to enroll at Anacostia and at Ballou, as they were pushed into housing projects across the Anacostia River. Anacostia was the worst integration-wise of all schools in the District. In 1954, forty-two black students were reassigned to Anacostia, which had an all-white enrollment. Later, the neighborhood demographics changed, as the Southeast area became mostly black. A wave of children were raised in poverty with little job training or hope. Those were the kinds of injustices I saw in the District that made me want to go into politics. I wanted to make a difference in Washington and I was not going to be denied.

B efore I ran for president of the Washington, D.C. school board in 1971, Thornell Paige, Jim Speight and I were involved in economic development programs in Southeast for young people. Thornell was the director of a large social services agency named Friendship House. His organization was focused on building the same kind of economic power for black people that we were interested in at Pride Inc. We both started out with small business projects that we wanted to grow into big visions around the District. I also joined the Black United Front in 1968. So we found we had a lot of common interests.

Thornell had several community service projects going on at that time in the Southeast, and we had our projects with Pride all over the city. We started working together on different projects and ideas for the Free DC Movement to shed the city from what we called "The Overlords," who ran the majority of the business around the District. At the time, about 80 percent of large District services and businesses were owned and operated by white businesspeople.

Well, Thornell and I were both confident guys with a lot of swagger and courage, who had a lot of ideas about how to make change, thought we knew everything about what to do to make change, and we realized the biggest change we needed to start with was the youth. The young people of Washington were the future. So somehow, we started having conversations about taking over the D.C. school board.

Thornell started having meetings with influential people around the District, and the candidate that everyone agreed to support for the new school board president was David Eaton. David Eaton was a well-respected pastor at the All Souls Unitarian Church, who counseled a lot of young people, and we knew that he would be great for the job of getting Washington's schoolchildren back on the right track.

Everyone in this education committee knew that I had a pretty good relationship with David Eaton, so they asked me to talk to him about running for the school board. The school board had eight ward seats and three at-large seats for eleven voting members, and there were six seats open that we wanted to fill with our candidates. We knew that if we could control the board with six voting members to five, we could vote in our own president.

But David Eaton said he wasn't interested in doing it because he had a lot of other responsibilities that would take time.

I attended the second or third meeting, and they were still trying to decide whom to support for the different seats. When David Eaton declined, the question came up: "What about you?" Thornell Paige started asking some of the others in the room what they thought about running for the school board, until he got around to me.

The group said, "Marion, why don't you run? You know what these kids need. And the community already knows you and respects you. They know you all around the District."

I was pretty popular around Washington by then. Thornell knew that I had taught chemistry to college students at Knoxville and had tutored undergrads while working toward my doctorate at Kansas. I would be qualified for the position.

At that time, I wasn't thinking about running for the school board. I had gotten used to being fully engaged running Pride, and I couldn't see myself sitting behind some desk all day. I still wanted to be out around the people.

So I told them, "I can't run for the school board. That's not my style of government. I'm not a bureaucrat."

But once Thornell asked me, everyone in the room became excited. They didn't see why I shouldn't run. They knew that I wouldn't be afraid to shake things up. So I got to thinking about it. Maybe it would not be a bad idea to lead the school board. I was already working with D.C.'s children with Pride Inc. But I also knew that we would need a campaign and campaign money to run.

So I said, "I'll tell you what. I got a vacation coming up in Jamaica, and if

Thornell agrees to run my campaign and the group raises ten thousand dollars by the time I get back, I will give it serious consideration. And by the way… I want to be the president."

The group consisted of Marty Swain, a white board member from Ward 6, Mattie Taylor, a black member from Ward 5, and other educational advocates.

I then took a vacation to Jamaica with Mary Treadwell.

I couldn't see myself taking any other position. If I was going to be on the school board, then I needed to be the president. I was always about leadership. So that's what they did. They raised $10,000 in campaign money for me to run for president of the Washington, D.C. school board, and Thornell Paige became my campaign manager. Ever since then, Thornell started calling himself the architect of my early political career.

We'd get together and Thornell would ask me, "Marion, what if I never asked you to run for the school board?"

I figure I would have gotten involved in politics eventually. Some years after that, I had gotten shot while serving on the city council at the old District Building, and Thornell was one of the first of my professional friends to think about me running for mayor, but we'll talk about that later. Some people felt I shouldn't run for public office at all. But it didn't make any sense for me to keep organizing on the outside if I saw a way to get in and lead the people from the inside. That's just another part of responding and stepping up in the times. If you see something that you can do better, and you have an opportunity to step in and do it, then do it. The promise in Washington was too great not to. I couldn't keep doing the same things that I did when I first got to Washington. I had to adapt to what the people needed.

So we ran six candidates for school board positions, while I ran for president. We used a campaign slogan to "Save the children and stop your bickering…" You always had to have a slogan for people to hold on to, and we all felt the bickering between the school board, the superintendent and the president of the school board was way out of hand and in the way of progress for the schools and children. Anita Allen was the incumbent president of the school board, and she was a part of the old guard with a powerful husband, the Rev. Andrew Allen, who was the pastor at First Baptist Church of Deanwood. But everyone realized that her leadership was known more for board members bickering among one another and with the superintendent than for doing work needed to improve education and the city's school system.

We then hired the public relations firm of David Abrahamson and Marvin Himelfarb to do political polling, and develop a winning PR strategy for my at-large school board race to the Washington media and the people on the school board who mattered in education.

At some point, David Abrahamson asked the question, "What happens if we don't win?"

By this time, I had built up a reputation around Washington as a hard-nosed Civil Rights activist with street smarts, a business sense and a Free D.C. agenda, while wearing a dashiki, an Afro, and sometimes carrying a gun. I carried a gun because I was around a lot of rough areas while involved in Pride Inc., but I never wanted to use it. It was more of a precaution. I wanted to use everything I could to my advantage. We were still in the Black Panther, fight-the-power era.

I had sold my gun by the time I ran for the president of the school board. But these two white men didn't know that. So I answered, "We better win." Then I told them, "Do you think you could outrun a bullet?"

My threat to win or else made the papers somehow, but I knew that David and Marvin were eager to work with me. They loved it! Bravado woke people up. It was all about maintaining a "take-no-prisoner" agenda. You don't raise $10,000 to campaign and lose; you campaign to win. And that's what we did.

We won five of the six open seats for the school board members, and I defeated Anita Allen 58 percent to 34 percent in a popular vote before the elected board members voted me in as president 11-0. I felt very encouraged by the victory. I felt it gave me an opportunity to really make a difference in the lives of the schoolchildren in Washington. But I didn't have time to gloat about the victory. We had a lot of work to do.

Washington, D.C. was at the bottom of national education lists in graduation rates and achievement, and our dropout rate was one of the highest in the country. I thought it was very important to raise the educational morale of the students and make the system more accountable for its progress.

I noticed particularly in Wards 1, 2 and 3, where white students attended public elementary and middle schools, by the time they reached high school, they would enroll in Catholic schools, private schools and boarding schools. White parents could afford it and they didn't trust the public school system to prepare their kids for college or for different trade schools. They even sent their kids to military schools.

A lot of the black students couldn't afford to choose where they went to school, and they didn't have the right connections for other options in education. I felt a great deal of empathy with the school situation to give these students a fair opportunity to learn. First, we needed a bigger budget and a raise for the schoolteachers. You couldn't make improvements without money. So I got the finances in order. And since we had organized the right team to run for school board members, we were all on the same page with what needed to be done. D.C. high schools, at that time in the 1960s, were worse off than the high schools in Mississippi. And you had some teachers who were progressive, but not progressive enough.

Then you had a lot of overcrowding in the classrooms, where there were thirty to thirty-five students to a class. We had Anacostia, Ballou, Spingarn, Roosevelt, Western and Dunbar high schools, but we needed more. We built H.D. Woodson High School in the Northeast, the Duke Ellington School of the Arts in the Northwest, and a number of middle schools and elementary schools all around the District.

The conditions of overcrowding had to be dealt with through a contract with school construction to create new schools and larger buildings. As the great Frederick Douglass said in 1848, "Power concedes nothing without a demand. Tt never has and it never will." So when I stepped in as the school board president in 1972, with Hugh Scott, an ineffective superintendent in place, I basically ran the school system myself and implemented more productive programs.

We had our schoolchildren repeat, "Yes I can! Yes I can! Yes I can! Yes I will!" to encourage them to have more confidence about themselves.

We were an urban area with low-performing students from low-economic backgrounds and families, where the history books called them two-thirds human, and they were basically less prepared to learn. Many of these children from low-income families had little or no support system at home, with uneducated parents who were struggling to survive by working a lot of hours—

if they could—to pay the bills and to make the ends meet every day. I mean, we're talking about families that could barely provide food every night, let alone help their kids with homework.

We had transportation issues for certain schools and households. We had children in second and third grades who still couldn't read. And in the more difficult courses of math and science, we had to deal with the issues of tutoring and more one-on-one time. Think about how difficult that was to do with overcrowded classrooms and no budget for assistant teachers. So a lot of the better schoolteachers were being overworked and underpaid, and they still couldn't get to everyone. It became a high priority for us to demand a bigger budget to create a much more progressive and efficiently run school system. It wasn't brick and water; it was what was going on inside the classroom that mattered—the quality of teachers and curriculum. The board began to look for a candidate who would focus on those areas.

The board, under my leadership, hired Dr. Barbara Sizemore in 1973, who became the first black female superintendent of a major public school system in the country. She was a breath of fresh air from Chicago, who understood what was needed to advance progressive ideas and increase the learning curve of the D.C. public school system. It was my idea to bring together students, parents, teachers and schools to create a new environment of concerned, caring and good people in our school system. That happened on my watch from 1972 to 1975.

But when Barbara Sizemore took the job, she had her own ideas about the curriculum and testing for students that didn't gel with the rest of the board members. She had undergone a six-hour public interview and was outstanding in her presentations. We couldn't get her to release the results of citywide test scores, because she felt they were unfair to black students. She had ideas that certain tests were biased against black schoolchildren who hadn't had a chance to learn certain things, but we still had to prepare them to take the same nationwide tests that everyone had to take. We couldn't ignore these tests simply because we didn't agree with them. That would have been irresponsible.

Barbara had a leadership style that rubbed some parents and students the wrong way. She would often disrupt the public school hearings that we had with the board members and create a lot of turmoil about what she felt was right, while ignoring the things that we still needed her to do. She often refused to give the board certain information. She was a decent person who really cared about the schools and students, but sometimes she had a problem communicating with me and other board members. Ultimately, the board members decided to fire her in 1975. By that time, I had left the board to run for the city council.

During that same term as the president of the school board, when positions were up for new elections, the Senate voted to withhold our annual budget while determining whether or not Congress wanted to continue paying for our partisan elections. I called a public hearing and commented that certain members of the Senate were holding up our budget because they did not believe a predominantly black school board could be fiscally responsible without a predominantly white Congress overseeing how our monies were spent. In government affairs, I learned early on that everything came down to the power over money, even in education. But after testifying on what we wanted to spend the money on, the Senate released it.

Ultimately, I wasn't able to do everything I wanted to as the president of the D.C. school board. We were able to make improvements on the test scores, graduation rates and deal with the overcrowding issues. We pulled the school system's finances and budgets together, and raised the morale of the students, but it was never enough; not for all of the things that were needed. It was an overwhelming task, and I felt that I had done all that I could do. The school system was a real taxing process to deal with. So when I saw an opportunity to run for the first election of District council seats, I left as the president of the school board to become an elected at-large council member. At the time, Walter Washington was still the mayor.

In campaigning for an at-large seat on the D.C. City Council in 1974, it was our very first election under Home Rule. There were eight members from each ward, four at-large members, and a chairman. While running for an at-large seat, I had to campaign all over the city. But since I had already run for the president of the school board, the at-large council seat campaign became easier. Voters around the District already knew me, and I was well liked. In my usual way of campaigning, I took my message to the people.

As an at-large council member, I became chair of the Finance and Revenue Committee and I was on the Budget Committee, chaired by Douglas Moore. While overseeing the budget and finance committees, I put the city's finances in order and became the voice of many people, including city workers and unions.

I felt as at-large council member, I would have more of a stake in affecting the lives of the people in the District and in the black community, not only in the school system, but within the much larger society. I wanted to be able to provide programs within the city budget to affect certain businesses and employment for the parents of the students and all of the people—old and young. I couldn't provide that leading the school board alone; I needed a bigger boat.

When I got elected to the council, I was thirty-eight years old and the youngest member, but I still possessed certain leadership skills that led me to continue searching for ways to effect more change in Washington. I wanted to be able put certain things in the budget for the school system as well, and to create a list to hire better schoolteachers, with more pay, assistant positions and a relevant curriculum with a concept of consciousness. I wanted to have it all in the city budget.

I needed the power to do more than talk and complain about it. I needed to make something happen. Up to that point, the federal government continued to dictate how much money we got and how we spent it in the District, and I wanted to put an end to that. But first I needed to understand how the money worked. Ultimately, I understood that the people as a whole needed employment, and through employment and better business, the community and the school system would be better off. Through increased city revenue and budgets, we would essentially create the money to be more effective with everything.

I figured working in the city council office would give me more opportunities to create change for the most people. So I was immediately interested in the roles of D.C.'s Finance and Revenue. Polly Shackleton, from Ward 3, was also on the Budget and Finance Committee. Being on the budget and finance committee gave Douglas, Polly and me three votes on any finance and budget issues.

We dealt with tax crunches, tax law revision, sales tax issues, the D.C. Gaming Commission, tax abatement for nonprofit organizations, and everything we did only marginally impacted the African-American community, which still was not getting a fair piece of the pie in Washington. I was the only one on the council who had come from the Civil Rights struggle, so I looked at these policies and the city budget differently. I was finally getting close enough to the decisions being made, where I could make the biggest difference for the most people.

I wanted to find ways to help the senior citizens with programs, and create housing programs, higher education programs for the District's youth, and opportunities for the Black-owned businesses. At the same time I did not want to increase taxes, but I wanted to ease traffic congestion and move the District of Columbia forward while understanding more about the economics and financing of the city budget. But while we organized ways to create more effective accounting practices for the city budgets, the federal government still held the authority to make all of the decisions. All of the District's income was put into the U.S. Treasury. There was no accounting system in place for the District; you simply asked for the money and got it without any accountability. Under the leadership of Mayor Walter Washington, with no accounting responsibilities, they had never asked for an audit to find out how much money was really being spent or what was in deficit.

In fact, once we started to organize the city's finances and understand the budget, the federal government was glad to have us do it. They didn't know what the correct process of accounting was either, and they wanted to support us in finding out. The idea of "Home Rule" was to eventually allow the District to become self-sufficient. We had to build a platform to support the development of more retail businesses, restaurants, movie theaters, centers for the arts, galleries, and citywide enterprises that would help Washington to create its own means of revenue.

We were the first elected council and none of us had political experience with legislature of a major city. We had to learn as we went along, but we were all committed to getting whatever we had to get done. It was the District's first detachment from the federal government, where the government affairs of Washington would no longer be directly tied to Congress.

During my years of serving on the council, I bumped heads with the older members on certain issues, particularly with the black middle class. I was a poor boy from the segregated South who wanted to spend budget money on the poor, affordable housing, fair taxes and senior citizen programs, and I was not going to be talked out of it. I figured a lot of the middle class were simply not used to the many changes that the District had to make for the majority of the poor people who lived there. But I didn't care what a lot of the council members thought about me as long as we could get done what we needed to do.

Of the thirteen council members, I was the youngest and the one who spoke up the most, but for the most part, they were receptive to me. Coming from the Civil Rights Movement and the Black Power era, with nationalism and respect for my African ancestry, I was also the most colorful dresser on the council. I had my own flamboyant style and way of expressing myself, so I would mix up colorful suits with bright ties and sometimes wear dashikis to the office. I didn't want to change who I was or what I liked simply because I worked in the government. I remember when I couldn't afford certain clothes as a kid and a college student, and I would walk into department stores and always look at the price first.

My dress style was unique and different from everyone else, and I tended to attract people from the media, the federal government, the District, the Washington community, and all of the organizations where I was invited to speak. I still had a certain charm that I would use when I needed to, and I always wanted people to know whenever I walked into the room.

Congressman William Natcher from Kentucky, used to ask me all the time when I was the president of the school board, "Hey, Mr. President, where do you get those, those, those ah…what do you call them? Dashikis. Where can I get one of those?"

But I never got him one because I doubt if he would have worn it. He was pulling my leg and probably thought of me as proud and colorful.

We only had two whites on the District council that first term; Dave Clarke from Ward 1 and Polly Shackleton from Ward 3. John Wilson from Ward 2 was probably the most experienced black man on the council. I had a lot of respect for him, but I also had a lot of ideas that were different from his. John

Wilson and I had worked in the Civil Rights Movement together and he had a philosophy that was similar to mine. He believed that the role of the government was to try and help those who needed help the most. So we got along great. By and large I got along with most of the members on the council, and I could count on most of them to support my ideas and legislation.

My experiences on the D.C. Council and with the school board allowed me to understand the inner workings of the government in every phase. The tax issues, working on the budgets, the city revenue, and my education in chemistry helped me tremendously in understanding the math and principles involved in city taxes and finances. With my leadership, organizational and analytical skills learned through SNCC, along with dealing with various groups of different people, I was prepared for the steep learning curve of running the District government. Most of the original council members had been activists in some form or another, and we were mostly Democrats with two Republicans. We didn't have too much dissension from the group, but some of the council members wanted to introduce different things.

The majority council members once supported having a Washington Gay Pride Day, but the Reverend Jerry Moore, who held an at-large seat, was the lone council member who was against it. He was a black Republican Baptist minister who strongly opposed it. That was back in the 1970s before the support that gays and lesbians have today was built, so you could imagine what some people thought about Gay Pride Day then.

Another time, Harry Thomas and I from Ward 5, wanted to support a resolution to bring Minister Louis Farrakhan to the District for a Nation of Islam event. It was an uphill battle, but, along with the majority of the council members, I prevailed. Minister Farrakhan was a firebrand for racial controversy, and the other council members thought it would have created far too much of an outrage for the D.C. government to support it.

It was while serving on the D.C. Council when I saw another piece of my big vision, but surely I wasn't able to implement as much on the council as I would be able to in my years as the mayor. Some of the council member seats were part time, and there was only so much that policy members could do without it being a full-time job. At that time, I wasn't thinking about running for the mayor's office; I was trying to be the best council member that I could be. My whole philosophy was to affect the conditions of the community city-wide. I became a strong voice for the black middle class, black-owned businesses, seniors, young people, and at the same time, I was the voice of the voiceless, and I was never afraid to speak up for what I knew was the right thing to do. I was smart enough not to fight a bunch of battles and lose the war, so I learned to pick and choose my fights on things that really mattered, like the tax reforms of 1974.

The District of Columbia had income tax laws, along with sales taxes, property taxes, tobacco taxes, and gasoline taxes. I wanted to reform some of those taxes, and particularly the sales tax because it disproportionately affected poor people.

Through the Finance and Budget Committee, we had to make sure that all District money was controlled and prioritized. We spent a lot of time on the budgets to account for the reckless spending and to get things back in order. We wanted to create a system that worked more efficiently moneywise. And we were able to change a lot of things that the Washington, D.C. government had done in the past under the three-commissioner system of old Washington.

By the second year on the council, we continued to be overwhelmed by a lack of structure on the new budgets that were presented each fiscal year, so we would ask for help from business executives who had some dealings with large corporations or large city budgets. We needed to talk to people who were familiar with the budgetary process, because we had a lot of programs and resources to cover: welfare, social services, property tax revenue. We had to identify what programs we really wanted to fund and what we wanted to cut out, including a bunch of costly project manager salaries that we considered excessive.

We wanted to not only educate ourselves on the government budget issues, but educate the people on the process, as well as set up a system where we could keep people from cheating it. We wanted a better streamlined government, which would allow us to do more and make better decisions with the money that we had and new revenue that we wanted to produce through a strengthened business economy. With Home Rule, we planned to bring the government back to the common people of Washington and do away with the old system of governmental ignorance that treated the black people of Washington like a plantation.

When I was reelected to the council in 1976, I began to figure out what I was doing. I had made great strides on the District council. Things were never perfect, of course, but we knew a lot more and were a lot further along than we were when we first started. We had a staggered council with a two-year short term and a four-year long term, and I had done a two-year term, so I had to campaign again. To decide who served two or four years on the council, in the beginning in 1975, we would pull straws. And nobody complained about it. It was the way we did it.

That was around the same time that I first met Effi Slaughter out at a park event on Fourth Street, Southwest. She was a very attractive woman; tall, intelligent and friendly. She was a field inspector for the health department. I met her on a Saturday and asked if she'd vote for me. She had just moved here from New York, and was not registered to vote. Later in the afternoon, I saw her again, and she was reaching inside of her purse, and I asked her if there was anything inside of there for me. And she asked, "What?"

And I said, "Your phone number." But I didn't have anything to write it down with.

She said, "I'll give it to you, but you're not going to remember it."

She thought her number was a hard one.

I said, "Give it to me anyway."

So I memorized it like I knew I would and called her up that Sunday. Effi was impressed, but I knew I wouldn't have a problem with memorizing her phone number. I had memorized thousands of numbers, including the city budgets. And back then, we didn't have cell phones to save everything for you. You had to do it all the old way, by using your mind.

By then, Mary Treadwell and I were separated. We had made a good team business-wise, but we were never able to separate our work from our personal life. You can't have two people of equal power in a relationship, you simply can't. I felt like I was trying to direct her or she was trying to direct me. I was either working for her or she was working for me. You just get tired of dealing with that every day. I think we wore each other out after a while.

Mary wasn't into politics, either. We had all kinds of success with Pride Inc., but then I left for good to join the city council, while she remained as the director of Pride. She rarely tried to help me with any ideas or come down to the city council offices. She never took the time to understand the city's

political arena. I didn't complain about it or anything. I realized that everyone couldn't adapt to new positions and situations as well as I could.

But Effi was different. She was the daughter of a young black mother and
an Italian father and she grew up in Toledo, Ohio. She had a very caring and
pleasant nature about her, and since she worked for the health department,
she didn't mind mingling at government events. We went out on our first
date about two weeks after I met her. The first thing I noticed was how well
she got along with people. She had a way of making people feel at ease
around her. She made people want to befriend her. We started dating and
became exclusive, which led to us eventually living together.

On March 9, 1977, during my third year and second term as an at-large
council member, I had no idea what was going on at the District Building on
Thirteenth Street, Northwest. It was a nice and sunny day and I was on my
way over to the offices. But if I had known what was about to happen, I would
have never gone in the building. I wasn't trying to be a hero; I happened to
walk in at the wrong time on the wrong day.

I had just come back from a speech at the Northwest Kiwanis Club, and I
remember stopping by the security guard near the elevators.

He said, "Be careful. There's a little bit of trouble up there."

I didn't know what he was talking about. People tell you to be careful all of
the time. So I got on the elevator and rode it up to the fifth floor to the council
chamber offices, and as soon as I stepped off the elevator to walk across the
hall, I heard gunshots ring out from down the hallway. I dove to the right to
get down and immediately felt a burning sensation in my chest, and I knew
that I had been shot.

I made it into the chamber office across the hallway and said, "I need a
doctor."

People were trying to calm me down, but I kept repeating, "I need a doctor."

I didn't know what my condition was, but I knew that I had gotten shot. I
didn't know who had shot me or what was going on. I didn't even see anyone
with a gun.

It turned out that a group of Hanafi Muslims had taken over the District
Building and they were holding eight to thirteen people hostage up on the
fifth floor. They were angry over what they felt was government mistreatment,

but they couldn't have known who I was before stepping off the elevator. They were shooting at anyone they saw and it just happened to be me.

The police and the fire department showed up and somehow made it to the fifth floor to place me on a stretcher. They then took me down to the fourth floor where we could take the elevator safely. The fifth-floor elevator wasn't safe to use.

It didn't take long for them to get to me out of there. It was a blessing. I figured that probably saved my life. But the small bullet wound was burning a hole into my chest and I was praying every second for God to save me.

They rushed me to the hospital, where the surgeon told me that I had been shot by a .22 bullet that stopped just inches away from my heart. The doctor said I was a very lucky man. But before he told me that, I didn't know what was going to happen to me. I didn't know if I would survive it. I had apparently escaped death by inches. A good friend of mine, Dr. Sam Mitchell, rushed me to the operating room, and found that the bullet had only gone in about a half-inch above my heart. The whole time I kept praying.

Then all of the news reports started to come out about me being a hero. I remember one of the reporters saying, "That's a crazy way to get elected mayor."

I wasn't even thinking about becoming the mayor at that moment; I was only thinking about still being alive.

The Hanafi Muslims held hostages for two days before they were talked into surrendering. Some other Muslim leaders helped us in that process. And I assure you, I wasn't trying to be a hero by confronting them. I repeat, had I known what was going on in there, I would have never entered the building.

After being shot, I was scared to death, thinking about assassinations and bullets. I definitely wasn't thinking about becoming a hero. The media created that story. I was scared like any other person would be. I wasn't trying to get any attention, and I wasn't thinking about running for mayor at that time. The shock of the shooting had me thinking more about dealing with my life than politics. God has a way of putting you in situations that you're forced to handle.

The Washington community showed me a lot of love while I healed in the hospital. And I didn't allow any of that hero talk to go to my head, but I did recognize how much the community cared about me.

Thornell Paige showed up and told me that he started thinking about me running for mayor as soon as he saw me in the hospital. Surviving a bullet wound and all of the attention had created sympathetic publicity that money couldn't buy.

Mary and Effi visited me at the hospital, too, but not at the same time. Mary and I were still friends, but we were going through a divorce. She still cared about me; we simply were not a couple anymore. When it was all over, all I could do was thank and praise God for saving me from potential death.

After recuperating, I went back to work as the finance and revenue chair, while continuing to serve the people. I learned early on during my Civil Rights activism that dangerous events can either slow you down or speed you up. But urgent times always seemed to speed me up, no matter how violent or stressful they got. I was up for the task and only became more determined to make a difference. I still had the necessary courage under fire to lead. I think I was blessed that way, and my getting shot didn't change that. However, being shot was still a scary experience for me. It actually led to me dreaming a lot about bullets.

I had been around violence, death and tragedy during the Civil Rights era, but I had never been shot. These dreams I started having with bullets in them felt so real that I would wake up in cold sweats at night. Now I knew what bullets felt like. And before that shooting, I couldn't really remember my dreams, but I could after that. They were very vivid.

You have to realize that a certain amount of danger comes along with the job of confronting change. That's part of the price you pay to lead a revolution. But I never believed that people looked forward to being a martyr. I wanted to fight and live another day, not die fighting. That shooting incident made me a little more aware of my surroundings and the importance of having security with me, but it never stopped me from the work that I was doing. You never let your fear stop you doing what is needed. If it's a worthy cause, you learn to fight through your fears. Nevertheless, you can still be more careful about it. So that's what I planned to do.

Right after the shooting, there was a lot of momentum and media attention for me to run for mayor. The conversations about it started to bubble up. But there wasn't any big moment where I said, "I think I'm gonna run for mayor now." Surely, I must have been thinking about it, and plenty of people were talking about it. Usually, I didn't pay the talk about running for mayor any mind, but the process happened naturally.

At that time, I made about $13,000 a year as a full-time council member, and I couldn't afford a lot of things I would have liked. It became a practical decision for Effi and me to live together. It didn't make any sense to pay two rents. I didn't really believe in talking people into doing things that they didn't want to do, and you had too many people in office without doing the work that needed to be done. I started to think about what kind of people I would hire if I had the power to choose the staff that I wanted.

Without me really knowing or asking, various supporters began to raise campaign money for a run for mayor at the end of that year. I remember the first thing I thought about was I didn't want to lose. If I was going to run, I wanted to win. No one wants to lose. In order to win, you must not fear losing. That's my philosophy. So as soon as I began to consider running for mayor against Walter Washington, and whoever else would run, I mapped out what I would need to do to win.

Washington, D.C. needed different leadership. Not enough people in the District were registered to vote or were even excited about voting. A lot of them still weren't used to it and didn't understand how much change their votes could make by electing the right city officials. We all realized that Mayor Walter Washington was part of the old guard. We needed someone new to break the mold and establish the freedom that we deserved in the District.

Those were some of the thoughts of preparation that went into my decision to run for mayor. You don't just jump into it; you have to be organized with a plan to win. We figured if we could register 20,000 new voters to support us, we could win the election. So we organized a campaign team with Ivanhoe Donaldson as the manager. Ivanhoe was another student organizer from my SNCC years in the early 1960s. We had worked together in SNCC in the South and I knew him to be a very bright organizer. I trusted him.

As I prepared to make my decision to run for mayor in 1978, I had a new decision to make. I had gotten a divorce from Mary Treadwell. I didn't want to campaign to run for mayor while Effi still lived with me unmarried. I didn't think Washington was ready for a mayoral candidate to live with someone. So I had to decide if I wanted to ask Effi to marry me and set a date before the campaign.

Effi was a huge asset to me. She fit right in with the social scene and was used to meeting and greeting a lot of different people. She was perfect for it, but she no longer wanted to be a girlfriend. I began to realize that running the city of Washington would be a huge opportunity to represent black leadership, not only for D.C., but for the rest of the country and for the world. Washington had dignitaries from all over the world living there. I consulted with a few of my political friends and strongest supporters to make my big decision. And I announced my run for mayor of the District that January in 1978.

Once I made it official that I would run for mayor, I remember many of my supporters were excited, but there were many people who were also opposed to my running. They didn't think I was ready yet. But I knew that I was. I was confident and courageous. I loved the people and helping them to achieve their goals. I wanted to give people hope and resources in their communities. I felt that I was the one who could make it all happen. I had a big vision of what could be done as mayor. And I was ready to take on the challenge.

CHAPTER 6
MY FIRST CAMPAIGN
FOR MAYOR

Washington, D.C. had never seen my style of politics. I would walk right up, knock on people's doors and tell them what they needed to do. I said, "You don't need to vote for people who've been doing the same thing in this town for so many years. That's the old leadership. We need something new to happen. So you need to vote for me, Marion Barry."

I kicked off the official campaign in January 1978, and we planned our announcement to have people look at us differently, so that's what we gave them. We had a kick-off rally at Kingman Elementary School at Fourteenth and E streets, Northeast, a few blocks away from where I lived with Effi. The event was well attended and lively. That's where I gave my kickoff speech of what I planned to do as the mayor with my big vision for the city. I talked about jobs, improving education, affordable housing, living downtown, neighborhood development, creating more black businesses, fighting crime and making Washington, D.C. a more livable place for all people and particularly for the poor.

After the rally, Effi, other campaign workers and I walked through the neighborhood in the snow. It was pretty dramatic, but we were dressed in coats and hats and were out in the cold. And we were warm with the spirit of taking our message to the people.

When Effi and I arrived back at home, we discussed the concerns we both had about us not being married and living together.

I said to her, "We either need to get married, or I'll have to get you an apartment, because the people in Washington are not ready for a person running for mayor to be unmarried and live with someone."

We both said we loved each other. She said, "I'll think about it. Give me a couple weeks."

Effi was a really sociable woman and knew how to relate to everyone. We both figured it would be a lot better for our image for her to be my wife rather than my girlfriend. She had been married previously to a musician, but they never had any children. And we both looked forward to starting a family.

Effi and I got married in February by Judge Luke Moore, who later became one of my advisers on legal matters. She was a great woman and was a natural conversationalist. With Effi at my side, and Ivanhoe Donaldson as my campaign manager, we all went right to work.

On the campaign trail, we knocked on doors all over the city. I was just responding to what the people needed, and I could see that the old way of doing things wasn't going to get much done. So if I needed to use a certain flair and style and flamboyance about me to get the people to listen, then that's what I would do. A lot of people were attracted to that. I gave the people confidence that I could get things done. I wasn't the typical old style of leader or politician that they were used to, who would talk about it and not do it. I wanted them to see me being active. I used everything I had learned during the Civil Rights Movement and my years with SNCC, and added some of my own ideas to lead the people of D.C.

I was used to organizing and fighting every day to get a quality seat on a bus, a good meal at a restaurant, the right to use the restrooms, to go to school, and freedom from being drafted into war, so campaigning for mayor was made much easier. It was a hard fight. I was an underdog. I don't think young people understand the great sacrifices we all had to make. They can imagine it in their heads, but they don't feel it in their guts. My job was to make some people feel it in their guts.

When we started our campaign, I had already been reelected for my council seat, I would have something to fall back on if I didn't win. But I didn't plan on losing. My team and I had a lot of new ideas and energy, and we planned to use it all. I was set on giving the people of Washington hope and leadership. I had gone to court earlier and won the decision that you could run for one office while maintaining the current office that was being served.

I attracted the young people, a lot of older people from different areas, the entrepreneurs who wanted more black business opportunities, the women who admired a black man who carried himself with pride and passion for his family, and the working-class people of D.C. who could relate to me. I also connected to some of the white people in certain areas. They were still a part of D.C., and I wanted to lead all of Washington and not only blacks. You can't cater to one demographic when you run for mayor; you have to serve everybody. So I was able to relate to people even when they didn't like me.

Politics is all about perspectives. Every community and person has their own goals and you have to understand their goals and their needs to properly represent them. Personal relationships are also very important in politics and in business. People want to vote for and do business with people who they feel they know and can trust.

I wanted to get the people of D.C. excited about new leadership. If we got them excited, we would get a lot more people out to vote. So our voter drives were always filled with young energy and excitement; we didn't know any better. Campaigning for the office of mayor was much bigger than running for the president of the school board or for an at-large council seat. You had a lot more people to think about. Whenever people saw Effi campaigning with me, she brought out a calm and amendable feeling from some of the women, who may have thought I was too tough or bigheaded. Effi softened my image for a lot of people. I was always popular for my community and political fights, but Effi opened me up to different groups. She was a Delta and had a lot of sorority sisters and friends who were in sororities. She was a popular and successful woman in her own right, who was also active an active mentor in the Jack and Jill organization. Seeing a bright and attractive woman beside me as my other half, made it easier for me to establish myself as more than a man running for office, but as a political couple. The people of Washington liked seeing that. Effi and I made a sexy young couple that kept the people talking.

Effi and I made a great team at these social events. There were certain segments of the population that she could relate to better than me. I would make my rounds in the room and talk to whomever I needed to talk to, but at a lot of these events, I would get there and pick up a drink. It was the start of a long and bad habit for me. Throughout all of my campaigns, policies and public appearances, I had a personal battle going on between the private

Marion Barry and the political Marion Barry. I was going back and forth between being a quiet and soft-spoken man or a firebrand forcefully fighting for the people. I always had those two sides of me. But I would always use these social events as opportunities to reach out to the people and get across what was needed or what we planned to do. I was very thankful and fortunate to have a partner like Effi campaigning with me.

We were out in the streets campaigning every day, knocking on doors, talking to people, handing out pamphlets and brochures and helping register people to vote. We went to the local stage plays and operas, even when we had bad seats. I liked *Porgy and Bess* as one of my favorites. It was a great stage play written by George Gershwin.

We also attended sports events and watched the Redskins games at RFK Stadium. The Redskins were pretty good back then, too. We even went to several Super Bowls.

But before I could become the mayor, I first had to win the Democratic nomination. The race was between three of us: Walter Washington, the first appointed commissioner and elected mayor, who was a grandfather figure; fellow at-large council member Sterling Tucker, the new favorite to take over for the middle class; and me as the young, upbeat and fiery leader of a new guard and era.

Both Walter Washington and Sterling Tucker were favored to win the Democratic nomination over me because of their experience. I was the underdog, but I didn't see the difference in either one of them. They were both part of the old days of bumbling and stumbling. So I started creating slogans for my campaign, calling them, "Tweedle Dee and Tweedle Dum. Pick one! They're just one and the same."

The slogan caught on around the city, and before I knew it, many started saying it, including folks in the media. That didn't mean I had everyone on my side though. You had a lot of the blacks from the middle class who didn't think I could win and didn't want me as their representative. Then you had Washington's popular radio personality, Petey Greene, calling me a "Bama." That was a word people in D.C. used for a country boy and outsider, who they didn't think was cultured or sophisticated enough to fit in.

I didn't like him calling me that, and Petey Greene was real popular on black talk radio back then, so I took offense to it. I figured if he knew so much, and the old Washingtonians were so smart, then I wouldn't have to do what I was doing to lead the city. I was young, bright, fearless and committed to the community, and I believe Petey Greene was a little envious that so many people liked me. But over the years, we got past our difficulties and learned to see eye to eye on some things.

I didn't see how reelecting Walter Washington or electing Sterling Tucker would effect much change in Washington, so I talked about their bumbling and stumbling every chance I got. I was the only candidate who gave the District a fresh perspective and something different from the usual. I viewed the position not only as an opportunity to lead Washington, but an opportunity for a black man to provide an example of leadership nationally. I don't think Walter Washington or Sterling Tucker thought of it that way, but I did. That was the difference between big vision and their little vision. You have some people who don't look beyond what's right there in front of them. But I saw Washington as one of the most important cities in the country.

Then they tried a "Midnight Caper," where Walter Fauntroy and David Easton invited me to a meeting to see if they could talk me out of running for mayor. The belief was that I didn't have a realistic chance of winning. They thought I would only deflect some of the votes away from Sterling Tucker, and they didn't want Walter Washington to win again by default. They made it seem as if my campaign was about free publicity and a ploy to make me more popular on the city council. But I wasn't just trying to make noise. Once I got involved in the campaign for mayor, I wanted to take my case to the people! I had organizers, supporters, donors, business owners and a lot of people in the community who had faith in me and who were counting on me to produce. I couldn't turn my back on those people. So when I found out what the meeting was about, I didn't go.

I decided instead to have a press conference that next day to discuss what was being plotted. I wasn't crazy enough to bail out of my campaign for mayor in a meeting with them, but I was crazy enough to use it for my momentum. The assumption was that Walter Washington could get behind Sterling Tucker or Sterling could back Washington, and that I was only in the way.

Herbert O. Reid, my well-respected friend, attorney, and outstanding

Howard University professor, was incensed. As a key adviser to my campaign, he said, "Well, why doesn't Sterling get out and have Walter Washington back you?"

Herbert O. Reid had a ton experience, and he was a lawyer in the original Brown vs. Board of Education decision in 1954. He taught constitutional law at Howard, and was a law graduate from Harvard. He was a dozen years older than me and more than qualified as a legal consultant. He was a brilliant and loyal man who was very knowledgeable about all that I was attempting to do. Everyone respected his professionalism and views, and Herbert thought that I had a real chance of winning.

We decided to reveal what this "Midnight Caper" was all about in a press conference with the Washington media. Walter Washington and Sterling Tucker were asking me to back out of the race, and I wasn't going to do it, which led the press to ask the question, "Why would you get out? Why not Sterling back out?"

The press didn't really care who won; they were only trying to sell more newspapers and increase their TV ratings with a good story. I was a magnet and a lightning rod for attention, and was always able to draw the news reporters for whatever I needed them for. But the "Midnight Caper" articles helped me to come up with a new slogan, "Take a Stand."

I said, "We need to 'Take a Stand' for new leadership and show that we are not going to take the same old, same old of do-nothing Washington politics."

You had to do something to make changes; you couldn't sit around expecting the best to happen. Nothing would change that way. That's how some of the old, established folks of Washington thought, but I knew better than that. I was from a younger, hipper and active generation who understood what creating new movements was all about.

We created posters and fliers with the new slogan and had them printed up and posted all around the city, while driving campaign cars with "Take a Stand" on the sides of the doors. We also had voter registration buses and vans. And whenever I gave public speeches, I always made sure to mix in pieces of famous poems and spirituals to add charisma and give people things to remember me by. I was always a colorful personality who could sell newspapers and television time. They even hired Tom Sherwood at Channel 4 on NBC Washington to be a political expert, covering my time in office. Tom Sherwood was originally from *The Washington Post* and was hired by NBC 4, being cited as a Barry expert. The women loved the way I spoke, and I made sure to fire the guys up, too.

When no one thought that we could win, we used the naysayers as fuel to work even harder. We campaigned ten to fifteen hours a day and on weekends. We had campaign parties with people enjoying music and dancing. We were the first campaign to patronize black businesses with a reception event at the Harambee Hotel, which used to be Ed Murphy's Supper Club. We even rented a double-decker bus and let kids and supporters ride on it with us, while passing out information fliers as we rode along, listening to popular music.

We got a whole lot of attention with the double-decker bus idea. Part of the philosophy was to make sure the people understood that we were with them and not just trying to get their votes.

All of the neighborhood kids would beg us to ride on the campaign bus. "Can we ride on the bus, too?"

It was a big, old, red and white double-decker bus, like they have in Britain, riding around in Washington. We would ride the kids around the neighborhood and back home.

I worked hard to spend time with people in their neighborhoods, so that the people knew me and what I pledged to do for them. I wanted to show them my personality, my character and big vision to move people forward. We wanted to strategically move the people to the polls, even busing them in if we had to, and if we had the money to do it.

We made our campaign a big, fun celebration and didn't know any better. We were all young and enjoying the process with tons of energy and excitement. None of it was hard work to us. It was our goal and mission for the people of Washington and we wanted everyone to feel included in it. No matter how secure Walter and Sterling felt about their supporters and their experience in Washington, ultimately, I knew that I had a better vision and a better idea of where I wanted to take the city. They hadn't organized from the grassroots of struggle like I had. I simply needed to get enough people to believe in my vision for the city and my ability to accomplish it, and I was destined again with faith, vision and perseverance.

We campaigned in and out of city buildings. We campaigned at art and cultural centers, to parents at recreation centers and playgrounds. We campaigned at restaurants and mom-and-pop shops. We campaigned in places where no one expected us to win or even get one vote. No stone went unturned and I remained gracious to every single citizen.

I did plenty of meet-and-greets and always talked to people about what was going on in their communities and what they considered to be their main issues. I was always in step and tuned in on the people's needs. I never turned away from a good conversation, even when folks had something negative to say. I was always listening and taking in information for later. That's what my detractors continued to get wrong about me. They had no idea how hard my team and I worked to listen all day and all night to the ideas and needs of the people around the District. We learned that my campaign had more energy, a better vision and more connectivity to the people. And my concern was always genuine. We wanted to find new voters and supporters everywhere.

We were also very inclusive in our campaign. Race and class didn't have any factor on whom we campaigned to. We opened up to the gay and lesbian community of Washington. We had the most women working in our campaign. It was always my goal to place women in key management and leadership positions. I knew how hard they worked and loyal they would be to achieving our goals. We reached out to young families and the seniors. We also involved the Asian, Latino and African immigrant communities of Washington, and the college kids.

We had a very diverse group of supporters and outreach all around, including various churches and pastors. And we had them all working with our campaign: gays, lesbians, the business class, the poor, the young, the seniors and immigrants to get me elected. David Eaton came on board to act as my spiritual adviser, while Herbert O. Reid was my legal adviser. Everyone who was involved in my campaign was on point and the best in their professions.

I even took campaign organizers with me to certain gay and lesbian functions around the city. It was the first time a lot of straight people had ever been exposed to those various cultures of the District. But I understood that we all lived there in Washington, and we all made money and paid taxes. So every voice needed to be included, and the community respected me for that. No one else had bothered to reach out to them, let alone attend their events. I wanted them to know that I was genuine. You don't really know a person until you can come where they live, and have a drink and party with them for a few hours. You can't ask to have a person's vote and you're never willing to come to their community events.

I made sure that no one felt left out, even visiting the Jewish synagogues and public housing projects that no one else would go to. Then we invited them all to a pool party, among our many events, and signed folks up, one-by-one, to help volunteer for campaign. These were all ideas the other candidates wouldn't be willing to do. I would outwork them, outthink them and out-campaign them, while they spent their time courting mostly the black middle class and the status quo of white businesses who didn't want any change in Washington. They feared change, but the city needed the big visions to become a first-class operation. So I moved to my own drum.

I had a lot of confidence going into the campaign and I wanted to win, but I didn't know that I would win. Some of the old guard of Washington and the middle class didn't think I was polished enough to be mayor. The old way of doing things was the reason why Washington was not yet a progressive town when I got here. So I needed to shake things to make a change, and I stuck to my convictions.

In our SNCC movement, as college students who traveled around the country, we learned to dress and talk like the locals do to relate, and in the big cities, we tried to dress the part and speak the right language to relate to them. Well, all of the people of Washington were not educated or middle class. In fact, a lot of them weren't. A lot of people in Washington had roots in the South like it was in Chicago. Southern people had moved up to the city. But since I understood the issue on class in our race and how it separated us, I wanted to make sure that the common people understood me, and that I understood them. So I made that common connection early and often. I was a poor but educated son of the South and I wanted them to relate to me.

I understood that Washington was a city filled with the haves and the have-nots, like many other cities in America. And 99 percent of the have-nots in Washington were black people. But because of all of the educated professionals that you had in the black community, you still had separation between the haves and have-nots who were black, more so than you had in some other cities. I recognized that the educated, professional black community of Washington was able to get some of the things done economically that they wanted to do, at least for their own families and neighborhoods, but not as much as I would help them to do with my policies. I imagined that they all would benefit from my big vision ideas and service as the mayor of Washington, and I wanted them all to respect me in terms of what I was prepared to do. I just needed that opportunity to prove it.

I also wanted them to like me. Sure I did. I loved it when the people liked and could relate to me. Who wouldn't? Any politician who says anything differently is lying. You walk around town and in your office every day and you're concerned about what people think and say about you. If you can't get used to that, or you don't think about it enough, it'll be much harder to get things done in office or to be reelected. As a public official, it's your job to care what people think. Otherwise, you shouldn't be in politics.

When *The Washington Post* gave me its strong and unexpected endorsement in August before the election, it really pushed us over the top, particularly with white Washingtonians. We were at a campaign meeting at a house in predominantly white Ward 3 with about twenty-five to thirty organizers when we got the news, and the room exploded with excitement for about seven or eight minutes until we could calm everyone back down. Personally, I was shocked they endorsed me for mayor over Sterling Tucker. *The Washington Post* had a significant influence of the white votes and political areas that I would need to carry to win. The editors agreed with me; I gave the community a new direction and fresh leadership, and I had put in my dues with public service. They realized that I was more than local and my ideas about providing proper leadership were much bigger than theirs.

The Washington Post endorsement agreed that I would provide a better image for the people of Washington, instead of having the same politicians who said nothing and did nothing. They saw that I would give the city a much stronger voice with presence that Sterling Tucker and Walter Washington both lacked. The paper agreed that we deserved younger and bolder leadership in Washington, and not just for the politics, but for the people to be proud to have a new example of an executive running local government affairs in his own way that would benefit more of the people who were not being represented. And their endorsement gave us a lot of new momentum.

Before the *Post* endorsement, we did polls to see how we would do with certain areas in the city, but polling was never the Bible. A guy looks at the different constituency to give you a snapshot of what you're dealing with and how to approach certain people. I understood that I was only liked in some areas, while not in others. We focused on the votes that we figured we were likely to get: the young, the poor, the elderly and many who had been left out, including women, gays and lesbians, liberal whites, the arts and culture community, small businesses and the blue-collar working class. We also campaigned vigorously in middle-class black neighborhoods.

You had some black Washingtonians who figured they didn't need civil rights. They had been educated, professional blacks who had lived and worked in Washington for years. A lot of them viewed my urgency for community activism as unnecessary. That's why we wanted to lean toward some of the voters who had been left out of Washington who did care what I had to say and to offer the city.

We did a three-way debate on television, where Walter Washington sat at the table on one side, I sat on the other side, and Sterling Tucker was the smaller man in the middle. Walter had the old guard of District supporters behind him with church pastors, Civil Rights loyalists, established businesses and the middle and upper class. But he was born in the South in Georgia himself. Sterling represented the younger new guard, who wanted to move forward, but with the same style of stagnant government without any new ideas or energy. He was from Ohio, and he was who the people considered stable and "safe." But I didn't see him offering the people anything new. I was the newcomer and young buck ready to change everything.

The three of us even lived in different parts of the city: me in the Capitol Hill area of the new political Washington; Sterling Tucker up on the black "Gold Coast" of Sixteenth Street, Northwest; and Walter Washington and his wife lived in the old school, middle-class area of LeDroit Park around Howard University.

Ivanhoe was a longtime friend from my days with SNCC, who was able to get along with the rich, white liberals and socialites that we needed to help us with campaign funds and influence in the white communities of Washington. We knocked on doors, went to a lot of different city meetings and events, and did a lot of campaigning together. We had a lot of fun in those days. We were campaigning the way we wanted with spunk and excitement.

When the primary vote was finally held that September, the *Post* endorsement helped us claim 47 percent of Washington's white vote in the Democratic primary, and just enough to beat Sterling Tucker by more than 1,500 votes. Walter Washington came in a close third. It took the voting board another two weeks to get an exact count. Some people like to bring up the fact that I only won my first election by a close margin, but I won. I didn't care about the final number; a win is a win. The rest doesn't matter. It's what I did in office and what I continued to do for the people that counted the most.

The Washington Post endorsement and our inclusion of all races, classes, sexual orientation and the business community helped us to win that first election. But I would never again get that much of the white vote. Even though whites had run a lot of the city departments, we still had more African Americans in the city of Washington, who needed more help from the government. So I had to keep my promises and do what I said I would do for the majority of my constituency.

After winning a close primary, I faced Republican candidate Arthur A. Fletcher in the general election and won the mayor's office in a 71 percent landslide.

Some people thought I would change once I got into office, but I wasn't going to do that. I had been organizing and leading for years, and I always knew what the goals were. You can't say you're going to do something for the people and then get elected and not deliver. I knew that much. That was what made me run for mayor in the first place. I wanted to do a better job than the people who were running, and I knew that I could do a better job than them.

You had others who felt that I should not have run for public office at all. Some of my Civil Rights associates were shocked by it. But it didn't make any sense for me to keep organizing on the outside, if I saw a way to get in and lead the people from the inside. That's another part of responding and stepping up to seize the time. If you see something that you can do better and you have an opportunity to step in and do it, then do it.

The promise in Washington was too great not to step up. I couldn't keep doing the same things I did when I first got to Washington. I had to adapt to what the people needed, so I adapted and ran for mayor. I didn't see the problem in that. A lot of people thought that I wouldn't be able to do it. A poor, black boy from the segregated South couldn't run for government in a big city. I was out to prove them all wrong. I had been studying the city budgets and different things that I would need to do and learn in politics, and I went right in there with a plan to do it. There was nothing to stop me from getting my goals accomplished.

Some people had their ideas about how I could say different things about certain groups of people before I became the mayor, and then negotiate with those same groups while in office. Sometimes, you say things to let people know that you hold them accountable. That doesn't mean that you can't come to new agreements and understandings with them. That's what the Civil Rights Movement was all about, new negotiations to benefit the people; right now. If you never call anyone out on anything, then you're not doing your job.

I understood that there were a lot of different people who made up the city of Washington, and sometimes different people had to be agitated for them to sit up and listen to what you had to say. Some don't listen to you the first time or when you say things too nicely. So you have to shake them up sometimes.

A lot of times, I would say exactly what the people thought. It wasn't as if I was saying things that others didn't agree with; they just didn't want to say it. I was the one who would, and then I would deal with a way to resolve the issue. I figure that's the kind of leader the people would want, instead of a leader who doesn't say what needs to be said and backs down from the issues that we all know need to be dealt with. I wanted to be a problem solver for the city, but you can't solve any problems without first identifying them.

I felt that people could really relate to me as a proud example of what you could do as a black man or woman, coming up from the poverty of Mississippi and getting an education, while always fighting for the improvement, wealth, health, education, freedom and opportunities for our people. I didn't see anything wrong with that. So I never paid much attention to anyone who would try to deny me from running or want to try and stop me.

Some people even criticized me for working with whites in the city, but I never had a problem with working with white leaders and organizing with them, as long as we all knew the goal. I had worked alongside white supporters in my days in SNCC, and while a student in Memphis and in Nashville. You work with whomever you need to work with to get things done. And once I held a position of power, I believed that it was better to make policy from the inside rather than to try to influence it from the outside.

Influence from the outside was the old method. The new method was having control. I didn't think that way initially about getting involved in public policy, but I evolved to understand the importance of it. We can beg and complain for changes while someone else is in power all we want, but we have to want that power and responsibility for ourselves to provide immediate and real change. That's what happens when you sign your name as the mayor, as opposed to someone else signing their name.

I always said that I was in the right place at the right time to lead in Washington. I wasn't going to be blind to incompetence. If you couldn't do the job, you couldn't do the job. We had a lot of people who did know how to work, who needed to be trained. So I surrounded myself with a strong team with know-how. The hardest part of the mayor position was finding the right people to fill the many top positions, where they were not only qualified, but were ready to help change the lives of Washington families. At the same time, you have to be realistic. You may not be able to change every single person's life, but it should definitely be your goal to change the lives of as many as you can, and that's what we set out to do.

Effi had campaigned hard with me. We had attended plenty of fundraisers together and I attributed part of my victory to her.

My mother, Mattie, and stepfather, Dave Cummings, flew in from Memphis, Tennessee a couple days before the election. They stayed with friends of ours who had more room. And my mother was very proud of me.

She told me, "Marion, you're about to become the mayor of the nation's capital."

She was with me at my victory party with tears of joy. All I could remember was all the hard work she had done to raise me. She and Effi were very proud of me. They both knew that I had what it took to get there.

Effi said, "Marion, we did it!" She was as festive and jubilant as me. We celebrated again at the Harambee Hotel on Georgia Avenue, African American-owned by Ed Murphy, and that made it extra sweet.

CHAPTER 7
THE FIRST-TERM MAYOR

was elected to office as the mayor of Washington, D.C. on November 6, 1978, and I was filled with excitement and optimism for the community. The first big call I made as the mayor was to U.S. Supreme Judge Thurgood Marshall. I wanted him to swear me in as the mayor after a big District parade when I was officially to take office on January 2, 1979. I had met and known Thurgood Marshall from the NAACP Legal Defense Fund. I was elated that President Johnson appointed him to the Supreme Court. I felt the circle had come full circle with the NAACP working to get me out of jail during the Civil Rights Movement, and now swearing me in as the second black mayor of Washington. Who would have envisioned a poor black boy from the Delta of Mississippi was now being sworn in by Thurgood Marshall, the first black Supreme Court Justice? This was history in the making.

Thurgood Marshall answered my call and agreed to swear me in. He said, "You got it. You got it!" He sounded as excited about it as I was.

I wanted to have the parade starting at Fourteenth and U streets, Northwest—U Street had been our mecca during segregation, and the parade would end downtown in front of the District Building, where we would address the people from a podium. We were so excited. Effi and I walked fifteen blocks in the parade and didn't realize how cold it was.

I had an immediate sense of loyalty and duty to the people of the District who elected me, and I knew I had to produce. So after a two-week break and a late honeymoon in Jamaica with Effi, I started to think about my transition team and how I could hire the best and the brightest young minds that we could find. That's the kind of people we wanted to attract to the District government. I wanted nothing but the best! So we attracted people who wanted to do the work, many of whom I knew and had worked with in other capacities, including my campaign. My belief was, "If you don't know enough about a situation, then bring in somebody who does." So I wanted great thinkers on my team who were unafraid to come up with bold, new ideas and solutions. We built up a strong professional organization and qualified black people and women.

We basically had to desegregate every agency from the normal policies and people that they were used to in the Washington administration, and let everyone understand what new direction we needed to head in. And we had to move fast and decisively to do it. When I first visited the mayor's office before moving in, many cabinet members had offices there, but I wanted more cabinet members to be close by me. I needed us to be able to work closely as a team, including budget, finance, personnel, city administrator, Corporation Counsel and the Chief of Police.

After restructuring the mayor's office and the entire D.C. government, we were ready to go and hire about 80 to 90 percent of the people that we wanted who were the best and the brightest, which we did. I already knew who they were, their work ethic, their professional capabilities, their loyalty to my goals, and more importantly, they knew me, my work ethic and what my visions were. I didn't want to hire people I didn't know. I wanted to hire a cabinet of people who were all in sync with the work that was needed, and I wanted a cabinet that looked like the people of D.C., with diversity, down to the fire department chief and the chief of D.C. police. Obviously, those who worked on my campaign knew what tremendous amount of momentum we had, so we wanted to get to work fast. Familiarity with each other could only help to speed up the process.

We had a lot of meetings with different candidates in my cabinets, and we were looking for bright, committed people with vision, who didn't have a problem with working hard with good work habits. I wanted people who were serious about the process of making a difference. I didn't want anybody there who simply wanted a job. I personally talked to every cabinet member before we hired them to see how committed they were. I wanted to know 90 percent of their ideas and personal politics, and that didn't mean I had to agree with all of them, but I wanted to know where they stood. They had to have some ideas, energy and a perspective of their own that I could use. They had to be able to bring their own vision and excitement to the office. I didn't want any dull, "yes" people. I wanted bright, young professionals, the best that I could find.

I didn't want anyone in my cabinet who lacked ambition or who was lackadaisical on the job. So we had think-tanks with people who worked hard and were smart, and I continued to gather information to understand everything people wanted and needed in the city. There was no written textbook on how to be the mayor; you had to learn while doing it. I had conversations and made friendships with the other black mayors around the country. Maynard Jackson, a Morehouse College man, became the first black mayor of Atlanta. Coleman Young, a U.S. military man and war veteran, became the first black mayor of Detroit. His family was originally from Alabama. Tom Bradley was the first black mayor of Los Angeles and his family was originally from Texas, like Maynard Jackson's family.

They all schooled me on how to conduct yourself or handle certain situations as the mayor, but for the most part, you have to get in there and do it! Coming out of the battles of the Civil Rights Movement, we all felt a common bond to the struggles of inequality, proper representation and more opportunity for our people. We all bonded as mayors and as black men, and I would visit and talk to them often.

At forty-two, I was not only black, I was also one of the youngest mayors in the country to run a major city and probably one of the most ambitious mayors. I set my own path with what made the most sense to me. I learned how to govern the District in my own way. I considered Washington to be one of the most important cities in America. By then, there were a lot more black mayors around the country. I became the president of the National Conference of Black Mayors from 1984-1988 and was very involved in the National League of Cities and the United States Conference of Mayors. But my priority was the District government.

Some of my new hires in government were not from the Washington, D.C. community, but they had come to the nation's capital with their own passions and ideas about building it into a first-rate city, and we were all excited about that. If you weren't excited, you couldn't work for me. Then we had the true

Washingtonians, who knew the ins and outs of different parts of the city to add their experiences on how to address certain issues with different communities. Like my campaign, my first cabinet was very diversified, with plenty of professional blacks, women, gay and lesbian administrators, many of whom hadn't had the opportunities to lead prior to my coming to office. I wanted to make the cabinet look and feel like the community of Washington, D.C. and not like a government that had been placed there by Congress. So I built a very strong relationship with the National Forum for Black Public Administrators (NFBPA).

I hired Ivanhoe Donaldson as my general assistant, and Elijah Rogers—who was headed for a position in Richmond, Virginia when I hired him—became my city manager. I hired Alphonse Hill from Chicago for the finance department. Herbert O. Reid was hired by the government as my adviser and general counsel. I had Stephen Harlan, an accountant and the president of the Greater Washington Board of Trade, as one my key business advisers, and Joseph H. Riley, the president of National Savings & Trust Co. He advised me on financial matters.

I hired a cabinet of high-energy officials, who were black, experienced and who shared my vision. I also hired Police Chief Burtrell Jefferson and Fire Chief Norman Robinson, who were both professional black men.

We then hired a bunch of young, fireplug professionals as I had hoped to do, and we were all bubbling with new hope, energy and ideas. I spent a lot of time and effort hiring the right people, particularly in management positions. I understood that Washington was a major business, and we wanted to make it the mecca of urban management and revitalization. We were probably the first major city in the country run by a minority management team.

I remember telling Herbert Reid, the older statesman in my cabinet, "If I want to jump off a cliff, try to talk me out of it. But if you can't stop me, then make my landing easy."

Herbert was a real powerhouse of a lawyer with a great sense of humor. He had been teaching law at Howard University for nearly thirty years, and had taught Virginia Governor L. Douglas Wilder, and the first female D.C. mayor, Sharon Pratt Kelly. In addition to the Brown v. Board of Education decision, Reid was involved in the "Chicago Seven" hearings, and helped Adam Clayton Powell to regain his seat in Congress in New York.

I could always count on Herbert to give me the truth and try to make sense out of things. You had to have someone on your side who knew what he was doing and how to navigate the boat with so many young people that I was hiring to major government positions. I also used Herbert to model my new dress code after. He and Jim Palmer—who was so light that he could pass for white—were both well dressed, and I needed to reform some of my bright colors and over-the-top fashion for more business blue suits, dark grays and a new collection of ties, shoes and overcoats. So I would go shopping for the office of the mayor with those two guys in mind.

I wanted to learn how to dress differently and carry myself more as a mayor, because your life changes and the perception of you changes with it. People want to see you differently as the mayor. So I made note of making grand entrances and exits. That's what you do when you want people to pay attention to you. If you don't want people to pay attention to you, then you slide in the back door and make no announcements. That would make it harder for you to get things done and for the people to know that you got them done. Yet, I still wanted to walk and talk with the low-income people, because I was still with them. I was regular people and something more than that at the same time, and I wanted the people to understand it. You can't always explain it, but you understand it. It's just a common connection that we share. God gave me a gift of being at the White House at 11 a.m., and then public housing with poor people at 3 p.m. I had the ability to bridge the gap.

Well, once I stepped into office, the times of black people and women only filling out minor roles in D.C. government were over. I placed plenty of young black professionals and women in positions of opportunity, power and responsibility to show what they could do in nontraditional jobs, and they were able to make some good money doing it.

The opportunities in government and all of the contracting that we began to provide in my first term as mayor of the District began to make a phenomenal impact on the wealth of Washington, D.C. and the surrounding Maryland and Virginia areas for black families for years to come. These opportunities for better jobs and incomes allowed black professionals and families to move into housing and neighborhoods in the District where they weren't allowed or couldn't afford to live in before, including the "Gold Coast" on Sixteenth Street, Northwest.

To this day, I remain proud of how many lives we were able to impact for so many black families of Washington, who were able to build new wealth and move up into the middle class. I just wanted to do the right thing for the community. Nobody had to push me into it. I had black folks hustling and bustling with confidence. Some of them moved out of the District to Maryland and Virginia: Prince George's County, Upper Marlboro, Bowie, Rockville, Bethesda, Gaithersburg, Alexandria, Arlington, Fredericksburg. In fact, Prince George's County is the highest suburban income of professional African Americans in the country. Part of my goal was to build and strengthen the middle class economically, meaning giving opportunities to people with salaries of over $50,000, with two people in the home. That's $100,000 in the house. That's building and strengthening the middle class.

I couldn't really complain about people moving out, but in later terms as the mayor, and with the Metro transit systems that we built in Washington, we went back and forth about a commuter tax and what it would mean to the residents who still lived and worked in Washington versus those who commuted. That argument continues to be a battle today.

I hired Florence Tate as my press secretary, an experienced press veteran who had a hell of a job on her hands, because I attracted a lot of media attention. I was the most colorful mayor the Washington newspapers and television networks could ask for. I always made the news because I was proposing new and innovative programs, but I was never all fluff and no action. I knew how to sell a good story. The guys are paid to cover you anyway, so I learned to use them when I could. The newspapers even hired extra staff and editors to cover me. The television networks followed my every move, too.

F. Alexis H. Roberson was hired as the first female deputy of recreation. She later moved into a director position in my second term, making her the first black female director of the Department of Parks and Recreation. She was one of many women who took over mostly male-dominated positions, mainly because the government would rarely seek them out or consider them as qualified. We had lots of new blood and lots of women. Gladys Mack became one of the first black women to run the budget office. Carolyn Thompson, at twenty-six years old, was hired in the licensing and inspection department. We hired Barbara Washington, who ran our intergovernmental relations office followed by Judge Judy Rogers, who later became a Superior Court judge. I knew how capable women were from my Civil Rights years with SNCC and I had no problems with seeing women in power positions, right down to my former wife, Mary Treadwell, with Pride Inc.

With black professionals and women, we had this saying, "It's not enough to be smart; you have to be bright!" In other words, you had to be energized and optimistic about what we were doing. You had to speak up, speak out and be confident, but not arrogant. I challenged my staff every day to be more than what they were on paper; they had to all be dynamic people who were about going to work for the D.C. community. That's what they were hired to do. Some of my cabinet members joked that while everyone else was sleeping, I was up planning my next moves. And they were right.

I hired Richard Maulsby as one of the first openly gay professionals in my first cabinet, and he remained loyal to my campaigns for years. I didn't care about his sexual preference as long as he could get the job done. I made him a director of motion pictures communications. I also attended a lot of openly gay and lesbian events and fundraisers in the Dupont Circle area and at the Lambda Rising bookstore, where attendees were shocked to see the mayor of the city accept them. But they were a part of the Washington, D.C. community, too.

During my campaign, I had given interviews to the *Washington Blade* newspaper and *National Advocate*, reaching out to the gay and lesbian community to support, and their advertising and businesses took off. The major business community suddenly decided that it was okay to court them, and they began to understand that gays and lesbians were a major economic force in Washington and a major part of the political process. So I was ahead of my time in supporting gay rights. I was one of the first major politicians in the country who was willing to go out on a limb to support and acknowledge them.

I had Richard Maulsby to help create a D.C. film commission to bring more film and television productions to the city. And when Robert "Bob" Johnson was trying to establish a cable television network, our minority contracting allowed him to get in and establish D.C. Cablevision, which later led to him forming Black Entertainment Television (BET), including providing him with land for the BET studio. Under my leadership, the city even sold him the property to set up the first BET studio off of New York Avenue, Northeast.

We hired Robert "Bob" Moore, a housing expert from Houston, as our housing director, as we began to pull together fair housing programs and implement citywide rent control and more building inspection. We implemented a strict policy to enforce the property owners to clean up their buildings for proper inspection or we would fine them and charge them twice if we had to clean it. There was a lot of apathy with the ownership of some of these properties when we first got into office. A lot of the owners were lackadaisical toward the upkeep, so we would lean on them, fine them and if they didn't respond to that, we would close a lot of the places down.

Our housing enforcement and rent control programs forced them to fix their properties up, make them safe to live in, and keep them clean or else. You also had a lot of fire code violations and vacant housing that we had to deal with in certain housing and in different communities. Whenever these houses cost too much to fix up, we had no choice but to board them up. Sometimes we had to deal with private owners who were not keeping up their houses. The majority of our problems were with investment properties and apartment buildings that were not owned by the people in the community, where they continued to take advantage of poor residents who had no means to fight them.

Those were the main violators we went after with standard property codes. You have a responsibility to keep up with the housing codes that are established to protect the consumer, and those who didn't do it paid the price until they got the message that we were no longer going to allow it. These neglected properties were not only a disservice to the people who lived there, but they were an environmental and neighborhood issue. Some of these places were close to downtown, and we couldn't have that.

I called him Bob Moore "The Hip Pocket Director." He was extremely effective at getting what we needed to get done in district housing. Anything we needed that we discussed at our community meetings, Bob would say, "We got it." Bob would go to the communities and promise about a million dollars. I would say, "Bob, stop shooting from the hip that way." I'd give him a hard time purposely, just kidding with him, but I would identify the million. He did this many times and got the people to believe in this administration.

I would say, "Bob, we need about a million dollars for this new housing program," and he'd say, "Let's go get it." Providing fair and affordable housing was at the top of my agenda of things to get done. At that time, we had far too many landlords who were overcharging people for rent and not taking care of too many unsafe and dilapidated housing and apartment complexes. We got tough on a lot of these delinquent property owners and got the council to pass a rent control bill. We let them know they were not going to get away with business as usual in the District. So we started fining them and taking properties away. The rent control bill that I sent to the council was one of the most effective in the entire country.

We established credit unions for public housing, where citizens could work toward buying and owning their homes instead of only living in them and renting them. We felt homeownership was their only major asset. It's more important to you when you own it. We also started the "Taking the Boards Off" project through our Economic Development and Public Housing Department, where we set up a trust fund to build or renovate some homes in Washington's rundown neighborhoods and enhance the quality of life.

We had one housing project on Bates Street that was a part of our Department of Housing and Community Development program. It was a very successful vision, but it led to controversy when opposing candidates attempted to paint the project with a tainted brush, claiming that monies were not appropriated properly, and that the Bates Street housing was never completed on time or up to standard. That was all a part of an unfounded game of politics that opponents would play with the media to try and throw as many darts on the board as they could to see what they could get to stick.

They would try and find disloyal, jealous people, anyone who had something negative to say to quote them in the media. But the residents who actually lived there said, "What are you talking about?" They lived in very nice and well-kept townhomes. We had city contracts while I was still with Pride, where we would clean up the same drug-infested Bates Street corridor several times during the summer. As the mayor, I helped to turn these three to four blocks into respectable and livable homes again. Nevertheless, competitors would team up with the newspapers to create these unfounded stories.

The fact is, building and renovating homes to finish and sell can take up to a year and a half to two years, especially when trying to qualify new home-owners. Sometimes they couldn't afford the 15 to 20 percent home loan equity, and in some instances, the city subsidized. And once they owned it, it was their job to take care of their new homes, not the city's. Those were the issues that were brought up in a game of campaign politics to try and discredit me and the things that we would do in office.

That first term, we had no real organized system of financial accountability and we had a large deficit that we had inherited from the previous office of Walter Washington. Under Home Rule, we had to establish our own bank accounts and I took the District money out of the U.S. Treasury, and put it in local banks. In the old system, the District would get the money from the U.S. Treasury without having to worry about balancing the budget for new workers or local government management. It was almost like writing a bunch of blank checks and printing money with no responsibility.

The District government had never been audited, so we did our first audit and found out that we had a $279 million deficit with a new $100 million budget for the year, which put us at $387 million in the hole. We had a lot of money to make in that first year to climb out. We wanted to reform the way we managed the government by utilizing bank loans to provide for more housing and residents in the District, and credit unions to bolster opportunities for black people to save money for houses, cars and better money manage-ment.

We were essentially starting over again, similar to the process I had experi-enced as a first-time council member. I was familiar with the process of starting over and took direct action to get our new systems and staff in order. I called for a lot of meetings where we went over the budget for each department. I wanted everyone to know what we were working with and I wanted no excuses. If you told me something wrong, if I didn't already know, I was going to find out. That was the accountability that I wanted. I wanted to make the leadership of the local government, the labor unions and the employees all accountable to the citizens they represented in the community.

I told them, "It's not about us, it's about the citizens." I wanted us to make the needs of the citizens first and for all government departments and services to fall in line and bond under that common idea to make it all work.

I remember government official George Harrod, the personnel director, who knew everything about the previous term of Walter Washington. He would say, "That's the way we've always done things," whenever we came up with needed changes for the old and no longer viable structures of running the local government.

I told George, "Stop saying how we 'used to do things' because we need to do them differently now."

I would talk to every department about ways to improve what we were doing and their ideas, including getting their budget numbers. If I was the one hiring all of these people, I figured I needed to know what they knew. People were always surprised when I would spring numbers and information on them in our monthly cabinet meetings because I had done my homework. I was the same hard-working man who had memorized a few dozen chemistry formulas and had tutored students on my basis of understanding. My years of education in chemistry had served me well, but people continued to not know, to devalue or to underestimate my educational background and experiences.

We wanted to use every means we could to effect change in the District for those in the dawn of life; the youngest people, the dust of life; the senior citizens, and the shadow of life; the poor and economically disadvantaged. That was our mantra of priorities as we prepared to organize our goals for office.

We hit the ground running and looked at a number of disparities in the District that we wanted to address immediately, including minority contracting. Washington had a population that was 66 percent African American, but white American businesses controlled 97 percent of government contracts. We wanted to put laws into place where the District contracts would be more equally distributed to allow opportunities for African American firms. We also wanted to provide subcontracting laws for the bigger firms that used subcontracts. These bigger firms would often hire smaller companies to do a lot of the work, and we wanted to include African American firms as a part of that subcontracting base.

The goal was to allow more economic parity for the people of Washington. And these were not handouts; these were professional people who needed the opportunities to work. I wanted a system in place to teach people how to fish rather than give them fish, but they still needed a chance to get to the lake. We couldn't have these major white firms locking up all of the routes to the fish. I wanted to open up the doors of opportunity and give people a key to the government. I wanted to build a coalition that understood the amount of courage and activity that was needed to get these things done. The people of Washington hadn't had that before. They were far too accepting and in-experienced in the process of fighting for freedom. That's why the strongest and most active minds needed to be in office to show them the way.

I made it mandatory that we have cabinet meetings every month to remain in sync as a group of department heads and city directors, and I wanted all of our cabinet members to know the city by meeting on or near the different project locations. In other words, if we had a new government project on Benning Road, Northeast, then I wanted to have a cabinet meeting on site so we would all know and understand the areas where we're effecting change around the city. I didn't want a bunch of bureaucrats sitting up in government offices every day. I wanted the cabinet and staff members to see and feel the city that we were serving. So if we planned to construct and remodel 125 recreation centers around the District, then I expected my cabinet members and department heads to be able to see some of them, if not all. It only made sense.

I then took the ideas that we developed with Pride Inc. with the summer youth employment programs and made sure we provided in the budget a mayor's summer youth jobs program. But instead of a thousand kids that we employed with Pride, as the mayor, I was able to provide a more substantial amount of summer jobs, where 25,000 to 26,000 youth registered all around the District and 21,000 to 22,000 showed up for work.

We also took the youth leadership model from Pride Inc. and the partner-ship with American University and introduced the program citywide, while seeking more college and university partnerships, including Howard and George Washington. The District government would then subsidize a budget for the universities to sustain the program. Our goal was to make the youth leadership program one of the best in the country for training the next pro-fessional leaders from the black, urban and female communities. We wanted to give these kids opportunities to learn what professionalism and leadership was all about at an early age. It was what we had done for ourselves in the South with SNCC.

We made sure to maintain a 50 percent balance between men and women, because we realized that a lot of young aggressive women would have taken over the program. We were getting far more applications from girls, where the program could have easily tilted to 80 percent young women. They seemed to have wanted it more and would show up in greater numbers. So we made it our mission to keep the young men involved. We paid the universities to provide room and board for the students in the program and everything. It was the first and only opportunity that some of these local students would ever have to experience living in a dorm for campus life.

The mayor's summer youth jobs program and the college leadership program were both highly successful. We inspired more kids to understand what work and being part of the employment system was all about, as well as provided a lot of senior students with the passion and confidence to attend colleges and universities after high school.

We started a boxing commission, where I appointed Cora Masters as the first female boxing commissioner. We held a multistate boxing tournament with Maryland, Virginia and North Carolina, connected through the department of recreation. We even had the Mayor's Cup Boxing Tournament at Howard University's Burr Gymnasium. We had a midnight basketball league at the D.C. basketball gyms, set up to give many teenagers and young men something to do at night that would keep them off the streets and provide a safe haven and alternative to gang and street violence. We even established a United States Youth Games event in Washington and expanded the games to involve young athletes from thirty-five different cities, while raising money for educational and athletic facilities nationwide.

We organized the first Washington, D.C. marathon in the early 1980s with 1,000 runners, who ran through every ward in the city for twenty-six miles over hills, around curves and everything you're supposed to have in a normal marathon. I remember we had football star Jim Brown to start the marathon by shooting the starting gun, and Coca-Cola and Miller beer were some of our sponsors.

I recall we had a Washington, D.C. New Year's Eve celebration down on

Pennsylvania Avenue on the federal lawn, where we had over 200,000 attendees show up. We had a large jumbotron with the countdown time on it, where we dropped a giant federal stamp instead of the Big Apple they had in New York. We were set up to rival New York's big celebration in a few more years, but then there was a murder inside the Old Post Office Pavilion and after that, we chose not to have it anymore. The crowd grew from 10,000 to 500,000 before we ended it.

We used to have a Riverfest every week for a month, where we would take private sector business people out on the waterfront and talk to them about politics and the District's various issues. It was budgeted through Parks and Recreation; we would have food, music and dancing and would end it with fireworks. We had a large segment of the community who came out and everyone enjoyed themselves, but some of the Southwest residents started to complain about the inconvenience of the event—attendees were tossing beer bottles in the yards. There were fireworks and commotion near their homes every week. Most of them were white residents, and we agreed to stop having them. The event grew to about 250,000 people over the weekend. I remember the neighbors' complaints. We shouldn't have ended it.

Looking back on it, I should have kept the Riverfest going. It was good to have people out on the water who rarely got a chance to go out on a boat. We could have had it once or twice a month and without the fireworks. Sometimes it felt like whites would complain about anything we did. They didn't want black folks renting boats to fish out there on the water, either.

One time I went out with a group of my black friends, whose boats were over fifty feet, and we took out five boats with about five people on each down to the Georgetown pier, which was frequented mostly by whites. We tied these five boats together in what they call rafting, and some of the white boaters, who were still on the docks, were overheard saying, "How did those niggers get those boats?" I thought that was really tasteless and uncalled for. So we still had a whole lot to do to create racial parity and respect in the District.

I continued to work hard to make the District government and the Washington community inclusive. We used to have great turnouts at the annual "State of the District" address at the new Washington Convention Center. The idea was to invite the citizens, the elderly and the Washington public school students to enjoy the building and to meet the city government workers and include them in the movement that we wanted to create in the city. I would speak to them all about what we wanted to do, answer a few questions and include a sound and light show to close it out.

We wanted to open up government meetings to the community with each department to explain what our project goals were and to hear directly from the people what their concerns were around the city. I wanted all of the department heads to have firsthand knowledge of what was going on and not be in the dark about the people they served in the community. Basically, I wanted to create a hands-on government that people felt would respond to them. If I could make rounds and have energy and an ear for the people in the community as the mayor, then my department heads needed to make rounds with the same openness and energy.

I told my cabinet members and staff, the Washington media and the public community that "I'm at home in the suites or the streets." And I wanted all of us to have the same hands-on approach.

I didn't want anyone slacking off on the job, either. If I would be a little late to get to our meetings, I would always call Ivanhoe Donaldson and Elijah Rogers and tell them, "You make sure we keep the trains moving on time."

I didn't want anyone using my late arrivals as an excuse, because whenever I got into my office for the cabinet meetings, I was always ready to go and I caught up quickly. I would always catch you if you were unprepared, especially since I spent the time to read everything. But I wouldn't let my staff know that until it was time to catch them sleeping. I always kept people off-balance that way, so it was better to be prepared around me than not.

Once I became the mayor, I had to watch out for people trying to take me for granted. People had a tendency to do that once they knew you really cared about them. They would tell my staff members, cabinet, directors, or anyone, "Mayor Marion Barry told me" he would do this or that. I had to give someone the power to counteract all of the name dropping, or else we would have chaos. That's why Ivanhoe became the bad cop, the drill sergeant, or whatever you want to call it. But you had to have guys on your team like that.

I would let Ivanhoe and Elijah Rogers set the tone of seriousness in our staff meetings, and we would get what we needed to get done with no nonsense. That included knowing what you needed to know, because I was always talking to people about what was going on in every department. And I was always prepared to call you out on it. But Ivanhoe and Elijah would keep folks in line when I wasn't there. They were my dealmakers and my deal breakers when they had to be. If I was the president, Ivanhoe was like my chief of staff.

I hired Tom Downs initially as my director of transportation in that first term, and he later became the city administrator. As the transportation director, the city was all over the place on where the Metro subway stations would be located, how much it would cost us, how much Congress was willing to allocate to the budget, and so on. At that time, we were working on the final decisions for the Green Line train. The Red Line was the first to finish in 1976, followed by the Blue, Orange and Yellow.

Well, the Metro lines were getting more expensive and tedious to build, so we were battling back and forth with Congress about the expense, especially with the Green Line crossing the Anacostia River to the black neighborhoods in the Southeast. It was the last one to finish, and it should have been the first one. The Green Line also slowed up traffic for a long time on the U Street corridor. But once we got it finished, the interstate connections from the Metro Transit created new ports of commuter money to utilize in the District. So it was well worth the fight and the struggle to complete them.

One of the biggest development projects we needed to undertake in the District was building the new Washington Convention Center between Ninth and Tenth and H streets, downtown. Some people say that the plans were already in the works when Walter Washington was the mayor, but all they did was talk about it for ten years with no construction plans, site or anything. We had a budget at the time allotted for about $86 million. We didn't have a Convention Center, and I felt that any first-rate city ought to have a large Convention Center downtown for events and functions, and to attract new business to the city. But when I got into office, we got it *done!*

There were previous building and construction regulations, with fire codes and such that forced you to wait five or six months to get a business license to build anything, which we thought was ridiculous. It made it easier to lock out new companies for old companies that already had their licenses and the money to wait. For new businesses, these restrictive provisions had the ability to do more harm than good. Well, I was not going to allow all the red tape to slow up the process. So we worked to create more cohesion with all of the different departments and regulations to move new building projects forward with a lot more urgency. Otherwise, it would have taken us forever to build downtown. And whatever we had to do to get new projects cleared, licensed and budgeted, we would work immediately to get it done.

The private sector built a lot of new attractions in Washington—office buildings, shops and businesses, restaurants, nightclubs, affordable housing, and the government did its share. We built up downtown Washington and made it what it is today. When I first arrived, there was nothing downtown but one FBI building on Pennsylvania Avenue. Very little downtown had been developed into major office space and retail.

When I came into office, we had 118 different business licenses and permits to pass, but the license investigation, inspection and compliance office was in another department and another building. I thought that was ridiculous. I wanted to organize all of the licensing and compliances in the same department and have them all work together in tandem. The previous disorganization is why it took so long for many small and big businesses and entrepreneurs in the District to establish themselves. So we wanted to create a one-stop business and permit center in one department to deal with everyone's needs.

There was also a problem with figuring out the citywide water bills in the office of public works. No one knew how to determine how the water use was calculated. We had thousands of District residents overpaying and under-paying for water bills. I told the department head of public works to find out a solution to stop the crazy water bill situation and over time, he did.

There were a lot of things—along with understanding the budgets—that we still had to learn in running a government. At the time, we still had to go to Congress for all of our budget approvals. William Natcher, the congressman from Kentucky, was more concerned about the District budget providing for more police than anything else. So he would keep pushing police numbers on us.

At one point, we wanted to start a DC Lottery to provide more revenue for the District and find more money outside of us asking for so much from our taxpayers. I wanted to keep finding ways to pay our own bills, but we had to get approval. To get the DC Lottery approved, we had a referendum in the city where the people approved it overwhelmingly. But we still had to go through Congress and they put many restrictions on us.

I also asked for a major economic development center at the corner of Fourteenth and U streets, Northwest. I wanted it there to reestablish an area that had been destroyed after the Martin Luther King, Jr. assassination in Memphis on April 4, 1968. I was actually there on Fourteenth Street the night the Washington, D.C. riots started.

Reverend Martin Luther King, Jr. had asked Walter Fauntroy and me to start planning a poor people's march in Washington, so Walter and I had been meeting up to discuss our plans. We got the news that Dr. King had been assassinated, and Walter called Memphis and found out it was true. Around 7 o'clock on the night of Dr. King's assassination, I looked out the window of the old Peoples Drug with Walter, and I could see an angry crowd starting to form in the street. I could tell they were about to do something to express their rage over Dr. King being killed. I also saw a few of my Pride Inc. people in green uniforms, so I went out and told them to go home.

But a lot of people were already riled up and very emotional. They started throwing things through storefront windows and burning cars and trucks and looting. They hit all of the stores, shops and businesses that we didn't own, or wherever they felt they may have been taken advantage of by the establishments.

I felt sorry for a lot of the white-owned, Jewish and immigrant businesses that got destroyed, burned down and looted that night. Sure, I wanted better treatment and fair business ownership for black people in Washington, but I didn't want to see anyone's businesses or properties randomly destroyed like that, no matter who they were. So I tried to stop it. But you can't stop a whole mob of people who felt angry and disenfranchised in their own communities. And there was nothing I could really do. I tried to stop some of the young Pride workers who were dressed in green.

The Seventh Street corridor, Fourteenth Street, Northwest, and H Street, Northeast were the major corridors being burned and looted. There were a number of neighborhood stores being broken in and looted that same night. It was a crisis in Washington. There was a foreign car dealer at Seventh Street and Rhode Island Avenue that had Triumphs and Buicks. The brothers hotwired the cars and could be seen cruising down the street. Several other major cities lost control in their communities that night of the assassination as well, including Memphis, Chicago, Detroit and other cities all over the country. So the federal government called in the U.S. Army, police and paddy wagons, and they arrested 12,000 people in Washington, overcrowding the D.C. Jail in Southeast and wherever else they could keep them. It was a real mess. The assassination was on Good Friday. The army came in on Easter Sunday morning, but never had to fire a shot.

Petey Greene, a popular local radio talk-show host, and many of the black media voices and celebrities, including James Brown, were trying to talk peace and calm into the people, but when the U.S. Army got involved, it potentially made the situation worse by angering the people more. I was up all night and all over the city trying to talk sense into the rioters and convince them not to try any counteraction violence that they were thinking. I was trying my best to help people to avoid getting themselves shot or arrested. The Army had M-16 rifles with bayonets attached. It was a very tense situation that could have escalated into something much worse.

After the riots, we organized a program with Pride Inc. and Giant Food supermarkets to distribute free food and supplies to the residents whose homes and neighborhoods were destroyed. I drove one of the trucks myself, delivering food to homes and housing projects that had been damaged throughout the city.

I will never forget those angry nights and that desperate time in the District. You could write a whole chapter alone on the Washington, D.C. riots. That's when I first became a board member on the city's Economic Development Committee. The committee was designed to help provide federal funds and seed monies to black-owned businesses that were challenged with the struggle of rebuilding after the riots.

A year later in 1969, President Richard Nixon declared a national day of honor for American astronauts who had landed on the moon on the Apollo 11 mission into space, right after he had opposed a national holiday honoring the work and courage of Dr. Martin Luther King, Jr. to end segregation and inequality. So I spoke out on it.

I said, "Why should blacks feel elated about seeing men walking on the moon when millions of poor blacks and whites don't have enough money to buy food to eat on earth?" I called the president out on his hypocrisy immediately. And the president didn't respond because he knew that I was right.

At that time, I told myself that if I ever got a chance to do something to inspire and impact that area of Fourteenth and U streets, Seventh Street and the H Street corridor, where the heaviest rioting broke out and damaged so much of the community, I would make sure to do it. That's why I was so determined to place the Frank D. Reeves Municipal Center for small business and economic development on that very spot at Fourteenth and U as the mayor, despite the disagreements from my cabinet members and advisers.

At the time, the U Street area had been decimated and was nothing like it is today. I had to stick to my convictions to create a ray of hope for the people who still lived in that area. The idea was to have the Frank D. Reeves Center to spearhead government-funded development of entrepreneurship through small businesses, with licensing and certification, financial services, community programming, security training, and a bunch of other government services and functions, where African Americans would be guaranteed a certain percentage of all new business. I wanted 35 percent of new contracts going to African American businesses.

The Reeves Center was a part of the new deal of equal opportunity employment for minorities that had been mandated by the federal government, and I was not going to allow anyone to talk me out of it. So as an executive decision, I overruled everyone in my cabinet who voted for the center to be placed somewhere else. I remembered when U Street used to be a mecca of the black community, and I wanted the greatness of U Street to return.

I saw the Frank D. Reeves Center as a monumental breakthrough of the promise that I had made to the people of Washington, D.C. who had elected me. I wanted the center to make a statement and be more than another government building. We also developed the government charity One Fund, which was for D.C. government employees to contribute to one pot to distribute to organizations and people in need.

Anchors like the Reeves Center were only the beginning to build neighborhoods like U Street and Fourteenth Street. We also wanted to build a living downtown, and help create plenty of opportunities for new businesses and for people to have a reason to come downtown. We wanted them to shop, eat at a nice restaurant, enjoy a movie, a stage play, an art museum, a nightclub, and have office buildings to attract employment to downtown Washington. So we cut through a bunch of red tape with licensing and construction, and created a more streamlined system where we were able to construct more than seventy buildings downtown, east of Fifteenth Street and above Pennsylvania Avenue. By 1982, we dropped from a deficit of $400 million in 1980, down to $224 million. The D.C. government allowed for these great gains by stringent financial control and new downtown revenue.

In my first term as mayor, I found that we had an atrocious child mortality rate in the District, one of the highest in the country. Far too many babies from African American mothers were dying as infants, mainly due to a lack of quality prenatal care, proper medical treatment and overall awareness. We went to work on providing more prenatal care information, distributing thousands of brochures, making them available at the free clinics, and cleaning up the general lack of execution and lack of policies at the hospitals that served impoverished areas. These young and mostly poor mothers were not getting the quality prenatal care and follow-up that they should have been getting. Overall health and wellness of the community was another priority of our urban revitalization movement. And in just a few years, we brought our infant mortality rate down to one of the lowest in the country.

Like the Frank D. Reeves Center and the H Street corridor, we wanted to continue placing government resources where we had the greatest needs, and that was often in the bleak African American communities. We wanted to show them that the new District government was working to give them hope. We weren't the same old Congress-appointed administration, which would continue to ignore them.

At the same time, I kept working ties with the former mayor, Walter Washington, stayed in touch with the council members and kept my working relationships with school board members. I was used to having many different professional relationships, and I viewed every one of them as valuable. I had a conversation and time for everyone, even the people who didn't like me.

CHAPTER 8
THE RACIAL DIVIDE

When I came into office as the mayor of Washington, some of the white Washingtonians claimed that our programs and developments didn't benefit them, but we had the hardest time getting any government buildings approved in their areas or keeping white kids in our summer youth and leadership programs. A lot of their neighborhood leaders didn't want the construction or added city traffic, and white parents didn't feel that their kids needed our youth programs as much. I suspect that a lot of them looked down on it as handouts, but we saw these programs as opportunities for the young people of Washington to learn how to grow into highly productive adults who were responsive to their communities.

Many white Washingtonians didn't see it that way. Some of them continued to complain about government programs, urban renewal projects and budget money that they felt didn't affect them. But I couldn't ignore the thousands of people in the District who needed help because they didn't need it. It was my job as the mayor of the city to provide the people with the proper services for a better quality of life, the same quality of life that whites could afford on their own. Simply put: a lot of white residents didn't need job training and placement, at least not in Washington.

I found that some white residents spent time in the white community and they didn't see the problems nor spend the time to see what black, poor people of Washington were going through. Some white schoolchildren weren't affected as much in public education, either. So they complained a lot about the amount of attention and resources that were allocated to the failing schools. I don't believe they expected me to have an agenda that was so useful to the black community, and it became upsetting to a lot of white Washingtonians.

However, with educational needs, there was only so much we could do to improve the individual learning at each school. After you hire and retain the best teachers you can train, it's up to everyone, including the students and the parents, to get the work done. I had already been though the difficulties of the school system when I was president of the school board and hired Barbara Sizemore. We all had to figure out a way to get along and agree on a policy that worked, then we could try and implement the curriculum for the schools and everything else. But it still came down to the kids and parents doing their part in the learning process.

Some whites only seemed to care about the three T's: taxes, trash and trees. So that's what I continued to provide for them in their neighborhoods. Some weren't interested in a lot of the inner-city programs and didn't need them. But when certain tax issues came up, and white businesses complained about them, I made sure to shoot some of the tax increases down. I knew that they cared the most about taxes, and I tried my best to be fair to everyone. I didn't agree with a number of the tax proposals.

Washington was a city with a lot of emphasis on city police. Washington was also still a police state when I got into office, with a bloated budget for city police. It was a holdover from the Republican President Richard Nixon's years, but the new Democratic president, Jimmy Carter, didn't get too involved as much with the local policies and practices. So I cut back several hundred jobs and made sure that we diversified the department from top to bottom without jeopardizing public safety. It was all a part of our tough management decisions, including assessments on what to do with property taxes, income taxes, sales taxes, and what all we needed to spend the new budgets on.

When you get serious about controlling the budget, you're forced to cut funds and reorganize in places where there is disorganization and overspending. The first thing we did was make sure we had more money going to the places where we needed it, and less where we didn't need it. At the time, we had too many programs that didn't work and too many people who didn't work, either. So we had the tough but necessary task of cutting back on many of the wasteful jobs in government administration. And I didn't get credit for those hard government cuts that we were forced to make, but we made them, and the city and the people of Washington all benefited from them, including the white citizens.

As a progressive and global-thinking black mayor, a lot of noise was made about my trip to Africa during my first term in spring 1979, but I made a key point to use Washington, D.C. as an example to the world that blacks could run their own city with excellence. My trip to Africa and other countries around the world was part of my outreach, not only to show the world what we could do, but to form new relationships. Our ancestral homeland was Africa. We had been brainwashed by Tarzan, Jane and Cheetah. A lot of people didn't see a connection to Africa as being as important as I saw it, but that's what I was doing. I saw a much bigger picture than most. Washington represented much more than a city; it represented a world philosophy of self-rule and determination. However, my aspirations of inclusion and fairness for people of African descent created a bunch of questions when I visited Africa. Some people asked me why I was going to Africa at all. Well, first of all, Africa is my homeland and I had been fed a lot of negative propaganda about the continent. All I knew about Africa was "Tarzan" and "Jane," and about African people being cannibals, which was untrue. So I visited twenty-seven African countries, met the presidents, spent time with the people and learned the culture. Most of the countries were colonialized from European nations, creating thirteen colonies in West Africa alone. As an African American mayor and dignitary, I wanted to learn about the culture and identify with them. And I did that.

After my return from Africa, I received calls from the U.S. Senate and the House of Representatives to explain the relations that America had with African nations and how the leaders in the different African nations received me. They had a bunch of questions about my trip to Senegal, Liberia, the Congo, and several other African nations and villages that I had visited. The American government was suddenly interested in seeing how new African and American relations could be utilized. That's what I had in mind when I went over there to visit. We had a lot of African immigrants and ambassadors in Washington, and we still do. So it made sense to me, with there being African American leadership in the nation's capital, to create new business ties there. Years later, I led an entire delegation of the National Conference of Black Mayors on a tour of Africa.

I also made a connection back home in Memphis. I wanted to inspire the Memphis community and the students at Booker T. Washington High School and at LeMoyne-Owen College. So I visited back home and told them all that I will never forget where I come from, who I am, what I represent, or what makes me who I am today.

I used to tell black college students in my speeches, "It's not about being anti-white; it's about being pro-black." I told them you had to be that way to continue to push for equality. Otherwise, you could rise to power only to continue hiring white people, which wouldn't change anything for the rest of the people who need opportunities.

I told them, "So, if you're ever in position to make a difference, you owe it to the people in your community to do it. You owe it to your family; you owe it to all the people who came before you and to the people who'll come after you."

And while back in Memphis, I made sure to order the biggest hotel suite I could get at the same Peabody Hotel downtown where blacks were not allowed to stay when I was teenager. So I considered it a good and very inspirational home visit.

As the mayor of Washington, I even pushed the business community to support the United Negro College Fund. My goal was to represent a precedent of productivity, courage and ideas to advance all of black America.

But Washington could be a very elitist city, with white-collar professionals, government officials and dignitaries from all fifty states and from other countries. There was a tendency to think more about class than the common good. We even had a serious issue with low-number license plate tags, where politicians, judges, federal employees and city officials would all call up and try to request low license-plate numbers as a status symbol while driving their cars around the District. I considered it ridiculous, but some of these officials would go to no end to acquire a "low tag," as they called them. They would try and call up anyone who worked in my office to get one. So you had to be careful of even the smallest things in Washington.

However, in my first term as the mayor, my progressive ideas and activity in local government allowed me to be named to a four-member board to advise the Democratic National Committee on urban policy in 1980. That position opened up connections and input in the DNC that year in New York City. It was at Madison Square Garden, where Jimmy Carter was named the incumbent candidate after beating out Senator Edward Kennedy in the Democratic primaries. I was very proud to be there, not only as a key board member and Democratic adviser, but as an African American mayor with roots in rural Mississippi, where the DNC had once rejected our demand to receive proper representation in 1964.

But my rise as the mayor of Washington was more than just politics and policies; I had to make adjustments for this new lifestyle. Effi and I had moved into a wonderful house in Southeast, Washington on Suitland Road. The press made a big deal out of it because it cost $125,000, and I was given a discount on the mortgage. Effi was a board member at Independence Federal, and she received a board member's rate on the mortgage. But I gave up the discount and went on to live at the Suitland Road house with Effi and our son, Christopher, for thirteen years. It was a nice, four-bedroom home, but nothing fancy. It had a basement family room, four bathrooms and a backyard. We had a lot of good times and memories in that house, good and bad.

Growing up in Memphis, I would have never thought in my wildest dreams that I could buy a $125,000 house like that, particularly since my parents only got $15,000 from the city to move to another town. Black kids didn't have the luxury of dreaming that big in Memphis. My mother and stepfather bought a house in Memphis for $15,000 and sold it for an upgrade to a $25,000 house. But my new home in Southeast Washington was on a whole other level.

It was never my goal to create individual wealth. I was much more concerned with creating opportunities and wealth—particularly for black people, and that's what I did. It was my philosophy not to buy a big house and all of that, but for safety reasons, you had to have certain measures of space to protect yourself and your family as a public figure. So we were forced to have a big enough space to entertain; that eventually included putting a fence up around the property.

Once I settled into the mayor's office, Effi began to work with incarcerated and embattled women. I created an office of the first lady right down the hall from mine. She became an advocate for a lot of different women's causes and continued to be very active with the Delta Sigma Theta sorority and with the Jack and Jill of America. Effi was helpful to everyone and was very generous with her time. That was one of the many qualities of her personality that made her perfect for me. I was so giving of my own time in politics that I needed someone who could understand that. It was why so many of my constituency loved me; I was always accessible, and that was to white and black citizens.

I still had to live though, and that included a life with my wife and the excitement of starting a family. At the time, I was over forty years old with no children. So after Effi and I were married, had finished the election process and had moved into a house, I figured we would have some kids. We hadn't been using prevention for some time after we had tied the knot, but Effi hadn't gotten pregnant yet. So I started searching around in her bathroom cabinets and found that she was taking birth control pills.

I knew that she had been using them when we were dating. But after marriage, Effi had told me that she was ready to start having kids, and that she had stopped using birth control. So once I found them in her cabinets, I brought them to her attention and asked her what was going on.

She said, "I don't want to raise kids by myself if you're not going to be here."

I hadn't thought about having kids with Mary Treadwell, because we didn't have the money or the interest at that time to start a family. I made less than $20,000 a year running Pride Inc., and Mary and I had made more of a commitment to the people and children of Washington than to ourselves. But as the mayor, I had the resources and I was ready to start a family of my own.

Effi was reluctant to have kids with me because of so much time I would spend away from home, campaigning and serving as the mayor. The job was all-consuming, so she was secretly taking birth control pills to stop from getting pregnant.

Effi was an only child who had been raised by her mother in Ohio, so she wasn't used to a large family like I was. I don't know if she even wanted a large family. But us not having any children became an issue for me. I wanted kids, so after I found her birth control pills, we had to have a serious talk about it.

Well, after we discussed it, Effi agreed to stop using the birth control pills and I got very excited about having my first child. But after a few more months of trying to get pregnant, I became suspicious again. I started digging around in the cabinets where Effi kept her things, because I was wondering about her taking more birth control. She told me she had stopped taking them, but she didn't. I found them again and had another talk with her about us having a family.

I really had to work hard to get Effi to feel comfortable about having kids, so we took a mini vacation and went up to Vermont to spend four days together at Senator Patrick Leahy's house. I had to get away from everything and concentrate on my wife. That's where I think we conceived our first and only child.

I was very excited and wanted to know the sex of the child, but Effi didn't. I wanted a boy, but she wanted a girl. So we agreed that if we had a girl, we would name her Christina, and Christopher if it was a boy.

Well, Christopher was born that next year on June 17, 1980. We decided to have a natural childbirth at the house with Dr. Charles Hall, who had an impeccable record of delivering babies. Christopher was born late in the afternoon around five o'clock, and Effi and I both cried.

I wish everyone could experience a natural childbirth and the power that we all have as humans to reproduce. Hospitals are only needed to make sure that you don't make any mistakes. But going natural was a beautiful and exhilarating experience for us. More natural childbirths, without anesthetics or spinal blocks or anything, would really allow people to understand the power of God. I really felt that way.

Effi was the perfect wife, mother and partner for me, and she didn't let anything disturb our home life. She didn't like the media coming around our house or around our son. In her mind, the family was off-limits, and Effi kept it that way. She was very secure and consistent about everything. I don't know if we would have lasted long in marriage if she wasn't.

There were always rumors about me womanizing and drinking as the mayor of Washington. That was one of the downsides of being a popular mayor. I was constantly being talked about in every which way. But Effi would ignore it all and never let it bother her. She wasn't a jealous woman.

I can't say that we never had any issues, though. Effi liked to shop and look nice, and money was never a real priority for me. I made enough to do what I needed to do to get by, but money was never a driving force, and I never made a whole lot of money as the mayor. We had three bank accounts. We each had one personal account and a joint account for bills or whatever we would need around the house. It was a miscellaneous account.

Well, one time, I went to get something out of the joint account, and there wasn't anything left in it. I said, "What the hell?"

So I went to Effi to ask her about it, and she got mad at me for asking what she had spent it on. But I didn't set up that account for her to spend it all on herself. She said she had bought some clothing and artwork that she liked for her wardrobe and for the house.

I said, "That's not in the budget, baby."

We were still pretty tight on expenses, so we had to figure out a better way to deal with the money, because I never really had a lot. As much as some people would assume that I made a lot of money as a community activist or a politician, I really didn't. I may have set up a lot of programs and policies to make some other people a lot of money, but I was never bothered much about making a lot for myself. We didn't come up that way in the Civil Rights era. The goal was always to sacrifice your personal needs to create more opportunities for others.

In that first term, we were fighting against a mountain of changes that needed to be implemented and a lot of hard work that needed to be done to make those changes happen. I never looked at it all as impossible; I knew that it would take a lot of planning and cooperation. And it would take time. You can't get everything done in just four years; nobody can. And no matter how much you try, you can't please everybody. There was always a group of people who felt left out, but I continued to try and work hard for everyone.

However, that didn't mean that I would become a pushover for things that I didn't believe in. And that included a teachers' strike.

We had a teachers' union strike against the board of education in 1981, where the teachers wanted more money. I opposed the strike immediately because it was illegal. Besides, when teachers were out of school, the kids suffered. So I called all of the parties into a meeting at the Hotel Washington. I told the management and the teachers that they couldn't leave until they came to a settlement to resolve this strike, and they did that.

The teachers' union leadership agreed that they would take the settlement back to their membership to ratify it, and it was done quickly. So they were able to get back to work and continue teaching the D.C. schoolchildren. That was the kind of active leadership I brought to Washington. I was not going to tolerate ineptitude or unfairness in the city government, from the business community or from any group of people who would try to box me in or intimidate my staff and me in what we wanted to do for all of the people of Washington. And I didn't care who you were—black, white or yellow. I was going to run the District government the way I believed it should be run.

We got a lot of things done during that first term, but sometimes you have things holding over. A lot of projects from Walter Washington's term needed to be followed up on and pushed through, which we were able to do. That happens a lot in politics; you get a rollover from one administration's list of programs to another. But I was still driven by a determination to make sure that more people were in better shape in 1982 than they were in 1978 when I first ran for office. And I wasn't finished yet.

CHAPTER 9

THE SECOND TERM

To win a reelection for a second term as the mayor of Washington, I had to run in the Democratic primary against two council members—John Ray and Charlene Drew Jarvis, daughter of Dr. Charles Drew, founder of blood plasma—who both served on the D.C. Council with me; and Patricia Roberts Harris, Secretary of Housing and Urban Development and Ambassador to Luxembourg, professor and former dean at Howard University Law School, and who was considered the epitome of the black middle classs. She had worked in President Jimmy Carter's administration in the 1970s. *The Washington Post* published another article endorsing me for my second campaign over everyone. The editors at the *Post* knew that we still had a lot of work to do in the city with so many good programs that we had started and the positive directions that we were already headed in. When you start a job as big as the mayor's office, you don't want to let it go in just four years unless you didn't do anything good. But I had greatly impacted and improved the quality of life for most Washingtonians, especially blacks and the middle class, and there was a lot more that I had to offer. And the candidates running against me were not experienced enough to take over.

At first, I considered it disloyalty that John Ray would run against me after being someone I helped get on the council, but I got over it. Charlene Drew Jarvis was pretty popular around certain areas of the District, but I wasn't concerned about her winning. She wasn't popular enough. And Patricia Roberts Harris was a pretty good woman, but it seemed to me that she wasn't used to being around the poor people of Washington. She had been the head of President Carter's Housing and Urban Development. I don't think she felt comfortable with the people from underprivileged environments. So we planned to play that up in the campaign.

Patricia Harris was not a people person and she didn't understand the *needs* of the people in the District. So during my campaign for reelection, I said, "We need a mayor of the *people* and someone who is *with us* and won't talk *down* to us."

I don't think any of the candidates really understood who I was as a leader, or they wouldn't have tried to run against me. But it was too late for niceties. The campaign had started and I planned to win a second term. Patricia Harris became the person I was most concerned about.

As the campaign heated up toward the final week, we were both at a campaign event at the United House of Prayer church. I used to visit three or four churches every Sunday. Winning the support of churches in government was important. The churches were a major part of Washington and their programming and services were good for the children and families. Having good faith was also necessary for people to have a certain belief in themselves, so it made *sense* for politicians to support the churches. But this meeting was very late at night at the end of our campaign. It must have been about twelve or one o'clock in the morning, and it was *jampacked* in there.

Everyone was waiting for Bishop Walter McCollough to give his endorsement of who they would support for mayor, and they were still taking church collections.

He said, "Well, people keep asking me if I want to endorse a new mayor to vote for or not, but I think I already like the mayor that I got."

He wrapped his arm around my shoulder in front of the congregation and the people in the church went *crazy*. They started blasting music with horns, organs, tambourines and drums, while shouting and dancing up the aisles.

"Yeah, Mayor Marion Barry!"

And the horns blew with the music, *"BLARRRNN! BLARN-BLARN-BLARN-BLARN-BLARN-BLARN! BLARRRNN!"*

It was a loud and exciting endorsement. And I was shocked, not so much because of Bishop McCollough's endorsement. We already had a good relationship, so I expected it. But I was more shocked how the people responded to it. I had really connected with the people of Washington, and they were letting me know how much they appreciated me.

Patricia Harris heard all of that and broke out in tears. She cried right there

A very young, confident Marion Barry
at 16 years of age Courtesy of Marion Barry, Jr.

Young Marion Barry and Dr. Martin Luther King, Jr. on the
campus of Shaw University in Raleigh, N.C. during Easter
Weekend, 1960 © Howard Sochurek/Time & Life Pictures/Getty Images

Leading a conversation with
Vice President Hubert Humphrey
on behalf of Pride Inc.
Courtesy of Marion Barry, Jr.

Ribbon cutting at Pride gas station
Courtesy of Marion Barry, Jr.

Discussing matters with Pride workers Courtesy of Marion Barry, Jr.

Marion Barry
runs for D.C.
Council citywide
at-large seat
Courtesy of Marion Barry, Jr.

Working with youth while
campaigning for the D.C. Council
citywide at-large seat
Courtesy of Marion Barry, Jr.

The famous double-decker bus that became so popular during the Mayor's race.
Courtesy of Marion Barry, Jr.

Marion Barry being sworn in as
mayor of the District of Columbia by
Supreme Court Justice Thurgood Marshall,
with wife, Effi, by his side
Courtesy of Marion Barry, Jr.

Mayor Barry's first cabinet
Courtesy of Marion Barry, Jr.

With Pope John Paul II during his visit to Washington, DC. Effi Barry presented the Pope with keys to the city. Courtesy of Marion Barry, Jr.

Mayor Barry meets with one of his most loyal constituent bases—seniors
Courtesy of Marion Barry, Jr.

Mayor Barry, with wife, Effi, and Baby Christopher in the Executive Office of the Mayor Courtesy of Marion Barry, Jr.

With Coretta Scott King and other Civil Rights leaders, including Reverend Walter E. Fauntroy (third from left) Courtesy of Marion Barry, Jr.

Mayor Barry, Effi and Reverend Jesse Jackson at black-tie gala Courtesy of Marion Barry, Jr.

Mayor Barry, the late Secretary of Commerce Ron Brown
(second from left), and other council members and
cabinet climbing the Great Wall of China

Courtesy of Marion Barry, Jr.

Mayor Barry all smiles with the Greater Washington Board of Trade
Courtesy of Marion Barry, Jr.

Best wishes to Marion Barry
Jimmy Carter

One of many
encounters with
President Jimmy Carter
Courtesy of Marion Barry, Jr.

With the King of Pop,
Michael Jackson,
backstage after the
Jacksons' Victory Tour
in Washington, D.C.
Courtesy of Marion Barry, Jr.

With Don King backstage after the Victory Tour in 1984   Courtesy of Marion Barry, Jr.

Among many visits
with Bill Cosby in D.C.
Courtesy of Marion Barry, Jr.

Marion Barry always in the middle
of things. This time, he tosses up
at the Washington Bullets game.
Courtesy of Marion Barry, Jr.

With the late James Brown at a black-
tie affair   Courtesy of Marion Barry, Jr.

The Barrys' official Christmas card
Courtesy of Marion Barry, Jr.

Mayor Barry during an international sister city mission to Africa
(Sister Cities International) Courtesy of Marion Barry, Jr.

Departing hotel after
prison release with
Reverend Willie Wilson
Courtesy of Marion Barry, Jr.

Marion Barry addresses supporters immediately after
being released from prison Courtesy of Marion Barry, Jr.

Campaigning down Martin Luther King, Jr. Avenue in Southeast D.C. for the Ward 8 council seat Courtesy of Marion Barry, Jr.

Marion Barry is flanked by a crowd of supporters, who accompany him to his D.C. Council victory party. It took nearly an hour for the crowd to walk one block. Courtesy of Marion Barry, Jr.

Being sworn in as the D.C. Council member, after returning from prison only months earlier. He's accompanied by his mother, Mattie Cummings; son, Christopher; and wife, Cora Masters Barry. Courtesy of Cora Masters Barry

With new wife, Cora,
and the late Betty Shabazz
on wedding day
Courtesy of Cora Masters Barry

Marion Barry and wife,
Cora, host a luncheon in
Washington, D.C. for the
late Nelson Mandela during
his visit to the U.S. after
his release from prison
Courtesy of Cora Masters Barry

Marion Barry and the
late Abe Pollin lay out
plans for the MCI Center,
now the Verizon Center.
Press Secretary
Raymone Bain is also
seen in the photo.
Courtesy of Marion Barry, Jr.

President Bill Clinton's Inauguration in 1996, seen here with wife, Cora, President William Jefferson Clinton, First Lady Hillary Clinton and Congresswoman Eleanor Holmes Norton Courtesy of Cora Masters Barry

The "Odd Couple"— Marion Barry and wife, Cora, with Speaker of the House Newt Gingrich in front of the Capitol steps
Courtesy of Cora Masters Barry

At home with Nation of Islam Leader Minister Louis Farrakhan and son, Christopher
Courtesy of Marion Barry, Jr.

Donald Trump, Congresswoman Eleanor Holmes Norton, Mayor Vincent Gray, Ivanka Trump and council member Marion Barry at the announcement of the Trump Hotel at the Old Post Office Pavilion during the summer of 2013

© Latest Mangum. Courtesy of Marion Barry, Jr.

Making of *Mayor for Life*: Council member Marion Barry, Jr. sits with coauthor, Omar Tyree, and his spokesperson, LaToya Foster   Courtesy of Marion Barry, Jr.

in front of everyone at the church. Bishop McCollough was that influential in city politics. He had a lot of respect in the District. And the majority of his church was low-income black people who could benefit from a mayor who looked out more for their specific needs. That's what a lot of political pundits and adversaries continue to miss about me. That's why I was able to do so well with so many segments of people. You provide them all with what is most needed.

I went on to win the Democratic Primary in a landslide with 58 percent of the vote. Anything above 57 percent is considered a landslide. Patricia Harris got 35 percent, followed by Charlene Drew Jarvis and John Ray. I then won the general election with 82 percent of the vote over Republican candidate E. Brooke Lee, who won only 18 percent.

We worked hard to get people who only went in one direction to become more diverse in their views and opinions, but the second term became significantly more polar. The black and white middle class went in opposite directions, where black people supported me more emotionally. In the white community, we still had some doubters, folks who wanted you to do more for them, folks who wanted to try somebody new, and others who didn't bother to vote at all. So I would invite white community leaders down to the mayor's office to try and figure out how we could move forward to create a more inclusive city.

Some of the white Washingtonians came to believe that I was too Afrocentric, arrogant and untrustworthy, especially whites in Ward 3. But I never said I would ignore the rest of the city for them. Up there on Connecticut and Wisconsin avenues, they wanted everything, and I couldn't do that to the rest of my constituency. So I picked up a lot of the loyalties from the black middle class on the second term. They saw what I had done for blacks during the first term. I had hired more professional black people than any city official had ever hired before, and it helped the black middle class to move on up, so they trusted me more on the second term. I wanted to do the right thing for the community where nobody had to push me into it.

While the news media began to question whether or not I had delivered the people what they had expected, I gathered new support from the black middle class, including hundreds of the city's black doctors and dentists. The black professionals of Washington confirmed that I *did* deliver and they had faith that I would continue to do so. They realized the other candidates didn't have what it took to qualify for the job. They had no idea what they would have been getting into. Under my leadership, Washington, D.C. was now big business, bigger than it had ever been, and I had done a commendable job of getting the budget in order with control over our spending.

We had a lot of campaign loyalists from my first term who were proud to be a part of that first big victory. They all understood the mission to not only give service to the community of Washington, but to be proud representatives of the city and of what black professionals could do. It was a real special time for us, but I wasn't done with the job yet. The problem was, how do you keep people motivated to do the hard work when they're emotionally drained?

We all worked so hard and long that first term that some cabinet and staff members were burned out and moved on to other things in life, including Elijah Rodgers. But that's normal with any office.

Elijah told me, "Mr. Barry, it was fun while it lasted, but I have some other goals that I have in mind. I'm not a government lifer." He left and went to work at the DeLong Civil Engineering Company, which was black-owned and based in D.C. So I couldn't hold him back from what he wanted to do.

In that second term as the mayor, our government staff got bigger, the budget was bigger, the deficit was bigger, and a lot of my first-term staffers were leaving office. We had to refill a lot of positions that second term. The energy and excitement wasn't as strong as it was during the first term. I hadn't realized how much we had done in those first four years. That was a very creative time. We did a lot of hard work, but we had fun doing it. But it's hard not to lose some of your luster the second time around.

There were a couple of mountains of new issues to handle during the second term, including millions of dollars in staff raises, Medicaid and public assistance programs, and property tax raises. On top of that, Congress wanted us to put aside $20 million toward the deficit.

There were so many decisions to make from the mayor's office in the second term, that I had to name Ivanhoe Donaldson as the deputy mayor to have the power to make certain judgments or decisions in my absence. The city policies and constant activity had grown to the point where a deputy mayor was needed. You had to reorganize sometimes to stay competitive and on top. So

Ivanhoe had to become my heavy right hand to make sure things continued to move on schedule and without so many people boggling things on me.

The federal government continued to resist control of a lot of our budgetary needs, but even Congress recognized me as a leader with a big enough vision to finish the job that we had started for better education, housing, employment, working policy and organization of the city budget. We had implemented some great programs that didn't need interruption; they needed more support and longevity.

I was far from ready to give up the fight. I figured if it's in your blood to lead, then it's in your blood to *do it*. There's nothing you can do about it. I still wanted to serve the people, particularly the black businesspeople who had been left out of the political process before I came to office. I wanted to continue to represent and support the gay and lesbian community who supported me, the people who lived in public housing, and the thousands of young people who benefited from our summer jobs, education and recreation programs all around the District. I wanted to govern again for the senior citizens and the folks who had invested a lot of faith in me. Those were the people I wanted to continue to bring hope and opportunity to, and the people who appreciated all that I had done the first term.

So we needed more support for a gladiator. That's how I felt. I felt like a warrior in the ring for the people, and I wanted to continue the fight, and Anita Bonds became my second-term campaign manager and general assistant. She had been director of constituent affairs during my first term, and another talented black woman to whom I had given an opportunity of power in the government.

My second term was all about moving all the programs forward that I had started in my first term—finishing the deal; that had been our theme and what I was coming back to deliver. We had election outreach teams of thirty-five people in each ward to reach out to our constituency and gather information on what they needed the government to improve in their lives. We paid about $50 a week to our workers who were seniors in the community. We had organized a rapid delivery pipeline to remain in control of the city. That's the organization that the pundits never realized.

But now I had to continue to create more outreach. I hired another woman,

Emily Durso, for my new staff of economic development. She had a George-town business background and had worked in business marketing departments. Emily became my transition officer for the major business community, where she built relationships with eighty or more companies to remain in sync with the business world. Emily liked to joke that I used her as my one acceptable white face at the business meetings. She created a likable buffer for the Washington corporate world, which was not used to dealing with such an aggressive and outspoken black mayor.

By that second term, I had earned a reputation of not going along with the status quo, and the business community was increasingly apprehensive about my aggressive governing style. Nevertheless, I couldn't be a successful mayor without working with them, and they couldn't get what they needed without working with me, especially with how much construction and building plans we had for downtown. The business community all wanted a piece of it, and I held the keys to the property. So we would go into these meetings with our staff, and we'd all make a good time out of it, knowing that we needed each other. I wasn't adverse to businesspeople. We needed businesses in downtown Washington. I just wanted them to know that we were going to play it *my* way, and that meant we would demand business contracts to be set aside for the 35 percent who lived and dreamed in Washington without being able to cash in on it. I was there to make sure that we all shared. They all hated it, but we all had to deal with it. We all can't get what we want without compromise.

A lot of times, you would have these large white companies that would complain that they couldn't find any qualified minority firms to do the work. They always complained about a lack of qualifications. There was always this excuse of whether or not someone was qualified for certain jobs.

When I was still a council member, white men would ask me, "Marion Barry, why don't your people lift themselves up by their own bootstraps?"

And I would tell them, "Black people don't have any damn *boots.*"

These white men kept forgetting that somebody has to give you an opportunity to *work* and then pay you for it before you can have any money to do anything with. A whole bunch of people think that the federal government takes care of black folks with welfare programs and food stamps, but they don't. These poor mothers and fathers find just enough work and money to survive, most of the time without help, and I wanted to give them the opportunities they needed to do *more* than simply survive. I wanted black folks to *live* like many white Americans were able to do and for blacks to have the same opportunities as white people. But these white businessmen refused to see the importance of these opportunities.

Luther Hodges, president of the National Bank of Washington, was a friend and an ally who attended many of these meetings with the key financial white men of Washington. He knew how hard it was to get through to them. He was more familiar with white businessmen than me. He could talk their language and ran in their same circles. He was a good ambassador for me to convey my visions to the business community. They just couldn't understand how much the opportunities meant to blacks and other minorities who had been locked out of creating wealth. Some of these men would act as if they befriended me in person, but then talk about me as soon as I left the room. That blatant disrespect and deceit is another ugly part of politics. It happens all the time.

So once I increased my position as the mayor, we were able to hire more people based on the qualifications that were needed at that time. It was all new, and we understood that black people needed that *chance* to see if they could perform the job. You don't always know who's going to be able to do the work when you first hire them. So we hired hundreds of excellent people who had held qualified and capable government jobs for the past twenty and thirty years. It's the same in any business. But when it's black people who hold these jobs, we're always being questioned about our qualifications.

I had to remind a lot of these white businessmen that when they hired a white student right out of college or promoted a white intern, nobody in their company said anything about it. So I already knew where this "unqualified" talk was coming from; it came from the same people who never would have elected me as mayor.

I continued to request that these major white companies find capable black firms to partner with or help to train. That's how we were able to create the learning model that we needed for more African American firms to acquire the experience they needed to compete for new opportunities. Once you did a few jobs and built a name up for yourself and your company, they could no longer call you unqualified. If you never get the opportunity to work your trade, how can you ever master it?

We did the same with black law firms when we entered the Wall Street market. We had black lawyers sign on to underwriting positions as junior counsels which qualified them in the Red Book of known names and law firms for future bond business. And we're talking about lawyers receiving commissions from multimillion-dollar deals!

I made it mandatory that we have black lawyers to integrate our business with Wall Street. We had qualified professionals in Washington who deserved those opportunities. I wouldn't let the city agree to do *anything* without black lawyers being involved. These Wall Street dealings helped to establish the major black firm of Hudson Leftwich & Davenport, which expanded its firm nationally. Dozens of other young black lawyers were then able to follow in their footsteps, gain experience and a name for themselves, while establishing their own firms.

The idea was to start with one qualified black law firm to partner with a white company and to eventually create *twelve*. That's what leadership, courage and big vision is all about. I was tired of hearing the excuse, "We can't find anyone qualified," about anyone. Those days were *over!*

We established the Minority Business Opportunity Center in Washington during my first term where we would list a number of minority companies and what we expected to share from government contracting. We would not allow any major white companies to get around it. It remained a part of our aggressive vision to make sure that we continued to move the city policies forward and not backward. That approach to city business was a totally new concept that created a lot of white resistance. We were asking for 25 to 35 percent mandates to minorities, and these white companies didn't want to give up *any* of it!

With something as basic as trash collection, you had major white companies claiming that black people didn't have the intelligence or the capacity to do the job. And we're not talking about in the *1960s*, we're talking about in the *1980s*. White companies still thought that way about working black people. That's what I was forced to deal with every day as the mayor of Washington. Our government-mandated contracts for certified minority businesses helped to create $185 million as the black share of the pie in the 1980s. It wasn't as if whites didn't get their share. They were still making double and *triple* what black firms made. But some of these white companies wanted *all* of the money! And I was *not* going to allow that to happen; not on *my* watch.

In the private sector, the white business community remained reluctant and was not receptive to hiring black workers inside the District. They hired from the suburbs, where a lot of them lived and socialized, and it was very hard to get them to break their way of thinking. We tried to implement a commuter tax for the people who traveled in and out of the District to work, effectively taking jobs and income away from those who lived in Washington. But raising taxes across the board became extremely difficult. We had to run a lot of government departments and services of state and county; including citywide healthcare, the D.C. Jail, and other local and state functions, even though we were not as large as a state.

When people started moving out to the suburbs, I felt it took a significant amount of income away from the District, and some of the professionals who used to live here and pay taxes. That's why it was so important for me to advocate a commuter tax on the travel back and forth to the District. So we tried to keep certain businesses opportunities here in the District to stop from losing more money to the suburbs. We made certain business permits for companies to remain in the District as well as ensured we let people know that we wanted them to stay here and flourish.

The majority of schoolteachers, after the residency requirement was knocked down, lived in the suburbs but worked in D.C. Most of our teachers are paid better than those in the suburbs.

Now we have a lot more Hispanic kids in the public schools of Washington, and a need for more bilingual teachers. We developed more schools that were specialized for certain trades or different student programs, and we had some students who did very well and other students who didn't. That all happens. Some of these schools do better than the others academically, but we've tried to make sure to keep the schools as safe as possible. However, if a kid decides to bring a gun after school, or around school grounds, we can have more police around the school and inside the buildings to deter them, but you can't stop them if that's what they want to do. As the mayor and the leader of the District, you get the responsibility and the blame for all of those issues, but you have to accept the bad with the good.

We spent a lot of time fighting against folks who were not affected by poverty, unemployment, homelessness, inequality or the citywide deficiencies in education. As the mayor and the leader of the local government, I saw that we could use budgets and more city revenue and resources to try and create more opportunities for those who did not have opportunities, while still managing a major city to do well. That was my job as the mayor, not to be satisfied with the status quo, but to build a much better Washington for everyone.

There were certain buildings that we wanted downtown or around certain areas in Washington that we felt would anchor the neighborhoods that surrounded them. Outside of the Frank D. Reeves Center on Fourteenth and U streets, we used the Hechinger Mall at Benning Road and the H Street Development Corporation, a nonprofit economic organization in the Northeast community, to successfully anchor those areas.

Another anchor for the city was the Convention Center downtown on Eleventh Street. But I knew that the first Convention Center was too small and would be obsolete in five years, so we put it in the public works creation budget to build a much bigger center on Seventh Street. The new Convention Center—years later—became the anchor of the Seventh and Massachusetts Avenue area to keep Washington in competition with other cities for big convention events.

I made it a point that citywide businessmen understood that. It's like building a mall; you always want to have an anchor store that brings most of the people to your location, then they can shop for food, clothing, toys and other items. And if you build a strong enough anchor, you allow yourself the opportunity to create business in more areas that need it.

We also had certain parking areas that were city owned or subsidized by the private sector, but it all added up to more property tax revenue for the city. All business was good business, and it worked hand in hand for all of us.

These neighborhood building anchors also served to bring people back to certain areas to live. After the Martin Luther King riots in 1968, a lot of people had left certain areas of the city, and some of them had moved out of the District, which meant less money for the city. A healthy and populated city meant more money for our budgets, and more budget money meant that we could do more to provide for the people who needed it. It all starts with having the capital and the ability to build. And with all of the new projects we put into the action, the city was definitely booming.

We built a relationship with Frank Raines in the Office of Management and Budget (OMB) to figure out what we needed to do to put ourselves in good credit standings during my first term. The District never had a relationship with Wall Street before, but we made it all happen.

We were treated as a federal agency, so we had to go to the treasury to borrow money. Initially, D.C. didn't have a bond value or ratings because our city budget accounting was so messed up. It took the District two years to establish a solid accounting system, where we could raise our bond ratings and borrow money from Wall Street.

Our bond market included the value of new downtown properties and the pension funds of hundreds of government workers, where we could borrow investor monies to keep the D.C. government operating.

I didn't want to owe the treasury anymore, so we had to learn how to balance our own budget with money in local banks. At the time, we had no credit rating in the District, which you need to have to establish credit. So we started to borrow money temporarily with the consultation advice of Frank Raines, just to establish a credit rating. We anticipated new tax money coming in to repay the loans.

Once Washington became the new hot place of urban development, more people wanted to visit the city. Since we had over fifteen million visitors annually, we had to develop more space for them to live while visiting, and they couldn't all stay in the Georgetown area. On our side of the White House, the East side, we opened business up to the hotel industry, building the Renaissance, the Grand Hyatt, the Marriott, Holiday Inn, and a bunch of other major and minor hotels downtown.

The private sector renovated the National Press Building between Thirteenth and Fourteenth and F streets, with an inside shopping center on the bottom floors. We built a major government office building on Pennsylvania Avenue. I was an influential board member of the Pennsylvania Avenue Development

Corporation, which was responsible for the Ronald Reagan Building. We built office buildings on E Street. We had department stores, bookstores, banks, restaurants, office service centers, and business building plans on Ninth, Tenth, Eleventh, Twelfth, Thirteenth and Fourteenth streets, all downtown. I was no longer talking about big visions; I was *doing it!* Downtown Washington, D.C. was coming alive as the "Nation's Capital"!

I even came up with a new slogan, "DC on the Grow," and we were growing *fast*. We were showing the people around the city, the business community and around the country that we were about serious development. And whenever we had celebrities or important people come into town, I made it my business to meet, greet and entertain them. I was the biggest and best host of the city and was proud to be the mayor.

I enjoyed meeting and greeting popular acts like Stevie Wonder, Patti LaBelle, Chaka Khan, Roberta Flack, Phyllis Hyman, the O'Jays, Donald Byrd and the Blackbyrds, Parliament and many, many more. They were all very inspired to be hosted by a black mayor in Washington.

George Clinton and Parliament called us "Chocolate City," where D.C.'s own Chuck Brown became famous as the "Godfather" of our homegrown, go-go music. There were other local go-go bands I hosted at events around Washington, including the Backyard Band, Junk Yard Band, Experience Unlimited and Sugar Bear, Rare Essence, Northeast Groovers, Trouble Funk and Little Benny and the Masters.

In my second term, we expanded the neighborhood arts academy in each ward and applied for national grants for the performing and visual arts. We understood that all kids were not interested in sports, so we wanted to provide more training in arts and academics, which included employment for professionals in the arts communities around the city and for college arts graduates.

I continued doing great things for the Washington community, but the problem was: I was too much. I don't think anyone expected me to be as creative—a visionary and have the tenacity and the courage to carry out these visions and plans, nor did they expect me to govern the city as strongly as I did. So as the Republicans began to sink their teeth into office with Ronald Reagan, with a Democratic mayor of Washington, I knew that I was in trouble. And it wasn't really from Ronald Reagan himself, because I had a good rapport when I met him in office. My concern was more with the Republican officials, and the U.S. Attorney for the District.

I served as the mayor of Washington, or either on the D.C. City Council, during many presidential terms: Gerald Ford, Richard Nixon, Jimmy Carter, Ronald Reagan, George Bush, Bill Clinton, George H.W. Bush and Barack Obama. And even though Ronald Reagan was a Republican and Jimmy Carter was a Democrat, I actually got along with them both. President Reagan once invited me, along with Vice President-Elect George Bush, businessman John Hechinger, and a host of other prominent businessmen and political leaders, to the F Street Club during his first trip to Washington and before he was sworn in as the president.

Jimmy Carter was a very progressive Democrat from the South, who was a peanut farmer with a great memory. I remember Pamela Harriman, the wife of former New York Governor William Averell Harriman, hosting a meeting for Jimmy Carter long before he had won the Democratic nomination. Among those invited were Polly Shackleton from Ward 3 and other local D.C. Democrats. Jimmy Carter wanted to hear our ideas of how to deal with large urban cities. Two months later, I met him at Chicago's O'Hare Airport and he remembered my name and the meeting.

But it was the Republican law enforcers and the U.S. Attorney for the District of Columbia, Joseph diGenova, who stepped up his efforts to discredit me and indict me. I was quite convinced that the District attorney and his wife, Victoria Toensing, who was in the criminal justice department, began leaking allegations about me to the Washington media that they knew they could never prove in court. And my second term in office was when countless and groundless allegations about my life and my staff began to come up in the media, nearly every week. The war to reclaim Washington for white people had been declared, but I was not giving up without a fight. I had been fighting all of my life for everything, and my position as the mayor of Washington was no different. It was time to put up my dukes and fight again.

CHAPTER 10

SOLVING D.C.'S PROBLEMS

Because of my insistence on minority contracting, African Americans suddenly had at least a 25 percent stake in the construction of all downtown business. With so many new revenue-producing properties, the District had equity for credit loans from private sector investors on Wall Street for the first time. This was all because of my resolve that we build a strong downtown and cut through so much of the red tape designed to stop us. Then the District started being bombarded with character assassination articles about my personal life, so-called "friends of Mayor Barry" business deals, and all kinds of other innuendo. *The Washington Post* even published a cartoon called "Marion Barry and the Marionettes," where they had an illustration of me controlling city council members on strings because we were so closely aligned on issues. Instead of the great business that we were doing, building up the city of Washington, the focus seemed to be on my personal habits, my cabinet's loyalty, and whatever corruption the Washington media could create around my administration.

When you're in office with 40,000 members on your workforce, any department can have some corruption in it, very easily. One thing about holding the highest local government position of mayor, you get held accountable for everything that goes on during your term, whether you have anything to do with every police officer hired, every city service contract, every government employee, agency, or anything else. I can't stop every individual from doing something corrupt, but as the mayor, you're held accountable for the environment that any corruption creates.

My mother always told me, "You don't take something that's not yours." So I had no excuses for the charges that arose during my second term; I understood that it was a part of the job.

I began to tell my cabinet members, "All y'all afraid of *The Washington Post*; y'all go to the other side of the room, because they don't like me." I didn't need or want people who were fearful of the media in my office, and it was obvious that I had a public relations war going on.

Most of the accusations that were held against some of my cabinet members and me by the media were not corroborated, so we implemented an Ethics Strike Force to investigate any wrongdoing among my cabinet. We formed a committee distinguished with trustworthy individuals with integrity to firmly examine any allegations. As it turned out, there were very few incidents of corruption in my administration. And a significant number of government officials who served in my first administration stayed on to serve in my second term.

One of the earliest cases where I was dragged into court for a grand jury investigation was with Karen Johnson in 1984. That was the first battle I had with Republican U.S. Attorney for the District of Columbia, Joseph diGenova. That was also the year I gave the presidential nomination speech for Reverend Jesse Jackson at the DNC in San Francisco.

The government subpoenaed Karen Johnson to a grand jury hearing and she refused to talk about anything. The judge then sentenced her to jail for eighteen months for contempt of court, and she still refused to talk. Through that entire period, I had no contact with her. As it turned out, the prosecutors produced a diary that allegedly belonged to Karen Johnson, who had a vivid imagination. The diary allegedly implicated me in having personal relationships with her and using drugs, none of which was true. That's what their case against me was built on: writings in a book.

To bring the mayor of the city into the courtroom based on writings in a book, first of all, was disrespectful, and made it seem it very likely that white Republican U.S. Attorney for the District of Columbia, Joseph diGenova, was attempting to discredit me and to minimize my victories and efforts in running the D.C. government with anything he could try.

During my first term as mayor, there was an accusation of doing drugs at a strip club after being invited to a Christmas party by Attorney Larry Williams in December 1981. Larry Williams was one of my strongest supporters, and he had called me over to a party at This Is It. It was a club on Fourteenth

Street right up from the old District Building. I called one of my aides, Sam Jordan, to go by and check the place out.

Sam called me back and said, "Everything looks good, Mayor. People are dressed in tuxedos and evening gowns. Come on over."

I took my security and walked across the street to the nightclub. I was then greeted at the door by Larry Williams, Sam Jordan, and the owner of the club, Hassan Mohammadi. I went in and had a drink, greeted people, and stayed for a while.

The next day, there were allegations in the media that I had either used cocaine or witnessed others using it at a strip club. But a police investigation revealed nothing.

I may have been guilty of a bad decision to enter the club that night, but there was no drug use or socializing with women from the club after I had left, as was reported in the media. *The Washington Post* also reported that Metropolitan Police Chief Maurice Turner had allegedly tried to cover up the incident and reprimand the officer who had already filed a report.

First of all, it's a security breach to reveal anything that I do out in the public when you're on duty to protect me. So when Chief Turner questioned the officer about it, he was doing his job to protect the mayor. But *The Washington Post* turned the case into this big scandal that kept coming up to haunt me. The media reports tried to claim that I may have done drugs and solicited several women inside the club, which never happened. There were constant reports in the media, but when they don't like you, they constantly write negative articles.

In reflecting on some of these issues, it makes you a little hesitant to say anything that might not be wholly accurate, because I know that my life in office can still be picked apart with everything that I include in this book. I just want my memory to be as sharp as I can make it when discussing certain things, right on down to my personal decisions off-hours at night.

There were stories, reports and rumors about me being at certain downtown nightclubs, strip clubs or whatever, where things were reported that didn't happen. I would read in the papers that I left the club with two women or did drugs or whatever, but no one would ever tell you that they saw me doing any of these things. However, if you're not careful, I do admit that Washington can be tempting. There's always someone trying to give you something or hang out with you. When you're in a position of power, people are constantly trying to make you feel bigger than what you really are. They attempt to cater to your ego. So the temptations were always there.

The media had created a climate where people wanted to make a big fuss about anything. I would ride around the city and visit certain homes of my supporters as a way of continuing what I had started. I had campaigned that way and had always dropped by homes to get a feel of how people were doing in Washington. It was my way of engaging them in political conversations in their own settings. Not everyone would come down to the public hearings to complain about policies. Sometimes you had to go out to them, and I was used to that. After elections, some politicians you never see. I wasn't that politician. Visiting and talking to people had always been a part of my daily operations as the mayor, so I didn't understand why the media was so concerned about it.

One time there was a report that my security detail cost the city a million dollars a year. I don't remember any other public official having to deal with reports about what it cost the city to protect them. I remember thinking, *whatever it costs, your life is worth it. Protecting your life and family is worth it.* I believe those concerns were only being used against me politically. They were constantly looking for excuses to try and diminish my effectiveness.

All of these stories would come out about everything I did or said in Washington, and if the newspapers and the media repeated it enough, you could begin to believe that it was true. They didn't want to accept that a black man could have a life and be friends with a woman in the community without them having sex. It was borderline racist and sexist. There were always reports about me womanizing and carrying on, but they were all unfounded.

These crazy accusations, news articles and negative spin campaigns directed in my second term led to U.S. Attorney Joseph diGenova getting involved in a witch hunt. He was trying to track down any and everything I did to see if he could find something corrupt or illegal to sock it to the mayor. In fact, when Joseph diGenova was first appointed the U.S. Attorney of the District in 1983 by conservative Republican President Ronald Reagan, as a black Democratic mayor, I knew I was in trouble. The whole climate of the White

House had changed, and we still had to go to the federal government to approve our budgets.

Suddenly, if it wasn't something I did personally that was being reported in the media, they would try to pin accusations and attention on the people around me. Obviously, these kinds of accusations and misrepresentations begin to get to you. It got so bad to where I was always concerned about what was being written about me, and I was always finding out about it late. Often I would begin my mornings reading the newspapers and watching the news to see what was reported about my administration and me. I was looking to read the newspapers before I started my days at the office, but that got me thinking too much about my perception in the media rather than focusing on running the government. I used to get the newspapers at home and read them at night or early the next morning, so I was usually late on what had been reported. I began to expect unfair reporting. So I personally stopped reading the newspaper. I told my public relations director that it was their job to read everything that came out in the newspapers or in the local news about me and then brief me on it, so that I wouldn't be blindsided. They needed to know what was going on in the media at all times.

Every angle of Marion Barry was interesting to the news media. Washington was the place to be, and as far as the media was concerned, I was one of the city's main attractions. Black photographers made a bunch of money covering my life in politics. Black columnists William Raspberry, Courtland Milloy and Juan Williams published hundred of articles about me for *The Washington Post*. It was an explosive time to be in the news, but you had to guard against it creating too many negative perceptions about you.

You have to remember that *The Washington Post* was very powerful. They had helped to take down President Richard Nixon with the Watergate articles in the 1970s. So this activity against me was *serious*. They tried to connect me back to Pride Inc. when Mary Treadwell got into trouble with the funding, but I had not been involved with Pride Inc. for years, and Mary told the investigators that. Mary denied the payment irregularities. These included Clifton Terrace, a 250-unit apartment complex owned by Pride Inc. Mary was convicted and spent time in prison, but there was always something the media tried to tie me to that I had to fight to overcome.

Effi lashed out at the media once, after they reported a story about her mother, Polly Lee Harris, who was arrested in accusations involving a fire where she lived in Prince George's County, Maryland. Effi felt the reports and accusations were politically motivated to slight me. She was furious that her mother was arrested, talked about and humiliated that way. She was not a public figure with an opportunity to defend herself.

That type of personal pressure on the family really made me think about not running for mayor again. It was one thing for the pressure to be on me, but when Effi and her mother were forced to deal with it, I had to really sit down and think about going forward as the mayor. Effi and I made the decision that the position of power would not be easy, and it wasn't meant to be easy. We had signed up for a tough road ahead for both of us, and for our son, Christopher. But we were not going to allow it to discourage the work that was being done for the community.

I have to admit that there were several occasions between Effi and me, where we had to sit down and discuss whether I still wanted to or should continue to serve in office. We never thought about not running again. There may have been conversations about it after the Vista sting, but that's much later down the road. There were a number of accusations, but nothing in my lifestyle backed the investigations. I didn't really live a flamboyant lifestyle where the media could tie a bunch of money or corruption to me. I was more overworked if anything, and I didn't let any of it stop me from what I was doing for the people of the District.

Effi and I were criticized for putting up a fence around the backyard of our house for protection and privacy, even after a disgruntled police officer had broken in. The fence was recommended and paid for by the police department for security reasons. The media tried to pull Effi and me into another issue with a fur coat that I had bought for her. We found that the coat had a rip in it, and I had a government secretary, Rob Robinson, to take the coat back to have it either repaired or replaced. He had it repaired, but he wrote out a government check to do it when I *knew* he wasn't supposed to do that. So I talked to him about it, but the media made it into a big deal as if I couldn't afford to buy my wife a fur coat.

I tried not to show it, but a lot of these *Washington Post* articles were pissing me off. That's when I had to stop reading the articles altogether, because you can get disconnected by thinking more about the press than the issues that you're in office to address.

To protect my cabinet members and staff, I used to tell them all of the time, "When you fight, fight back to back so their divide-and-conquer tactics don't work." I said, "Because I'm not going anywhere!" Back to back means two people standing back to back and either way you turn it, they're together, so it's hard to break them apart.

I didn't want all of the media stories pulling us apart, but we had far too many reports about government administrators and their personal problems with accusations of embezzlement and all of that. I considered it a smoke-screen to continue to deny us the confidence and the people's trust that we needed to be a productive government. I'm not trying to say that we didn't have problems or that anyone was perfect, but we had so many good things we had done, while the newspapers and reporters decided to focus on the few instances. And it was only the start of a continuing effort by the U.S. Attorney to get me out of office. These efforts began after I gave some black contractors legitimate contracts and opportunities to do work in the city.

Then *The Washington Post* dragged Ivanhoe Donaldson into an investigation. They claimed he had a constituency fund set up with payments to his bank account that he paid personal bills with. From what I know, I believe it was for $190,000 of stolen city money in 1985. It was a painful investigation because I had known Ivanhoe all the way back to our early years in SNCC. I had worked with him in the South and in Mississippi. But as the U.S. Attorney Joseph diGenova released reports of government abuse, where Ivanhoe was alleged to have separate accounts, I had to deal with it all. First, I had no knowledge of what was going on. And as close as I was with Ivanhoe, I was surprised that he hadn't discussed anything with me. It was an embarrassing and painful time for both of us.

Ivanhoe was convicted and went to jail. And it was very regrettable what happened to him because he didn't have a history of taking money.

After my friend was no longer in office with me, it was still obvious that I was the man in the hot seat that Joseph diGenova was really after, so the news-papers and networks continued with their reports. All of these stories leaned heavily toward the greed of the white business community and the power structure to be back in control of Washington. So they dragged another friend and ally, Jeff Cohen, into the picture and accused us of improprieties.

Jeff Cohen was one of the largest developers for inner-city projects. He had been very successful before he got involved in government contracts. He was also a good friend of mine, and one of Christopher's three godfathers. He was one of the original organizers of my campaign for mayor, along with Max Berry, Stu Long and Ivanhoe. In politics you always expand your friendships and hope that they are good people. But occasionally something goes wrong.

I didn't feel any particular way against the newspapers or the U.S. Attorney for the District for all of the dirt that they tried to stir up against me. I knew I had to keep the city running to protect the interest of the Washington community. But I was convinced that certain people in power positions wanted me out so they could have *all* of the downtown business and construction without having to share it with black folks and other minorities if I wasn't in office. They were trying to find any way they could to get around having to deal with me and minority contracting, to the point of assuming I had personal relationships with every African American who owned a business.

I had to joke in my private cabinet meetings, "I guess they think black people are all cousins and go to the same churches."

I was from Mississippi and Memphis with no relatives that I knew of in D.C. Although, I did have a lot of ties to the churches and the business community of Washington; that's to be expected as the mayor. A mayor was supposed to make rounds in the city. I participated in parades, celebrations and events in Wards 1, 2 and 3 as well, and knew a lot of the white citizens of the District.

However, certain people in the business community could not get over their resentment of a black man being in control of a $2 billion industry, especially one who wouldn't bend over backward to cater to them. Sometimes you had to be fearless as a leader to make sure you gave everyone a fair chance to make a living. We had cleaned up a lot of the systematic disorganization, organized the budget, handled the deficit and finance problems, and created a much more streamlined government that allowed us to have such a rapid success rate, and now they wanted me out, but I wasn't leaving. We still had work to do, and I wasn't backing out or backing down to anyone. The white business community was less concerned about how much more efficient I had made the local government in my first term; they focused more on the rise of black contract business in the District from 3 percent to 15 percent, 20 percent to 35 percent, and eventually to 47 percent.

In 1986, I proposed a $240 million construction budget to improve the city streets, aging bridges and buildings, and improve conditions at Lorton Prison in Virginia. I wanted to make sure that in the next twenty to fifty years, the city of Washington was not falling apart and that sewer lines would not be breaking all over the city because of poor street conditions. I also wanted to improve the conditions of District housing and the prison system.

With these new city construction needs and minority contracts, I had secured black firms and workers with nearly *half* of a $2 billion a year corporation, while producing seventy-four new buildings all over downtown and through-out the District. Black people were suddenly getting a major piece of the economic pie and some people were *hot* about it, so they started focusing more and more on my personal life.

I believed strongly in having the power to make a difference; that's what the Civil Rights Movement was all about. We hadn't gone to jail and fought all of those years because we liked it; we knew that it was necessary. Nobody likes going to jail and having to struggle and fight for everything. The students and leaders from the Civil Rights era believed in having the political and eco-nomic power to make demands and to *take* what we needed to have to survive. My time in office was all about providing people with their basic human needs, whether it be physical with food, good health, clothing and housing; mental with a quality education, proper leadership and hope for tomorrow; or eco-nomic with employment, jobs and different programs of minority advancement.

Because of the bigger budget in the second term, we had to lay off 200 government employees, mainly in the community service departments and in various management positions, while creating new jobs that we had promised. We were basically making room by creating flexibility for jobs in other aspects of the government. When things happen that are unexpected—and there's always something—the budgets are usually not enough to cover the expenses. Typically, the budget is barely enough to cover program expenses in the first place, so any unforeseen situation forces you to crunch numbers again. Our goals were always presented with instances where we were not in position to completely fill our needs.

I looked at any new positions from A-Z that could be cut to free up more money for programs, including administrative positions that many times were in excess. One time I thought I had found 2,000 job positions that we could cut from proposals presented in Walter Washington's term as mayor, only to find out that the positions were never funded. You can't save any money by cutting positions that never had any money in them to begin with. But I thought I had found something.

Outside of all the negative reporting, in 1984, we had the first wellness and fitness program in the nation for government workers who wanted to remain fit or healthy. So we had physical wellness programs and workouts. We did it to send an example to our youth to stay involved in healthy and active living practices, while using the government workers to set the example.

We also became one of the first major cities to have a government crisis center set up for HIV/AIDS. We had testing programs, where you could get tested in five to ten minutes. The next effort was in compliance. We had medicine coattails that slowed down some of the ailments, and if you could not afford it, the city would pay for it. Our response to the disease was immediate and comprehensive. We even set up an Effi Barry AIDS Initiative.

AIDS programming was one of Effi's passions. The programs enabled thousands to get tested and many to get treatment. AIDS hit the country out of nowhere, but since we were already involved in the gay and lesbian community, we had the contacts and staff to become very proactive in providing information to help fight it. We had always been serious about the rights of gays and lesbians, with antidiscrimination and basic human rights policies.

We also called to get advice from San Francisco Mayor Dianne Feinstein. San Francisco was considered the mecca of the LGBT (Lesbian, Gay, Bisexual and Transgender) organizations. But after a few years of hitting the District, African American women became the fastest-growing community that was inflicted with the AIDS virus in the country.

On the educational side, we introduced a provision to fund and run the University of the District of Columbia (UDC) like a state school. We had the idea to combine three minority schools in the District as one, where we could keep the price down for students to attend. But the budget was too expensive to run it, so the federal government killed the idea and would not help to fund it.

I told people all the time, "Education is the key to eliminating poverty. And if they can't make it, they'll take it."

But education is expensive, and we were trying our best to make it much more affordable for more of the citizens of Washington to attend and learn professional skills at the college level. UDC is one of the few urban land grant universities in America. At one point the university had 8,000 students, and it dropped down to 2,000. I pushed and pulled to get the university back to its original grand glory, but the city could no longer afford what UDC needed in the budget.

However, in my second term—not that I was perfect in the first, because no one is ever perfect—I started to make more personal decisions that may not have been the right thing to do for me politically. Without ever addressing my drinking as a problem, I would drink a lot of alcohol at these parties and events.

Effi noticed that early on in our relationship and she would always warn me about it. "Don't let them give you too many drinks tonight."

I would go to many events and pick up a casual drink. I didn't realize it, but it would be one event after another, where I would be offered complimentary spirits. That's what you did at a lot of these events; you would drink and socialize and drink some more. I think in a lot of ways I was still a quiet man from the South, but I would force myself to step up and to meet with the people I had to meet with. I had that battle going on all the time between the private Marion Barry and the political Marion Barry. The personal Marion Barry was quiet and soft-spoken, but the public Marion Barry was known for being the fire-breathing hell-raiser. I always had those two sides of me. So I would use these social events as opportunities to reach out and get across to the people what was needed or what we planned to do.

Effi knew that drinks were passed around like water at most of these events. She had been there with me. As the mayor, I was invited to more events than I could count. At each one, you could pick up three or four drinks, *easy*, before the night was over. My favorite was Hennessy or Cognac and Coke. And if you weren't careful, you could get used to it. It was all a part of the socializing.

As a result, I developed a drinking problem that it took me years to deal with. I would be invited to events all over the city, where the drinks would be free. They would either give me drinks or someone would buy me one and then another without me even thinking about it. Effi would always tell me that I drank too much at these functions. But you continue to go to them because it's the nature of politics.

Washington will suck you up if you're not ready for it. I had moved into a lot of different circles in my first ten years in Washington, and I was still moving. I amazed myself with how far I had risen and how I was able to stay on track with it all. Sometimes, I would stand around at a party with a drink in my hand, while everyone was buzzing around me, and I would think, *Damn! I did all of this shit? How did I do it?* But I didn't have time to be *too* proud or introspective. I had to keep doing what I was doing, and what had gotten me there.

The problem was, my personal side wanted to enjoy some of it, and I always had this curiosity about what more could be done. How many more people could you talk to? How many more things could you learn about your community and what's out there? That curiosity was what would get me into trouble when you start making bad personal decisions that affect your political career. So I found myself having a hard time getting to sleep at night. I was the consummate night owl, and never a morning person. But at night, that's when a lot of the wrong people can invite you out to the wrong things and get you involved with the underbelly of the community; folks who wanted to be around you and impress you.

"Hey, Mayor Barry, you want to come to this party?"

That's how it always started. People always wanted me to be somewhere. *Everybody!* And I was never one to turn down a good party or gathering. I thought all the way back to my graduate school years at Kansas, where there were no parties. Now I was the mayor of the nation's capital and there was a party every night.

There were always rumors in the media and around the District offices about me being involved with different women in the government, but Effi wasn't bothered by any of that. Since I had hired so many women to my cabinet and to high department positions, the D.C. government had become woman-friendly. But that didn't mean that I was sleeping with them. That was your typical view of sex and chauvinism that was a part of city politics. But I continued to hire women in prominent government positions in my second term, with some of them who climbed up the ladder, including Carolyn Thompson, Maudine Cooper, Alexis Roberson and Carolyn Smith, who became the first woman to head the department of financial revenue.

However, I do think some women tend to gossip and talk more about what's going on in people's personal lives. Men didn't talk about their personal lives as much. It's not something that men typically do.

My second term was naturally more challenging than the first. The budget kept getting bigger and much harder to balance, and the commitment to get the work done was not the same. I no longer had Elijah Rodgers and I later lost Ivanhoe. I had to work even harder to get the effort we needed from the staff and the different departments. There was this never-ending feeling that we needed to tighten things up. Our responsibilities kept growing: the city's healthcare, property taxes, licensing, transportation, hospital needs, housing and the homeless, city recreation, educational budgets, the private sector; it all never stopped. And I'm not complaining, I'm explaining. That's the world of responsibilities I had stepped into as the mayor.

The second term also forced us to deal with the rise of the drug epidemic and rampant prostitution. In the 1980s, white Americans were openly using powder cocaine, mostly in the privacy of their homes or in the restrooms of their private parties. But the people in the inner cities and the streets started using crack, which was a much more addictive and deadly form. You were also convicted much more harshly for using it. White folks would get a slap on the wrist for using powder cocaine, but the federal government started giving people five to ten years of jail time for using crack, and it was disproportionately black people.

The unemployment rate, mixed with inflation and the rising cost of living in the 1980s, made the poor people of Washington ripe for the drug and prostitution rings. It became a very lucrative business for people who figured they couldn't make a living any other way. As I said before, there's only three ways in which you get money: you can inherit it, you can make it, or you can take it. And there were too many people taking it. That caused more people to demand more police involvement.

Everybody wanted more police patrolling the street; 3,000 or more, with twenty difference police agencies involved. It was a big hit to the city budget to hire so many new police to try and curb what was going on, but we had no choice. By the mid-1980s, crack had exploded everywhere, and not just in D.C. The federal, state, county and local governments and police forces all had their hands full all around the country. So if the feds couldn't stop the drugs from coming in, how could we?

We had problems with police corruption and the internal affairs office. When we were forced to hire so many new people, we didn't have sufficient time to do all of the background checks. From 1982 to1986, we were on the job to do the best we could to stop the drug trafficking. I viewed hiring more police as the last resort, and it didn't seem to work. When you have more police working inside of offices instead of out on the streets, it's not going to change anything. We even had issues with emergency 9-1-1 calls. The dispatchers were not contacting the police squad cars fast enough. And overall, we were ill-prepared to handle the onslaught of drug trafficking that was yet to come.

N o one was prepared for the drug culture and the violence that took over the streets in the mid-1980s with crack cocaine; it simply took over. And it was not only happening in Washington; it was all over America: New York, Florida, California, Philadelphia, Chicago, Detroit. The police weren't prepared for it and the federal government wasn't ready for it, either. There was no amount of money that we could toss on it with more police to make it go away. You try to cut money in one area to make more available for something else, and you find that it still isn't enough to make that much of a difference.

The culture of unemployment and the increasing cost of living made the time ripe for a lot of young men who fell right into the fast money that they were making out in the streets. That was the quandary I was in. You could never stop people from wanting to take or sell drugs unless you had enough jobs or treatment for them. That was undeniable! Once they started making thousands of dollars selling drugs out on the streets, a lot of the kids didn't want my jobs anymore. You were not going to make thousands of dollars a day in the mayor's summer youth jobs program.

I continued to think about more ways to help people to find employment while creating more opportunities for them in Washington. I felt the improvement of the people's lives was the most important thing and the only way to make a difference. But the violence of the drug years was so brutal that it took precedence over everything. We started having more murders in one year than we had in *ten* years. We had over two hundred murders in 1983 and the numbers continued to escalate.

That was Police Chief Maurice "Big Mo" Turner's solution: "Let's lock 'em all up." Police chiefs all over the country were struggling. Mo Turner, whom I appointed in my first term, had been on the force for many years. In the beginning of his career patrolling, he couldn't arrest white folks. He could only detain them. He worked his way through the ranks from officer to sergeant. He was one of the few blacks who could pass the test at the time, until he finally made the rank of captain, where the mayor could appoint him to any position above captain. He finally made it to assistant chief. He was a police-man's policeman. He was D.C.'s second black police chief.

Mo Turner was in the same dilemma other police chiefs were in—locking up drug dealers and drug users. That was Mo's recommendation to me. He called it Operation Clean Sweep. There were over 12,000 people arrested over the years fighting the drug wars. In hindsight, this was not the solution. If police arrested twenty in one night, there were twenty more to take their place. Then there were the federal crack versus powder cocaine laws.

It was the beginning of a really tough and agonizing situation in D.C. and in the neighborhood communities. These young people were the *children* of the community. They weren't somebody else's kids; they were *our* kids. And they were more prevalent in the lower-income communities. Like I said, if they couldn't inherit it or make money, then they were prepared to *take it* by any means they could.

We tried to organize a "Police and Citizens Together" campaign to fight the epidemic, but that didn't stop it, either. The citizens were scared to death of the violence prevalent among young people.

I said, "These are young children. How are you going to be afraid of your own children?"

But we were dealing with a lot of young people who hadn't grown up with their fathers in the house, with overworked mothers, a lack of discipline and very little respect for school, their elders or each other. They were growing up in environments where it was kill or be killed, eat or go hungry. Some of these kids didn't care about anybody, even their mommas. That's the kind of children we were dealing with. So the issue was not going to be solved easily. I still try to help and speak for lower-income mothers to this day, who continue to pray to find a helping hand to raise their sons and daughters. It's a long inner-city epidemic that came to an ugly head once you had so much money involved on the streets.

In the Southeast, the drug boys were in charge of whole neighborhoods. They had lookouts on the rooftops of the buildings, and it was like we were in a real war zone. Powder cocaine, crack, marijuana; it all took us by surprise with the volume of it. In the past, you would always have somebody selling something, but not young people and whole neighborhoods selling at all times of the day and night. Then drug boys started killing each other over the turf, and who wanted to make more money in whatever area.

We had this one area called Hanover Place, Northwest, where it was a 24-7 drug market, and the young guys were ten deep. You lock ten of them up and there would be ten more there the next day. They had fire power too, so we had cops who were worried about getting killed over there. D.C. police were doing a bunch of overtime and starting to ask for days off. It was a bad era in Washington, but we didn't know what to do about it. We were constantly trying to find solutions. We had never seen anything like this, where ten- and twenty-dollar rocks of crack cocaine caused so much chaos in the community.

The federal government finally arrested Cornell Jones, one of the master-minds that it said was behind Hanover Place, but that didn't stop anything. It only slowed it up. They would arrest one big dealer and slow down one drug market only to have to deal with another big dealer in another hot area.

Hanover Place was one of the worst areas, but there were other bad drug turfs all over the city, where they sold drugs and had drug wars over territory and money. These young guys were fearless about their turfs, creating life-or-death situations for the police. No matter what we did, these young guys kept finding ways to continue their drug markets all throughout the mid-1980s and into the early 1990s.

There were drugs on Connecticut Avenue, too, but it was powder cocaine that whites were selling to other whites.

We even had the first "D.C. Drug Summit" to try and discuss the epidemic and come up with answers. But the epidemic of drugs was obviously economic. Some of these young dealers were making thousands of dollars and they were spending it in *cash*. You would hear stories about these young guys buying cars, gold jewelry, clothes and treating their friends to expensive wine at the different nightclubs around the District. It was big business and no one was complaining about the money that was being spent, even in the Georgetown area. Or they would drive out to the malls in Maryland and spend lots of cash.

A lot of these young guys became very popular on the streets, like Rayful Edmond, who rose to be one of the most powerful young dealers in the city, and on the East Coast, according to the federal government. I first met Rayful at the basketball leagues in Southwest. He was a young, likable guy, good-looking, with a good personality, and a lot of his friends he played basketball with had no idea that he was involved in drug selling. He was basically pulled into it from his family. That doesn't make it right, but Rayful had a lot of people who liked him and were very loyal to him.

Once Cornell Jones was off the streets and in jail, according to the federal government indictment, Rayful Edmond took over most of the D.C. market, and he was still in his early twenties. According to the federal government, he had young guys all over the city, who would live and die for him. During those years, he had "mules," or what the federal government called dope carriers, who made enough money in a week to buy extravagant clothes, shoes, jogging suits and cars. Back then, they liked the Mercedes, the Nissan sports cars, Bronco jeeps, Jaguars, or anything that stood out. But once the police started locking so many of them up for being so easy to spot, they started driving more "hoopties," or older, beat-up cars to go unnoticed.

A lot of new laws were implemented with mandatory minimum sentences for crack cocaine as a means of trying to punish and curve this new epidemic. The federal government passed laws where possession of twenty-eight grams of crack cocaine got you a five-year mandatory minimum sentence for a first offense, but it took five-hundred grams of powder cocaine to get you that same five years. With black people selling and using crack cocaine and whites selling and using powder cocaine, there was a disparaging treatment of the offenders. There was nothing that I could do about it. A lot of these guys were making the wrong choices, and young black men were getting killed and locked up in jail from coast to coast.

Rayful Edmond was finally arrested and convicted by the federal government in 1989. It took the government years to find anything to pin on him, but, according to the indictment, they finally succeeded through a series of wiretapping with informants who helped to put Rayful away with several people from his ring. Then they said he figured out how to run his organization from jail. But once he was sentenced to a long jail term, the streets of D.C. became even more violent. It was a "one man down, next man up" mentality.

We started breaking new murder records every year. That's when the news reports around the country started calling us "The Murder Capital." The city of New Orleans had the most murders per population the years before that. There were a lot of young black people caught up in the struggle of trying to figure out life, while dealing with unemployment, stress and the effects of racism.

Police Chief Maurice Turner was forced to initiate an "Operation Clean Sweep" that arrested thousands of people for different drug-related charges and violence. And once the D.C. Jail was overflowed with arrests, we had to send the prisoners down to our state prison in Lorton, Virginia.

Every big, urban city was experiencing the same thing, but in Washington, with the federal government being here, it was more of a white-collar city than a blue-collar city. So the stakes were much higher in Washington than they were in a blue-collar city like Baltimore, and we got a lot more news about it here. *The Washington Post* and other media reported drug and gun violence almost every other day.

Once the prison population began to overcrowd in Lorton, we were all facing some desperate times, including the prisoners, who continued to complain about their conditions. That's how some states ended up getting more budget money to build larger prisons instead of public schools. But these young guys, with all of their violence and drug selling, and after all of these arrests, the concept didn't make much of a difference.

Then we had the HIV and AIDS problem with a huge infection rate inside the prison system. We set up some voluntary and involuntary testing of the inmates, but it was very expensive to deal with. Then we started to have problems with infant mortality again, with low-weight babies from crack-addicted mothers. So we had to continue to implement educational health programming for medical advice, transmittable diseases, protection options, proper nutrition, medical care and all of the things that are needed to birth and raise a healthy baby.

Throughout the crime and drug waves, AIDS, infant mortality, the rise of inflation, the lack of available jobs, the budget issues and everything else we had to fight through, the majority of the people of Washington continued to support me as the mayor of the city. Despite the government's witch hunts against me and my administration, I continued to do an outstanding job against so many difficult odds. And I won a third election in 1986, gaining 61 percent of the general vote against a white Republican, Carol Schwartz, who won 33 percent.

Carol Schwartz was a white moderate Republican who had served several years on the board of education. Some people were not sure if she could really govern with a sense of fairness. Other people viewed her as a great person and she had a significant amount of support in Washington. However, I had *more* support.

We knew that a lot of the white business class would probably vote for Carol to replace me, but I had always looked to increase the progress of business in the District and I never lost sight of a strong business community. Nevertheless, there were still some white residents who felt that I hadn't done enough for them. They continued to want more in their favor and to rebuff our citywide programs. The District could not be all about them. But you still had a large segment of white companies who were very angry about the minority contracts that shifted 3 percent of black business to 47 percent by my third term. That was unprecedented for black businesses anywhere. So people continued to complain of kickbacks, "Friends of Barry" and all of that nonsense.

We had over one hundred volunteers for our third-term campaign for mayor, and we really felt unstoppable. But the public demands were getting higher with each new election. Everyone was asking for something: jobs, educational needs, new homes, a way out of poverty, building contracts, *everything*. The work never stopped for progress. So I hired Maudine Cooper as the new chief of staff along with the leadership experience of Carolyn Thompson as the city administrator.

Maudine Cooper was formerly from the National Urban League, and I had previously appointed her as the head of the D.C. Office of Human Rights. She was a no-nonsense manager, and I liked her because she took care of business. Carolyn Thompson, a native Washingtonian, had worked her way up through the ranks. One of my first tasks for Carolyn Thompson was putting together all of the permits into the Department of Consumer and Regulatory Affairs and she did a great job of heading the department.

While I fought the doubters and naysayers, we had a large number of my constituency from the black middle class, who profited from my leadership, which increased the black middle class. Some, for personal reasons, moved out to the Maryland and Virginia suburbs. The economic and political climate grew hectic in the District, and the suburbs of Maryland and Virginia served as calmer and more spacious surroundings. Meanwhile, the media and the U.S. Attorney continued going after everyone around me, including Alphonse Hill, who was one of my young, smart city managers.

Al Hill was indicted by a grand jury on charges of extortion, fraud and income tax evasion. He was very good with numbers and he got caught up. I didn't know anything else about it. People make decisions based on their own access to opportunities and they may not always be the right decisions. I couldn't account for everything Alphonse Hill did on the job or during his free time. But I was sorry to see him go. He paid his debt to society, and now he's teaching at Howard University. He's a great example of how people can make mistakes and still become successful.

There was always something unexpected that you had to prepare for as the mayor. I remember that January of my third term in office in 1987, I was invited out to San Diego, California for the Super Bowl to see the Denver Broncos against the Redskins. I was invited by Jack Kent Cooke, then owner of the Redskins. Doug Williams, one of the few black quarterbacks in the league, threw his first touchdown from the snap. He went on to throw four more. Tom Downs was the D.C. transportation chief at the time, and we ended up having an unpredictable snowstorm that same Sunday night of the Super Bowl. Tom was caught in the middle of it and everything in the District was shut down overnight. I mean, it snowed like hell, and Tom was overwhelmed. I tried to hustle to get back to Washington, but there were no flights available because of the snowstorm cancellations. The people of the city were clamoring for me to return.

When I finally arrived, it was a couple of days later and the D.C. government workers had plowed the snow all up in front of Pennsylvania Avenue, like a big white mountain. It was crazy. We had never dealt with that much snow, and we didn't know what to do with it. So I held a press conference where I said, "We are not a snow town."

I was only being honest about it, but the response to my comments made some critics have a fit, mostly because I was out of town when it happened.

There was no way of me to know we would have a snowstorm like that. Not even weather forecasts had predicted that much snow. So I apologized and we ended up having the federal government help us to dump the snow into the Potomac River. That first month with a snowstorm was a forecast of the many challenges that I would have to overcome during my third term.

Our successes had been good over the first two terms. However, there were still people who needed more help, so we had to continue working with the federal government to hammer out all of our budgetary needs to assist more people in Washington. As the jobs and employment rate continued to rise, we continued to meet these challenges day in and day out to provide a bunch of folks with opportunities to make a living.

We had to continue pushing extra hard to provide employment for a hungry workforce. I created opportunities where people who wanted to work and were able to work could work. I still wanted to make sure that the elderly could get their health program benefits, but we didn't have enough money to do everything. We had city functions, county, state and a bunch of government officials to account for. So it was a constant juggling act to fit everything in, or as much as possible.

In the middle of all these other city issues and drug territory wars out in the streets of D.C., we fought to continue budgeting for progressive programs. The local funding for job training increased dramatically with government jobs for adults and youth. We also had programs and legislation to reestablish returning citizens from the correctional facilities and to reinvolve them in society. We had far too many unemployable men who needed to be useful when they returned to the District. That would have helped our economy, helped the families of the young men, and also reduced the drugs and crime rate. We all know that unemployed men are more prone to get involved in illegal and criminal activities. What else would you expect them to do if they can't find jobs?

Because of many growing needs, we faced a number of budget challenges. The unemployment rates continued to increase, hundreds of impoverished citizens were losing housing, and drug addiction was on the rise. Warren Graves, who served the District and continues to serve the District as the chief of staff to City Administrator Allen Lew, was the chief of staff, and Mitch Snyder was a homeless advocate at the time. The homeless explosion happened suddenly. I proposed to the federal government to start a program called "The Coalition for the Homeless" to house and feed the homeless for free. The Community Partnership for the Prevention of Homelessness was run by Sue Marshall, and is one of the most progressive programs in the country because of my leadership. So we had homeless people from not only Washington, but people who showed up from the surrounding areas of Maryland and Virginia.

Everything happened all at once! A number of homeless people flooded the downtown area, where the hotel management had to deal with paying customers who didn't want to be around the homeless staying in the same hotel rooms that they were still *paying* for. The District government paid for rooms and breakfast, lunch, and dinner for the homeless. We even took over a few of the hotels for the D.C. Department of Human Services to run them, but it became too overwhelming. There were homeless families with babies, pregnant women, drug addicts, some who were mentally disturbed, and we didn't have enough staff or expertise to deal with it all.

On top of the financial challenges and the homeless, we began to have a high level of prostitution downtown. With everything else that was going on, prostitution enforcement wasn't as high on the priority list for us to stop it. Every city had its prostitution areas to deal with. But the level of it increased in downtown Washington because of the desperation of everything else at that time. There was so much to deal with on a daily basis in government management and in serving the people of Washington that I failed to realize how it all began to affect my personal life. The good part was that no matter how overwhelming the issues were, I knew that I could overcome them. But the bad part was that when you're in office so long, your personal decisions as a man can begin to affect your political and public life while in office.

Because I was an active mayor, I would work twelve to fourteen hours per day, and this kind of schedule would wear anyone down. Some mornings I would go into the office late in the morning, but we still had a government to run with rapid turnaround on some of the issues.

I make no excuses about my third term in office, but that's when my bad personal decisions really started to compromise my political career. Over time, you get caught up in the moment of everything.

CHAPTER 12
UNWISE DECISIONS

Being mayor of a big city like Washington, it's difficult to have a private life.

There were a lot of people in Washington for me to get involved with, and sometimes they had bad intentions. A lot of folks offered me things for free, invited me to a lot of different places, and wanted to be around me. I could have easily turned a lot of these invitations down because politically, it would not have been wise. Since I attended evening affairs, Effi and I had an understanding. She would go to bed early, and if I came in too late, I agreed not to wake her. So, as a result, I would spend a lot of time in the lower-level family room when I arrived back at home late.

She would often say, "Don't wake me up when you come here late." She'd wake the next morning and make breakfast for Christopher and me.

A friend of mine had a renovated house on Eleventh Street, where my friends would have parties and get-togethers. I had been around drugs in the 1980s. Sure, I had. There would be parties and get-togethers where you'd be at a private location and you'd see people going into the bathrooms and coming out sniffing and all of that. However, despite the stories people told about me, I had never gotten involved with any of that until later on in my career. I was more of a social drinker.

On this one night, I ended up with a group of three women and four guys at the place on Eleventh Street, where I became separated from the rest of group with this one woman. The rest had left, while this one woman stayed behind with me. I don't remember asking her to stay or anything; she ended up being there alone with me. Maybe she asked them to leave; I don't know.

So I was left with this pretty woman and occasionally she went into the bathroom. I knew what she was doing; it was the 1980s and I had been in places where people were using powder cocaine recreationally. But I had never touched it.

Well, after about her third trip to the bathroom, this woman came out and said, "That's some good shit." She asked me, "You want some? This makes my pussy hot."

That's exactly what she said to me. And I was *shocked*.

Of course, I had been around pretty women with sex appeal before, but not women who had been so vocal about it. There were plenty of women who wanted to be around me as the mayor of Washington. The attraction of power was one of the many perks of the job, but most women had been more tactful, so it wouldn't go any further than flirting. Attracting women was never my reason for wanting to lead, but it was a trap that any man in power can get caught up in. And this woman had me in a compromised position.

At first I hesitated. I had never done anything like that before. But this woman's comment excited me. I was used to being around respectful women who would never say anything so bluntly—at least not to my face. Women could say anything when you're not in front of them. So I was curious. If cocaine made this woman feel that hot, I wondered how it would make *me* feel.

I had already been drinking that night so my judgment was not as sharp, especially with a pretty young woman in front of me. So I told myself, *What the hell? Why not?*

I said, "Yeah, I'll do it." But I didn't know how. So when she put the powder on a business card and I raised it up to my nose, I exhaled instead of inhaled and blew all of the powder off the card.

She got mad and said, "What the hell are you doing?"

People take their cocaine supply seriously. But I didn't know anything about it, because I had never used it. But she had more of it, so she gave me a business card to practice with. She didn't want me to waste any more of it. She fixed the card right and put some more powder on it, and I snorted it up one nostril and then the other. That was my first time ever trying cocaine, and it felt like I had ejaculated. The cocaine was a powerful stimulant that went straight to my penis. I could see what this young woman was talking about.

What happened next? I had sex with her. She would have never done that out in front of me if she didn't want to tempt me, and I would have never agreed to take cocaine with her if I didn't want to try it for sex. It was my bad judgment, and I blame no one but myself. It was a mix of power, attraction, alcohol, sex, and drugs.

From that point on, you chase that same high and sex that you felt the first time. But I never considered myself addicted to anything or having problems with substance abuse. Cocaine use was a part of the times in the '80s, and it didn't matter whether you were black or white, rich or poor, or whether you lived in the city or out in the suburbs. Cocaine use touched all of us, and if not you personally, then a friend, a loved one or a family member.

It was around that same time in the late 1980s when I first met Hazel Diane "Rasheeda" Moore. Most people called her Rasheeda, but some of her family members still called her Hazel. We met in the fall of 1987.

Her mother, Mary Moore, was a member of the Nineteenth Street Baptist Church and was the choir director. She wanted me to meet her daughter and see if I could talk to her about the ideas and talents Rasheeda had to teach young schoolchildren around the District. For whatever reason, her mother continued to call me down at my office about meeting up with her daughter, so I finally agreed to give Rasheeda an appointment. Our meeting was mainly because of her mother's persistence.

When Rasheeda showed up at my office for the appointment, she was a tall, very attractive and articulate woman in her early thirties. She had been a model in New York with several *Essence* magazine covers under her belt, and I really liked to talk to her. She had a lot of life and spirit about her, but she also had five kids from a marriage to a guy from overseas. Because of Rasheeda's previous issues, I guess her mother was trying hard to get me to do something with her to give her a new life opportunity. It seemed like everyone was getting caught up into something or another involving drugs in those days.

I didn't know everything about Rasheeda at the time; I was just meeting her. But she had picked up a drug habit that probably started during her modeling career in New York. I don't know why, but models were known for taking drugs. I guess that was a part of the lifestyle. And I can't be certain, but I'm assuming that her mother most likely knew about it. She may not have known the *extent* that her daughter was involved in drugs, but I'm sure she knew Rasheeda had a problem.

Rasheeda had gotten mixed up with a lot of the wrong things and the wrong kind of people up in New York. She didn't tell me everything, but she told me enough to know that she needed a fresh start back in Washington. Who knows all that she could have been through while modeling up in New York? I didn't. But when I first met her, it was out of genuine appreciation for what she could offer the District schoolchildren through our arts programs at the recreational centers.

Rasheeda had a lot of experience in fashion, design, marketing, etiquette and modeling that she wanted to teach some of the impoverished girls in the District. She wanted to teach them how to walk, talk and carry themselves to be successful. She was a very convincing woman who knew how to charm people, so she tried to talk me into it, but I told her to come up with a proposal. I couldn't do anything with her ideas without a proposal, and I told her that. So she finally wrote out a proposal, and it was *fabulous!*

At that point, we had a strictly business relationship. I gave her a few numbers to call to look into providing grants and funding for a children's program to teach young people the concepts involving fashion, etiquette, acting and modeling. We ended up putting her program under the summer youth and recreational center budgets, and she had a grant to run the program. So I stopped by a few times to see how she was doing with it. She was set up in a classroom at Fletcher-Johnson Middle School in Northeast.

She had these children designing evening dresses and clothes out of paper bags and plastic trash bags. I had never seen anything like that. If you could make clothes out of trash bags, you could make clothes out of *anything*. She was teaching them how to walk and interview and how to carry themselves. They were doing presentations, acting, modeling and they were learning how to do their own makeup. It was a great program.

Needless to say, I was very proud of Rasheeda. She had put her plans into action and the children in the program loved her. We were thinking about expanding the program and I was glad that I had given her the opportunity. That's when I started inviting her out to lunch to talk.

I was really fascinated by Rasheeda's conversations. With her modeling experiences and creative ideas, she always had a lot to talk about. She was very sharp, well dressed and she knew how to carry herself out in public. So I got used to being around her. It was really comfortable.

Rasheeda was very aware that I was a married man with a family, and she was very respectful of that and my obligations and commitment to Effi. Effi was extremely popular around Washington and everyone knew about her. Rasheeda and I even talked about that, how to keep black families together and teach them tact and good social habits. It wasn't like we became involved right off the bat. We were friends. And we would mostly meet at evening events and social affairs around Washington. She sometimes knew where I was going to be and she would show up there to lend her support as a professional and a friend. A few times, Effi would be there, but there was no reason for her to be alarmed or to suspect anything between us. Effi wasn't like that anyway.

Eventually, Rasheeda and I grew so fond of each other that our relationship naturally evolved into something more. I started thinking about us having more than just a business friendship, and I'm sure she felt the same. By the fall of that year, we had both reached that point.

So I called her up one night to meet up and see me on more of a personal level, and she said okay. I remember we decided to meet at the Channel Inn at the waterfront in the Southwest area. My friend's Southwest condo was nearby.

We met up and had a few drinks at the bar and we both knew that we would hook up later. We had already evolved to that point, so Rasheeda agreed to follow me to the condo in her car. That night was inevitable. We arrived at the condo and had a very good time that night. No drugs were involved, just the alcohol from earlier.

I can't remember how we started using drugs, but we evolved. I became very conflicted about the drug use. You get comfortable enough with a person where you're willing to try more things socially and sexually. That's what happened between Rasheeda and me; we became very comfortable. But I was very conflicted about the drug use. I didn't want to do that anymore, but Rasheeda did. I had no idea how strong her craving was, so I started to worry about her.

At the time, I still didn't view myself as having a drug problem. I had only done it on and off on occasion, and I didn't want to do it anymore. I found that Rasheeda wanted to do it most of the time, and that's when I first decided to pull back from her. I still had a city to run and a family to look after. I couldn't be walking around taking drugs.

By that January and February of 1989, I started to really get worried about her drug use. I had talked to Rasheeda's mother and had a conference with them. We all agreed and arranged for Rasheeda to go to a rehabilitation and counseling center to do what she needed to do to get herself right. I couldn't be around her anymore with all of the drugs that she was doing.

Rasheeda had a big family, too, with two sisters and two brothers, nieces and nephews. I think she was one of the younger kids, and her mother was glad that I had taken on the effort to work with her and to help her. But Rasheeda was very crafty about fooling us and not getting herself the help that we all thought she was getting from the counseling. I started to ask her how things were going with the rehabilitation and she would say, "This is just what I needed. This is great!"

I was somewhat suspicious of that because she sounded a little too happy. You don't get that happy about going to rehab. Rehab is generally hard for people to accept. So I called up the program organizers and they said that she had never even been there. She had been bullshitting us all for *months*. I arranged for her to go to a rehabilitation center. We had another conference call on the Monday evening after she entered rehabilitation.

The next time I saw Rasheeda, she started talking about how great the program was and how much it had helped her.

I said, "Stop it, Rasheeda! Stop the bullshit, *right now!* I called the program counselor and she said she hadn't even *seen* you."

This woman had the gift of gab and she would try and con you if you let her. I had to let her know that I wasn't going for it. After that, I didn't see her for a while, and she called me for about fourteen or fifteen days *straight* to get me to respond to her. But she never tried to contact me on my personal phones or during my family time. She called mostly during my office hours. This was around April 1989. I found it was a waste of my time trying to help her, so I stopped seeing her.

When I finally answered her phone calls and began to talk to her again, she kept telling me how badly she valued her relationship with me and that she never wanted to do anything to jeopardize it. Looking back on it, I should have seen a lot of the obvious signs of a challenging relationship with her.

One time I arranged for her to have a birthday party for one of her kids at the L'Enfant Plaza Hotel, and she ran up a tab to $1,500 on what she called "just having fun." I was thinking more in the lines of two or three hundred dollars or so. Otherwise, I would have never made the arrangement for her. Everything was that extreme with her.

Since Rasheeda had been a model, she was still a dynamite dresser who would always look her best at events, whether she took drugs or not. She was also well-behaved out in public, but people had no idea what kind of demons she was battling behind closed doors. However, it all came to an end at an AIDS awareness fundraiser featuring Dionne Warwick that summer. She called and told my secretaries that it was a matter of life and death that she needed to talk to me. It wasn't life or death. She wanted tickets to the Dionne Warwick show. I told her I'd think about it. I eventually decided to get her the tickets. The show was on June 11, 1989. Rasheeda was decked out appropriately as always. She socialized with the people and had a good time there. Then she wanted to join me for an after-party event, which I reluctantly allowed her to do. I had a big executive suite at the Grand Hyatt hotel that night. After everyone left, she asked to use the bathroom to freshen up before she left, while I waited out in the room for her. It took her fifteen to twenty minutes.

After a while, I got curious and knocked on the door. I still didn't trust her drug habit.

I said, "Rasheeda, are you doing drugs in there?"

I could smell that she was smoking something. I knew the smell of the powder. I also knew how people would go into the bathrooms and do their drugs. So when she started stalling and wouldn't answer me, I told her that if she didn't open it, I would kick it in. She opened the bathroom door and I caught her with a crack pipe.

I said, "What the hell?" The bathroom was filled with smoke. I looked around to find out where the pipe was, and I found it behind the commode. I wrapped the glass crack pipe in a bathroom towel and smashed it up so I wouldn't cut my hands with it.

Rasheeda grabbed onto my arm while I broke it. She started screaming, "Don't do that! Don't do that! Don't do that!"

She was freaking out over me taking her drugs away and breaking her crack pipe.

I did it anyway and told her, "Pack up your shit and go." I was *pissed*. Rasheeda had promised she wouldn't bring any drugs. Then I checked her purse and found that she had five more crack rocks. So I took them and went to flush them down the toilet.

Rasheeda had never tried to do that out at a public event with me before.

We had only done drugs privately and in private settings. But I would never go out to an event like that on drugs, and I wouldn't allow *her* to do it. People were expecting me to show up that night and be the mayor of Washington. Dionne Warwick was there with a bunch of other influential people. Dealing with drugs was the last thing on my mind!

The next thing I knew, Rasheeda started to wrestle me to get her drugs back.

"Give me my *shit*, man! Give it back to me!"

It was like Diana Ross in *Lady Sings the Blues*. I wasn't a violent person. I had never hit a woman in my life, but I had to smack Rasheeda upside her head and push her down to get her off of me.

She screamed, "Why you take my *shit*? Why you take my shit from me?" But I had already flushed it down the toilet. I was *not* fooling around with her that night. This was a major event that she was trying to *fuck up!*

So I told her, "Rasheeda, you gots to go now!"

Then she ran out in the hallway and started yelling up and down the halls, "Marion Barry! Marion Barry! Marion Barry!"

I ran out there and grabbed her back inside the room.

"Bitch! Are you *crazy?*"

She wanted her drugs that badly. She was ready to make a big scene right there in the hotel.

I said, "I'm getting out of here." I had intended on staying at the hotel that night. But I didn't want to be seen with her acting like that on drugs. So she stayed while I left. That was the last time I even *spoke* to her.

I didn't talk to Rasheeda again after that for *months*, but she kept calling me and trying to apologize. She was harassing me and trying to get back in with me, but I didn't want to hear it anymore. She would always try and use her charm. That's what desperate people do on drugs. So every day she called me for about a month, leaving messages with business associates that she was trying to reach me. She was very careful with how she approached things, while making sure to respect my position. She knew that I was still the mayor, and she respected that, but that didn't stop her from acting out on drugs. So I was *through* with her! I didn't see her again until January 18, 1990.

CHAPTER 13
THE VISTA HOTEL

I don't want my life and legacy to be all about what happened to me at the Vista Hotel. That's why it was so important to write this book. I want people to know all of the details of my life and the battles that I've won for so many thousands of poor, underrepresented and left-out black folks in America. My life is much more than that one embarrassing event on January 18, 1990. But that's all that some people know about me, and that's what they judge me on.

People who are not from D.C. are always asking the question, "Why would they keep voting for this man for mayor?" Their attitudes are based solely on what happened to me at the Vista, and other negative, untrue stories in the press. What they don't understand is that the hard-working residents of Washington already knew that it was all a set-up. Washingtonians already knew what the government was trying to do to me because they lived in the District. What appealed more to them were the jobs that I provided for them and their children, their husbands and the care for their grandmothers. The people of Washington cared more about the houses that we helped so many families to move into. They cared about the government jobs, construction and security contracts, trash collection services and all of the other major opportunities that we provided for so many African American professionals and women.

Black lawyers, judges, middle managers, political activists and thousands of working class all benefited from the opportunities that we opened up, including dozens of executive positions that were rarely offered to blacks or women. I was the first mayor who had the courage to make sure that it all happened. If you were qualified, then you deserved the opportunity not only to apply, but to actually *get* the job.

We also gave hundreds of young, minority student leaders their first opportunities to go to college. That's what people outside of Washington don't understand. They don't know the work that I've done. It was never about what I did for myself, or *to* myself; it's always been about what I've been able to do for the *people*.

Washingtonians never allowed the federal government or the FBI to determine what my legacy would mean to them. So when they got a chance to vote for me as mayor again in November 1995, they voted for the Marion Barry, Jr. who had come to Washington, an optimistic and charismatic fighter from the South, who did all he could do and as *much* as he could do to benefit the majority of the people. I wanted to give Washington a much better today and tomorrow than what they had yesterday. I wrote this book to inform the people who don't know my whole story. Now you'll have a chance to know what really happened.

After the hotel episode with Rasheeda Moore at the Grand Hyatt, I didn't bother to talk to her again. Once she finally stopped calling me, people who knew her from our inner circles started telling me they saw her in California. We had a few people we both knew in common. But at the time, I didn't care. That hotel scene was the end of my relationship with her.

With Rasheeda out in California, she eventually got arrested for a traffic violation in December 1989. At the time, she had a bench warrant for not attending a grand jury hearing back in D.C., and the FBI agents told her they would put her in jail if she didn't cooperate in a case that they were trying to build against me. She had been subpoenaed for a hearing back in D.C. earlier that year, but maybe she had missed it because she was out in California. But when she got arrested in California, the FBI was able to pull up her records and find her to bring her back to the District. I had not been talking to her during this period and knew nothing about it until the trial.

I didn't know if she was out in California when the court system sent out a warrant for her arrest in D.C. or not, but they couldn't send her away for that. She just didn't know her rights. So she panicked and agreed to go along with their plans to set me up. That was the only way for the government to try to bring me down. They couldn't find anything corrupt on me, because I had never taken a dime. So they became desperate to attack me for my personal life instead.

In the months before the sting, I was preparing to campaign for a fourth run at mayor. With all that was going on with the city government and with me personally, I didn't know how to give up. There was still a lot more work to do. There were still too many people out of work—too many who needed affordable housing, people who needed additional jobs—black businesses needed more opportunities. Downtown neighborhoods needed a lot more attention and development. All I had known how to do in my life was how to *fight*, so that's what I was prepared to do. I would fight through all of my adversities and accusations, and continue to fight hard for the people. I was going into my final year of the third term, while the FBI was busy trying to build a case against me. My personal, political and family life were all suffering from the stress of my life in service. I didn't confide in a lot of friends at that time. I kept pushing forward, even as the FBI began to look through my bank statements, telephone records, credit card bills and anything they could find to try and nail me with something. Before anything went down, someone at the bank told me about the FBI's subpoena of my records, but they couldn't find anything. So I knew that something out of the ordinary was going to happen. Sometimes, you can feel it in the air. You feel like somebody's watching you with evil intentions.

Effi told me, "You need to watch yourself out there with the wrong people, Marion. The snakes are around."

She told me that all of the time. But she never rubbed it in my face when I was wrong. Effi was above that. If she ever thought about or suspected that I was involved with other women, she never told me about it. She never even asked me. Not that she was naïve; she had a lot of faith.

The FBI had no cut cards. I remember noticing a Hertz rental truck that was always around me or in front of me, but I didn't pay much attention to it at the time. There's a whole lot of different things going on in a busy day. Sometimes it would be nine or ten o'clock at night when this truck was around, but I never panicked and questioned it. You don't see the significance of things like that until it's too late, unless you're already looking out for it, and I had no reason to do that. I later found out that the FBI and some under-cover D.C. police were both involved in staking me out.

So they brought Rasheeda back to D.C. to set me up. They put her up in the Vista Hotel, placed the cameras in the room, supplied the drugs and told her what to say. They even babysat her kids. Then she called my office several times on the afternoon of January 18, 1990. On the final call before I responded to her, she said it was a matter of life and death. That was the only way to get me to answer her phone calls, because I hadn't talked to her in *months* and I didn't want to.

I was skeptical about anything Rasheeda had to say to me. So I asked her, "Rasheeda, what is it? What's up?"

She said, "I gotta talk to you! I gotta talk to you!"

I said, "Okay. What do you need?"

"I really would like to see you to talk about it in person. I'm staying at the Vista Hotel."

It was around five-thirty or so when I finally answered her call with my office hours winding down. I told her I had a meeting after work that day. We had a housing raffle at the Carnegie Library around six-thirty, seven o'clock.

Rasheeda said, "Well, why don't you come to see me afterward so I can tell you about this situation."

I didn't think it would kill me to talk to her. So I went to the housing raffle at the Carnegie Library and made it back over to the Vista Hotel to see what Rasheeda was talking about. I arrived at the Vista around eight o'clock and called her from the phone in the lobby. I had my security detail with me, and I was not planning on going up to her room.

Rasheeda answered the phone and said, "Come on up."

I said, "Rasheeda, I'm not coming upstairs. You can talk to me right here in the lobby."

I had not seen her in a while and I had not talked to her, so I was not interested in being that social with her. I was only there to see what she needed in this so-called "life-and-death situation," so I was already skeptical. The last time I saw this woman she had acted out on drugs.

She said, "I just ordered a bowl of soup, but once I finish that, we can come back downstairs. Now come on up."

I didn't have any premonitions of what was going to happen that night. All I knew was that I wasn't going to go upstairs. I should have stayed in the lobby and let her eat her bowl of soup and come down when she was ready, and none of this story would have happened.

Against my better judgment, I said, "Okay." So I took my security with me on the elevators to the seventh floor and went up to room 727 to knock on the door. I wanted my security with me in case something crazy was going on. I still didn't trust her.

Once Rasheeda came to answer it, she opened the door and said, "Come on in."

I don't remember her wearing any particular clothes or anything that looked different from what I had seen her in before, so I told my security to go back downstairs. As far as I could tell, everything looked normal.

I said, "I'm not gonna be too long."

But as soon as I walked into the room and Rasheeda closed the door, I saw she had a dresser filled with bottles of drinks, glasses and ice, including Hennessy and Coca-Cola. I didn't think about it at the time, but everything was set up just right to get me to drop my guard. I didn't even think about looking for her soup. I looked over to the dresser at her set-up instead.

Then I walked over and said, "Let me have a drink."

I went to take off my jacket, and I don't remember if I put it up in the closet, over a chair or on the bed. I only remember taking it off to get comfortable.

I got a glass to pour a drink of Hennessy and Coca-Cola, I put the ice in it, and I sat on the bed beside Rasheeda with the drink in my hand. At that point, I don't remember asking her what her problem was. She obviously wanted to get me in the room for intimacy, or at least that's how I thought about it. I started thinking sexually while sipping my drink. But every time I reached to caress her breasts, she pulled away from me.

Then she said, "Let's do something." That was Rasheeda's code word for drug talk. "Let's do something." But I wasn't planning on taking any drugs. That was more of Rasheeda's problem. I wasn't into drugs like she was. I was only interested in the sex.

I said, "What are you talking about? I don't do that anymore."

I didn't have any drugs on me and I wasn't thinking about it. So we went back and forth over it, but we didn't have any drugs anyway. I didn't think about whether Rasheeda denying me sex was normal or not. That didn't really run through my mind. I only knew that I was more interested in sex and she was more interested in setting me up.

At some point, Rasheeda told me she had a girlfriend who had some. So she called up her friend, and this woman stopped by the room in a matter of *minutes* with the supply of drugs.

Again, I wasn't thinking about all of the details at the time. In retrospect, a girlfriend popping up in the hallway of the hotel out of nowhere, with a supply of drugs, was definitely suspect. She was in and out and only there to make a fast delivery. She was obviously working with the FBI and the sting, but I just wasn't thinking.

Rasheeda took the drugs over to the dresser, and I noticed that it was more than powder cocaine. It looked like *crack* with a glass stem! I had learned what crack looked like and its devastating effects while fighting the crack epidemic in the city.

I said, "I'm not doing that." I had never smoked crack cocaine in my *life*, with *anybody!* But Rasheeda had. I saw how irrational the crack pipe had made her act the last time I was with her at the Grand Hyatt. I knew how addictive it was, and I had heard nothing but terrible stories about it. It was a hard street drug that thousands of people were strung out over.

So we went back and forth again. I had no interest in the drugs, but I figured Rasheeda would have some good sex with me if I agreed to do it with her. Drugs and sex went hand in hand with Rasheeda. I held up the glass stem and said, "I don't even know how to use this thing." I told her, *"You* do it." I wanted to see her use the stuff first to make sure it was all right. I was still skeptical and wanted to make sure nothing funny was going on.

Rasheeda said, "No, you do it first."

I was foolish enough to start thinking about how good the sex would be. Since I had never gotten addicted to powder cocaine—or at least I didn't think I had—I figured the crack would be a one-time thing that I would move on from. I didn't consider myself a drug addict in any shape or form. It was only a means to an end that night.

I went into the bathroom and started practicing how to use this glass stem with no drugs in it. I had never done it before and I didn't want to look foolish like I did when I first tried powder cocaine. So I practiced.

When I came back out with the stem, Rasheeda put the drugs on top of it and had a lighter to light with it. I didn't have any of that.

I asked her one more time, "You try it first," but she refused to.

She said, "Why don't you do it?"

We went back and forth again until I decided to try it. As soon as I began to inhale it, the FBI broke in the door.

Rasheeda started screaming, hollering and acting surprised.

"AHHHH! AHHHH!"

She ran around the room like a cheap horror movie.

The FBI told me, "You're under arrest," or something like that. I can't remember their exact words. I was just *pissed* at the whole thing. I never even wanted to go up to her room.

They ran Rasheeda out of there and sat me down on the bed with no handcuffs. They had a paramedic there with them instead. He was prepared for me with emergency equipment.

In no case in history had a drug sting ever allowed a person to actually *consume* the drugs. Usually, they would break in and arrest you *before* you did it. So I was thinking that they were really trying to *kill me*. That's why they had the paramedic there with them to cover their tracks. Why would they bring a paramedic with them unless they *expected* me to have an overdose and die?

Whatever they had put into the drugs gave me a strong rush with my heart pounding. And the paramedic was right there to try and calm me back down. That's when I sat there and screamed out the words that became infamous, "The bitch set me up!"

I was stunned and didn't know what else to do. The paramedic gave me an EKG right there on the spot. Then they read me my rights.

I can't remember the exact order of everything; you would have to look at the tapes. I think they're on YouTube now. They definitely won't show you everything that happened or what was said that night before they busted into the room and caught me with the pipe in my mouth. Needless to say, I was beyond embarrassment.

Then they handcuffed me and took me out of the room to the service elevator. They wanted to take me out of the back of the hotel instead of taking me through the front doors. They took me straight to the FBI headquarters at

Ninth and Pennsylvania Avenue, the same downtown building that was there when I first arrived in Washington in 1965. That's ironic, ain't it?

I called my lawyer, Herbert O. Reid, from the FBI building to come get me out. I don't remember anything that was said between us on the ride back home. I was pretty much numb. I just wanted to get back home to talk to Effi and see my son, Christopher. That's all I could think about was how much pain it would cause them. That was the only thing on my mind.

I called Effi up and heard crying over the phone. She had heard about the sting on the news already, and she was worried to death that she couldn't get in touch with me. She was more concerned about where I was mentally and spiritually, and how I was taking it, than anything else. She was also concerned about Christopher. We could only imagine what people would say to him at school with all of the media attention about his father. So Effi called Carlise Davenport, who was the owner of Tots Developmental Center that Christopher attended when he was younger. She was a friend of the family who came right over to the house to get Christopher that night and take him to her house to get him away from the media storm that she knew was coming.

By the time I got home to Effi, the sting was all over the national news and media people were already outside the front of my house. So I went inside the back door as usual.

As soon as I got inside, Effi embraced me and kissed me, feeling more empathy for what she knew I was going through. She wanted to respond to my need to affirm the human spirit more than anything. When you have challenges like that, you need to have someone who can get around all of the accusations and blame to get to what's needed at that particular time.

Effi asked me, "Marion, are you okay? This is gonna be all right."

I held her there and asked myself, *How could I have been so stupid?* I knew that they were out to get me, and I walked right into it.

Obviously, the FBI had been preparing to send this Vista Hotel tape everywhere. How else could you explain how so many media people had gotten a hold of it so fast? It was all over the news before I had even arrived home that night. The FBI tipped off several local newspeople about what had happened.

After everything settled down, Effi asked me, "Who was she?"

I had to explain my relationship with Rasheeda and how it had started. But

Effi remained fiercely protective of our family, our marriage and of our house-hold. She had never seen me do any drugs because I never brought it around her and Christopher. I knew how much she and I both believed in family. But I had committed *tremendously* bad decisions with my drinking, and Effi was aware of that.

I explained to Effi that I was not in love with Rasheeda and she was not in love with me. It was a relationship of access more than anything. We were around each in a way where we both satisfied a need. She wanted someone she could talk to who believed in her and whom she respected, and I enjoyed Rasheeda's company, her conversations and occasional sex. She may have fantasized about something more than that, but I didn't.

Effi spoke about it all in an interview later on that year, where she said she didn't want to kick a dog while he was down. That was her way of explaining to the media and the public why she didn't leave me. Effi was willing to move forward and forgive me without further indignation.

Now that I look back on it all, Effi was a *blessing* to be so strong and sup-portive, even in my darkest hour. I don't know how many women would have been able to do that. That's what made her so incredibly special. She was so giving, poised and understanding. She always led by example and knew the right things to say. She kept her poise through it all, even in the heat of the night.

But I couldn't sleep much after that. The ideas rolled around in my head of how I had allowed the Vista sting to happen to me. I kept asking myself what I could have done to make better decisions that night. There were so many elements of that night that I could have said *no* to, starting with Rasheeda's invitation to the hotel. I could have forced her to tell me over the phone or nothing.

With the Vista Hotel sting occurring on a Thursday night, Effi kept Chris-topher out of school that Friday. As expected, that next morning, the story was all over the news. And people were selling T-shirts from vendors all over the city. *"Goddamn bitch set me up!"*

I have no idea how they were able to print those shirts so fast. It was like someone had tipped them off and they had their machines ready overnight. I knew a guy who printed up 500 shirts the same night of the sting. I should have printed them up myself. I would have made a ton of money. The next thing I knew, these T-shirts were all over the country. This sting was unprecedented in history for a public official.

The first night I had at home after the Vista, I had not left my house all day. My friend, Dick Gregory, the Civil Rights activist and health expert, heard about the Vista sting on the news like *millions* of other people. That tape was shown all around the world. The U.S. government sent the tape to all of the presidents, ambassadors and U.S. embassies. Dick Gregory was always hanging out in D.C., and one of his daughters went to Howard, so he stopped by and made some kind of a concoction of liquids to pour in the bathtub for me. He told me to relax in the tub and cleanse the alcohol and whatever else Rasheeda had given me at the Vista out of my body.

"You sit in here for a few hours, you'll be all right."

I sat in that tub with whatever he put in that water and felt sick as a dog, and was still thinking about drinking. Dick Gregory had a lot of faith in me and was confident that I would pull through. But my son, Christopher, didn't feel the same way.

Christopher was around nine at the time. And I remember trying to pour myself another drink in the basement family room, when my son ran over to snatch the bottle from my hand.

He said, "You drink too much!"

I hadn't really been paying attention to whether Christopher had noticed it or not. Sometimes you forget what kids are able to take in because they're so young. But it was obvious that my son understood what was going on. We hadn't really sheltered Christopher away from anything. He was right in the middle of a lot of events and things that were going on around him, and you took for granted what he may have been thinking or what he was able to understand.

Christopher was in the fourth grade at the time of the sting. He was a student at St. Albans School, and his experience there was a disaster. St. Albans was a school where a lot of the kids of federal government officials and wealthy white businessmen attended, and Christopher was right up in the middle of it.

They had no black instructors at his grade level there, and it was not a great place to send a black student in need of nurturing and culture. The neighborhood school where we lived in Ward 7 was Anne Beers Elementary, but Effi was reluctant to send our son there. As the son of the mayor of Washington, Christopher had a privileged life and had been around wealthy and powerful people ever since he was born. Once he was old enough to talk about his feelings as a child, he told me he felt like a *Cosby* kid during my early years as the mayor, but he said that some things changed after the Vista.

Christopher had been a part of the Washington middle class for all of his early life, even if he didn't want to be. He was a part of the black middle class and had to deal with racism and kids telling him what their parents said about the mayor. It got him into a lot of fights at school and frustrations at home. He was always around celebrities and special events and was protected by security detail like Effi and me. Christopher found it very difficult some days to deal with his position in life. So that night at the Vista didn't just affect Effi and me; it greatly impacted the life of our son. I knew that before I ever arrived at home that night. Everything you do can affect your children.

The U.S. government sent the video everywhere, to every embassy and every country to make an example of me. It was definitely race-related. They wouldn't have done that to a white mayor. And the people who saw it on the news, they didn't see it as the government or an FBI set-up; they only saw it as me in a hotel room with a woman to do drugs.

I felt miserable and frightened of what people were thinking about me with the substance abuse. I had to hold my head up high out in public, but I couldn't sleep. I was up tossing and turning and asking myself, "How did I get myself into this? What could I have done differently?"

The smartest thing would have been for me never to have gone to the hotel to meet Rasheeda in the first place.

What made it so bad was that the media members were already being fed information on the sting before and after it happened. I found out during the preliminary court hearings that the FBI told the reporters, photographers and media people exactly where they had Rasheeda staying so they could get pictures and report everything while it happened. They knew that she had been flown back to Washington, and they knew that her kids were being babysat by government officials, while they forced her to do their bidding.

They had Rasheeda set up like some kind of guinea pig. As I found out more about it, I felt sorry for her. But I didn't want to go to jail for her, so I was prepared to do what I always did: *fight it.*

In the fallout of the Vista Hotel, a number of people came out and asked for my resignation from office. Sharon Pratt Kelly led the charge, with BET owner Bob Johnson. Bob Johnson should have been ashamed. When he came before the council's Economic Development Committee, chaired by Wilhelmina Rolark, he only had six hours of programming. The cable award was about to go to Percy Sutton, but a good friend of mine convinced Ms. Rolark to let Bob Johnson get the franchise. He was a programmer and not an operator. He had to hook up with a company called TCI, a national operator, out of Denver to establish District Cablevision and build its infrastructure. In less than two years, Bob had grown BET into a 24-7 cable station with millions of viewers. The newspapers and media were quick to get their opinions. I actually helped Sharon Pratt Kelly as her campaign manager to become a national committee woman from the District for the Democratic National Committee before she ran for mayor. And prior to the Vista sting, Bob Johnson had helped to raise $100,000 as the finance chair for my fourth run for mayor. And everyone knew it.

So a lot of people felt it was wrong of both Sharon and Bob to come out so strongly against me after having such close ties. I had advised Sharon and helped in her political career. My minority contracts and business programs had helped open the doors and the climate of opportunity that allowed people such as Bob Johnson to build his cable television empire, including the land to build his first studio from the ground up in Northeast D.C., off of New York Avenue. I was very upset with them. Everyone had their opinions about me, but I still had a city to run, so I didn't pay Bob or Sharon any mind. All of my thoughts were on the city's management. With all these opinions, it didn't stop me from effectively running the city.

However, when Sharon Pratt Dixon ran for the mayor's office later that year, she started a slogan saying, "Clean house with a shovel, not a broom," while holding up a broom. I didn't like that. I felt it was a bit over the top and insulting, particularly after all of the positive things that I had done with the D.C. government, and all of the hard work of the D.C. government employees who worked for me.

Some of my supporters were very upset about the whole thing. They knew how bad the government had been out to get me. But I told them we needed to focus on continuing to do our jobs. I told them, "Us bickering and getting too distracted by this is what they would want us to do.".

As the mayor, I had no time to wallow around in the mud; official documents still needed to be signed. City contracts still needed to be executed. And all of the normal duties of the mayor's office needed to be carried out. The city government didn't stop because of me. So I had to delegate to the cabinet members who were prepared to take over.

I asked Maudine Cooper and Carolyn Thompson to run the city operations with Maudine Cooper as the chief of staff and Carol Thompson as the city administrator, along with the various department heads and assistants who all accepted their responsibilities. The city was still in business no matter what, and I had no problem with two women running it, because I had been around capable women my entire life: in my household, in SNCC, the Civil Rights Movement, the formation of Pride Inc., and during my early years in Washington politics.

I had hired the right people, who were able to handle the job because they were all prepared. It was very special to have African Americans in positions of power who were able to get done what was needed, particularly in positions with money and a city budget. That's why it was so important to appoint deputy mayors to share the responsibility and understanding of government policy. Some people devalued how hard it was to run a city from the bottom up, because we did it so well, but the next mayor in office would find out.

In the meantime, I had to deal with going to court and facing up to things in my personal life. I had a great run of years as the mayor with much more ups than I had downs, but at that time, I wanted to be by myself and clear my head with no one around me. Dick Gregory and others were there to support me, along with Effi, Cora Masters, my attorney R. Kenneth Mundy, and a lot of other political allies, close friends and family. And the national media was all over the place. We had reporters, television cameras and network and cable stations that I had not seen or heard of. They were taking pictures, recording footage, asking questions and getting in the way of the courtroom during the preliminary hearings. But it would be months before we started the actual trial.

My attorney, R. Kenneth Mundy, told me that I needed to get treatment immediately before the trial proceedings. I didn't really feel that I needed to, but he insisted. I was still in denial about my drinking and drug challenges.

He said, "You need to go to treatment before the trial."

He felt that that we would alienate ourselves from the sympathy of the courtroom if I didn't at least make an effort to get help. The people would want to see that I was taking action to work on my issues.

He said, "You have to realize that everybody is dealing with *something*. They can all relate to self-improvement." But I still didn't like the stigma of confessing that I needed help.

At first, I thought about the Betty Ford Center for drug and alcohol treatment. But that may have been too public of a place. I felt I needed to get away from all of the media attention and people trying to report on everything. We found a treatment facility in West Palm Beach, Florida that was close to Cora Masters' oldest brother, Thomas Masters. He was a pastor who lived and preached in nearby Riviera Beach, a nearly all-black town adjacent to West Palm Beach.

For me to even get to this rehab center in Florida for treatment, my security team had to arrange for me to dodge the media. Jim Vance, a local television news anchor, did one of the best interviews and really humanized the issue. It was on that Friday, where he showed the home with the aroma of greens and dinner being cooked with family all around. He didn't sensationalize it. He helped to keep the media people away from coming to my house. They were following me around everywhere at that time. So the plan was to go to Florida for treatment and get away from D.C. on a Monday morning.

I arrived down at this drug and alcohol treatment center in Florida with Effi and Cora and met up with Pastor Masters.

The first time I participated in a group session there, they had addicts from all over the country, but I still didn't consider myself to have a problem. They all announced their names and what they were struggling with.

"Hi, my name is…and I'm a grateful, recovering alcoholic or drug addict…"

Well, when the introductions got around to me, I couldn't say anything because I still didn't consider myself an addict. We then watched film of different cases and all the effects of addictions, but I wasn't ready to admit that I had a problem. I thought those who had addictions had no kind of profession or place in life. I told the counselors there that I knew about addictions from reading about them, but that I was not an addict.

The counselor told me that most addicts had a hard time admitting to it. I told him I used drugs and alcohol more as a recreation, but by the night of the Vista Hotel, my judgment was clearly poor. I knew I was drinking too much at receptions and parties, but I didn't realize how much it had gotten to be my normal routine, even at home.

As a special privilege, the counselor of the center in Florida allowed Effi to stay there with me overnight. We all had dormitories with televisions and privacy, but I continued to be scared about opening up. I didn't want these people thinking a certain way about me, and I didn't know any of them. I didn't even want a lot of people around me. I needed more one-on-one counseling.

This rehab center was really peaceful and away from everything and had Southern home cooking. They had several dormitories all on one floor with several patients in a room. When you first arrived there, they put you in a room with four people, and over time, they would move you to a dorm with two people. They had meeting rooms, a cafeteria and the facility could hold up to fifty patients. But this place was no grassy resort with beach water and swimming pools; it was still a treatment facility to get yourself right.

Most addicts—when they know they're about to go into treatment—try to binge and get as much as they can before going cold turkey. I didn't do any of that. While I was there, I learned that an addiction to heroin is physiological and affects your body, where a cocaine addiction is more psychological and affects your mind. But most people can't afford a quality treatment facility. It takes a lot to care for, house, feed and treat addicts for weeks or months at a time.

Cora's brother, Thomas Masters, gave me some tapes that helped me a lot. They were recorded sermons where he preached about the Prodigal Son who had hit rock bottom before coming back into the favor of the Lord. I could really relate to those stories. They picked up my spirit and allowed me to accept what I needed to do in rehab. Thomas Masters provided a bridge for me to feel comfortable down there in Florida.

When the doctor there sat down with me and saw the physical impact that using drugs and alcohol had on my body, he asked me how I got involved in it and what I planned to do about it. I was very determined not to let the other patients see me sweat, so I gave the doctors a lot of grief by not opening up. I started off by telling him about my drinking problems in another group session.

I thought I was beginning to open up to the group, but after the first two or three days, the doctor asked me, "How come you didn't just say it? 'I'm an *addict*,' because you *are*."

I said, "I didn't think I was." And I didn't.

It took me about three days to admit that I could possibly be addicted to cocaine and alcohol—especially alcohol. It was really a tough thing for me to do. You think that you're invincible sometimes because you *have* to think that way as a leader and as a public official. I had an entire city to run with thousands of people counting on me, so I trained myself to fight through all of my own personal issues and keep going instead of getting any help.

I remember Jesse Jackson tried to come down to visit me in Florida as a pastor, but there was a mix-up, where Thomas Masters was already on the list and the facility wouldn't let Jesse in to see me. Most people still didn't know where I was.

Carolyn Thompson and Maudine Cooper came down to visit me and to report on the government affairs in Washington, and they did a good job of not telling anyone. We spoke on the phone every other day. I had total confidence in both of them to do what was needed to run the city. And I was very proud of them.

I ended up in this Florida rehab facility for twenty-eight days, and I still didn't want to be there. I had to go through a twelve-step fellowship program of breaking your addiction. But they can't really keep you there if you don't want to be there. It's not mandatory like prison. And you can't go to appease other people; you have to be comfortable with yourself.

I found out that a whopping 80 percent of patients in rehab would go into relapse and end up back in treatment after coming out. I then went to a South Carolina facility for fifteen more days and a total of forty-five days away from the D.C. offices. But I needed to do it. I had to clear my head from all of my government duties and get myself right.

Some people were hoping that my cabinet would all fall apart in Washington, but it didn't happen. My cabinet cared deeply about the city and the functions of the D.C. government, and all worked together and continued to ask, "What can we do for the city and the mayor?" Nobody resigned. Nobody gave up. Nobody left. My answer was always to do their *jobs*. That's what I would have done as a leader; you continue to work through the adversity. There were still hundreds of decisions that needed to be made from the office of the mayor that they had to focus on. I wanted to lead and serve the community of Washington myself, but I was forced to admit that it was more important at that time to get my life together. I had to let it go and have faith.

I attended this new treatment facility in South Carolina that was used for soldiers. They had a transition program there that was co-ed with mostly whites and mostly women. But there was no way I was getting involved with them. That was the last thing I needed was a rumor of getting involved with people in treatment. I was there for a purpose.

When I finished the program in South Carolina, my security team came down and arranged for me to travel by train on the sleeper car, where no one would recognize me on the way back up to D.C. Nobody knew that I was back. I had to stay low and was very careful about the media people being all over me again. When I arrived in D.C. on my first night, Effi cooked a big meal and was very loving. She was still the perfect wife and mother and the First Lady of D.C. Effi never missed a beat. She was always supportive of the struggle and the big vision. And instead of alcohol, we drank apple cider.

Effi told me, "Don't worry, Marion. This too shall pass."

I remember my mother used to say, "Every ball of twine has an end to it."

On my return from rehab, I went to Alcoholics Anonymous and was tired of alcohol and drugs. I went to AA sessions two times a week at the Simplicity program at Thirteenth and East Capitol streets, as a part of my transition.

I had kicked the habit of smoking cigarettes in Jamaica way back in the 1970s. Now it was time for me to kick the habit of alcohol and drug use in the early 1990s.

Before my trial, I became so conscious of how the media could create a story with imagery, that I made sure I was never photographed or it was ever assumed that I had a drink in my hand. I would also tell the reporters what I was drinking, whether it was water, juice, soda or even Kool-Aid. I didn't want anyone to assume anything.

Ironically, CBS-WUSA-Channel 9 news anchorman Bruce Johnson told me years later that a lot of the media professionals were going through the same issues that I was going through with drinks, drugs, alcohol and women.

He said, "Shit, Marion, we had our own struggles and addictions to deal with. That's what made your case so strong and hypocritical for a lot of us."

Bruce Johnson had always been a straightforward guy, off the record. I trusted his political insight and opinions. But he said that at the end of the day, the reporters all had to do their jobs, whether they liked what was going on or not. They could all see that the Vista Hotel sting was entrapment, but they weren't the ones in political office who had to deal with their personal lives being opened up to the world. And Bruce was right; there's a lot of vulnerability involved in being a public official. Your personal life is followed and scrutinized like no one else's, except for maybe popular entertainers and athletes.

All of the FBI and police preparations for the Vista Hotel sting were yet to come in the trial. But it's not like they were going to let me know that they were trailing me. Sometimes, the FBI will track someone for *years* to find something on them. In my case, they had teamed up with the local police to build whatever case they could against me. There was another report that the DEA was pulling together its own sting against me before the FBI stopped them. They wanted my case for themselves. These federal agents had been following me for two or three years. And it took them that long to pull together something desperate enough to stick me with, while spending millions of dollars to do it.

A lot of Americans had drinking and drug problems. That's why we had so many problems with drugs and violence in America as a whole. That's why we had laws against it. The drug culture would not have been such a big problem if no one got addicted. It was like the Prohibition Era of alcohol in the 1920s and '30s all over again. And it wasn't only inner-city black people and the dark alleyways where there was drug abuse. It was the white middle class, the upper class, the entertainment industry and a *lot* of different people.

I want to emphasize cocaine is not grown in the U.S. It's brought here and a lot of folks believe that the federal government is complicit in this.

But America still liked to chase the "lock-'em-all-up" stories, where the trials were full of young black men, standing defenselessly in front of an old white judge. Those are the most common images that we see in American courtrooms, and I was getting ready to become another one.

CHAPTER 14
THE LONG TRIAL

I was a public official and defendant standing trial in federal court on fourteen charges, including eleven for cocaine possession and three for perjury. The trial lasted for eight weeks. All the cocaine possession charges were misdemeanors. Because you've been charged doesn't mean that the information is true.

After my arraignment, the first thing we had to do was choose the jury. The prosecution could remove six prospective jurors and my defense team could remove ten. The prosecution team for the District included Judith Retchin and Richard W. Roberts, my defending attorney was R. Kenneth Mundy, and the District Judge was Thomas Penfield Jackson. Cora Masters called him a red-faced white man and I couldn't argue with her. The judge looked like he was angry from the moment the trial began and as soon as he walked into the courtroom. In my opinion, the judge had already concluded that I was guilty. The late Kenneth Mundy, who was black and one of the most brilliant defense attorneys in the country, was on my defense team. I had known him over the years, but I didn't have a need for him to defend me until then. Sometimes you save the best for when you really need them. And after the Vista Hotel sting, I *definitely* needed him!

In the jury selection process, the members of the jury were identified by numbers that the prosecution and the defense would call out to remove. Of course, the lawyers on both sides went back and forth over whom to keep or whom to remove on the case. But after being elected mayor for three terms, a lot of the jurors already knew me. I thought the case would be a hung jury immediately.

We eventually settled on the twelve jury members; nine women and three men, and all of the women were black. All three of the men on the jury were white and five of the women were seniors, who all became my strongest supporters during the case. I later learned that they were my strongest supporters in the jury room.

Without my knowledge or approval, at one point, my longtime friend, Reverend Jesse Jackson, called for a plea bargain deal for a lesser charge. We later met for lunch where I rejected the proposal. Rather than drag me through the court proceedings, his idea was to have me pledge not to run again for reelection of mayor in exchange for the U.S. Attorney for the District Jay Stephens to accept a lesser charge than a felony. But the U.S. Attorney wasn't going for that. He wanted blood. They hadn't spent all of that time and money simply to have me step away from office with a slap on the wrist. They wanted to make an international example out of me, and the process had already started.

On the first day of the trial, I ran the gauntlet through an army of news reporters from all over America with microphones, cameras and shouting questions. Without my security detail, I could have been *harmed or hurt* out there. They were that aggressive. The trial itself was set up to break my spirit and to make me look bad in the eyes of the people. You had white Americans lining up to convict me based on the image of the Vista Hotel tape alone. But black people wanted to defend me. They understood what was going on, based on a history of black men being brought down in disproportionate numbers. It had happened to many of us in a lot of different ways, whether it was political, personal, criminal, economic or outright assassinations. I had been involved in the Civil Rights Movement, during suspect shootings, police raids, water hoses, dogs and horses, and plenty of lies, cover-ups and entrapments, so I *knew* what the government was capable of.

The government needed me to take the drugs so they could go after a much bigger conviction.

During the proceedings, Kenneth Mundy told me to trust *no one*, where anything I did or said to the wrong people could be used against me in trial. One of the challenges for prosecution and defense was to choose an impartial jury, which made it difficult because a lot of the jurors knew me or thought positively of me.

The commotion outside of the courtroom was *crazy*. There were cameras and newspeople from all over the country, with national television personalities that we had never seen in Washington. Jesse Jackson, who lived in D.C., flew in and out of town from Chicago to support me. Dick Gregory was there, several pastors and reverends from around the District, and the prosecution tried to keep the Nation of Islam's Minister Louis Farrakhan out of the courtroom altogether. When he showed up to lend his support, they thought his presence would intimidate the jurors. So we had to appeal to the judge to even allow Minister Farrakhan in court. After the trial began, Judge Jackson wanted to ban Farrakhan from coming to the courtroom. The Nation of Islam went to court. The Court of Appeals overturned Judge Jackson's ban and allowed Farrakhan to reenter and stay as long as he wanted to. I got to know Minister Farrakhan while on the council. I had followed the work of the Nation of Islam. He called me at home and said that he supported me, and to expect to see him there. And he came. That brought him and me even closer together.

Outside the court, the Reverend Willie Wilson had a prayer tent for me during the entire trial, and he was offering his spiritual support to anyone who wanted to join him. I really appreciated that. Reverend Wilson was showing the whole *world* that he supported me with all of those national cameras and reporters out there.

It was a real hectic atmosphere outside the courtroom, so Effi and I agreed to keep our son, Christopher, away from it all. The judge even held the case in a smaller courtroom on purpose to keep some of the people out.

Everything the jury and the people in the courtroom heard about my case was conflicting from day one. Bringing Rasheeda all the way from California to get me up in a hotel room to allegedly smoke crack was the highest form of entrapment. The members of the jury could clearly see that. They couldn't even agree whether or not the substance they had in court was really crack cocaine. None of the evidence was clean, and none of the witnesses were trustworthy. They all had something to gain from my conviction—especially Rasheeda and most witnesses. The entire sting was set up off of Rasheeda and the FBI's deal.

Kenneth Mundy's line of questions to the witnesses went right after the government deals that were being offered and the lack of facts to corroborate their stories. The FBI had offered many witnesses package deals and immunity, including Rasheeda and Charles Lewis, who had earlier drug accusations from the 1980s. He was the first witness.

Charles Lewis was the liaison for the governor of the U.S. Virgin Islands, and he also worked in the personnel office of the D.C. government. At one time, the governor of the Virgin Islands wanted me to send people from my administration there to help him to overhaul his personnel system as we had done in Washington.

Charles Lewis had been under investigation and was convicted for drug possession, and he alleged that I had used drugs with him in the Virgin Islands. The prosecution also had him to allege that I was with him at a Ramada Inn in D.C., where he propositioned a maid to get drugs. I had met him there for lunch and had been long gone before he propositioned *anyone*. But those were the kind of stories that people would link you to when they were offered deals. So the prosecution continued to ask about different meeting places with Charles and my connections and trips to the Virgin Islands.

Charles Lewis lied so much on that first day of court that I found it difficult not to react. I couldn't believe the extent of the lies that came out of his mouth, and it was easy to pick him apart for the jury. He tried to exaggerate everything to paint a deceitful story, and it got so bad that my attorney asked the judge for a five-minute recess.

Kenneth Mundy pulled me outside the courtroom and said, "Stop showing your reactions to Charles Lewis. Now go back in there and sit, smile and don't react to people's testimony."

He was concerned about my reactions to the lies, but it was incredibly frustrating for me to just sit there and listen to that. Imagine someone making up stories on you inside of a courtroom full of people, and you couldn't speak up about it.

The prosecution was digging as deep as they could to try and create a mountain of evidence out of lies. They desperately wanted to paint my cocaine use into something much more than it ever was. I had never used cocaine as much as they tried to say I had. Once a person catches your hand in the cookie jar, they'll try to say that you ate *all* of the cookies. And that wasn't true.

Kenneth Mundy decided that it was best for me not to take the stand because he realized that none of the testimony against me would hold up. All they had was the video of the set-up at the Vista. Everything else was suspect with a million holes in the stories. So my attorney told me that all I needed to do was show up in court and let the jury witness what they were trying to do to me, and that their character assassination wouldn't work.

Our strategy was to keep the prosecution guessing on whether or not I would take the stand. But because the contradictions from the witnesses were so obvious, we decided that I didn't need to. They had a list of people who attempted to paint me as the biggest drug abuser and womanizer that you could imagine, and it wasn't true. I decided to hold press conferences after the court hearings daily at four-thirty, where I would talk about the misleading information that was presented during the case.

I felt it was important to inform the public of my side of the story. We also knew that some of the jurors were getting out and reading the papers and watching the news. But I didn't do it for them. I held these press conferences for all of the people who weren't inside the courtroom and who still wanted to follow the case. I wanted to keep them updated on what was going on in there. For the people who wanted to read it, they read it, and for those who didn't want to read it, they didn't.

The prosecution lawyers didn't like me having press conferences after court, but it was working for me. Who cared what they liked or didn't like? They were trying to send me to *prison*. So I told the press how badly they were lying and exaggerating things in court. I had consultation with my lawyer on what not to tell them, but I gave the media enough of the basic information to paint a good idea of what was going on.

As more information on the sting came out, there was a report where the FBI failed to consult with District Police Chief Isaac Fulwood about the sting. Isaac Fulwood was an outstanding policeman who came through the ranks the hard way. He had nothing but integrity. But the FBI went on with the idea anyway. That's why they included a paramedic that night.

Lead prosecutor U.S. Attorney Jay Stephens and his staff grew increasingly *irate* as more of the details of the sting came out and swayed the jury. He was trying so hard to get his trophy and convict a high-ranking black man and public official, even though the evidence was stacking up against it. So he kept trying to get the jury to execute the law without prejudice of all that the FBI and the police had done to set me up, but no one could do that. Math was math and the numbers were adding up to entrapment.

I didn't feel bad about Rasheeda or hold any grudge against her during the trial. I saw her as a victim of a system that had used her weakness against her and had used my weakness against me. I understood what they were doing and what kind of pressure she was under. So I forgave her. I only called her a bitch as a direct response to what happened that night. In fact, I was more upset at myself than I was with her. I should have never gone up into that hotel room.

Rasheeda stayed with her family in Washington during the trial, but with FBI and police protection. I had forgiven her for what she had done, but I couldn't speak for everyone else. I don't believe she was that well liked in the District at that time. I would never wish anything bad on her, but there was nothing I could do about how the people felt. Rasheeda might have been harmed by someone, especially with how emotional some of our people can get. But I couldn't worry too much about her; I had to defend myself from what they were trying to do to me.

I couldn't speak to Rasheeda's mother, but imagined how Mary Moore must have felt in all of this. Understandably, I had to keep my distance from her family, because anything I said to them could have been used in court against me. They could have tried to charge me with obstruction of justice.

During my time away from the courtroom, I liked to spend time with boxing promoter Rock Newman, who was promoting big fights for heavyweight champion, Riddick Bowe, who lived in Fort Washington, Maryland. I had been to several of Bowe's championship fights, and being around the boxing training camp helped me to relax. It took me back to my own roots in boxing in Memphis. I had first met Rock Newman years ago when he worked on Howard University's campus as a dorm room adviser. He used to oversee the dorms for the football and basketball players, and he was inspired by the boxing tournaments we used to have at the Burr Gymnasium with Cora Masters.

I remember he told me one time, "Politics is just boxing; everybody wants to be in your camp when you win, but it gets like a ghost town when you lose."

Rock told me that I had given the city an identity for progress, business, pride and advancement for black people. There were few cities in America that had so many blacks in charge, and Rock understood that black power always posed a threat for whites.

I really bonded with him. Rock said the boxing tournaments at Howard with Cora Masters had inspired him to get involved in managing and promoting fights. I even went up to the Catskills with them to watch them train in New York.

After eight weeks of going back and forth to court, when we got close to the verdict, I didn't know if I was going to jail or not. It was August of that year in 1990, and I was *terrified*. Dozens of newspaper articles had been written about it, the television news was all over the place, and my supporters were all sitting there *nervous* along with me: Effi, Cora, Rock Newman and a bunch of good friends and allies.

I also believe that Effi had a huge impact on the courtroom and the jury. They saw her come to court every single day and show her support through all of the misinformation about me and the lies that were being told. Even some of the *truths* that were exposed in court were painful. And for *eight weeks* every single day she came to court and sat there in rain, snow or shine. Effi actually cried in court a few times at some of the things that were being said about me, especially with us not electing to take the stand. She knew that some of the things they were accusing me of were not a part of my character. They were things that Effi *knew* I would never do. So she called it a public castration. But I had opened myself up to be picked apart and lied about in court like that because of my unwise decisions.

Once the jurors were sequestered during the deliberation process, they were not supposed to watch the news, talk about the case to outsiders or anything else to guarantee us a fair trial. But that was impossible to do because the news about the case was everywhere. We all *knew* that while they were going home before being sequestered, they were getting more information about the case. It was *impossible* not to from all of the newspaper and television reports. At that time, there were police barriers to redirect the traffic with so many different media people trying to get into the courtroom and report the story. They were also at my house, and they were there from *day one*, during the pretrial and the whole thing.

At the end of this long process, no one had any idea what this jury would do. We were all sitting there in the courtroom to find out. One of the jurors gave me the thumbs-up. I didn't know what that meant.

The jurors were deadlocked on all of the fourteen charges but one, illegal drug possession, a misdemeanor. All fourteen of the charges were subjected to deliberation. Five black members of the jury reportedly voted for acquittals on all but one charge. That one charge, for drug possession, was not even at the Vista, but at the Mayflower Hotel with a lady named Doris Crenshaw. Even though she'd been given immunity, she testified during cross-examination that she brought the drugs to the hotel. The U.S. Attorney combined all of these charges, even those unrelated to the Vista. The three white men on the jury voted guilty of all charges. Evidently, racism still lived that strongly in America. These three white men were not swayed by anything they had heard in court. They only voted in accordance with the tape from the Vista Hotel, but they were not my peers and they had not been continuously persecuted in America like black people had been.

Ultimately, the jury and the residents of Washington did not want to see their mayor behind bars after *knowing* that the government had gone out of their way to set me up. It left a bad taste in their mouths. None of them had ever seen me out in public, asking for or taking drugs. It was a personal and private issue that was being flushed out into the open for political gain. Most of Washington had known me as a fighter who would do all that he could for the benefit of the people, not as a drug-addicted crook that the prosecution tried to make me out to be inside the courtroom. And the jury apparently realized that yanking me out of office through such a strategic and personal attack on my character was unacceptable. After hearing weeks and months about the trial with constant reports from untrustworthy witnesses, many of whom had been given immunity by the prosecution, the people of D.C. had seen and heard enough of the condemnation of the mayor's office. They knew what that FBI sting and court case was designed to do, and they also knew what my record was in the community. I was not some raving, rampaging and out-of-touch mayor, running around on drugs. There were thousands of residents in the District who had grown up in the programs that I had provided for them and their families that had helped them to improve their quality of life. They were not going to allow a campaign of destruction to taint their tremendous amount of respect for me. I was overwhelmed by their support and appreciation.

The jury was hung on all charges but the misdemeanor conviction of drug possession, which happened at the Mayflower Hotel. So the judge had no choice but to declare a mistrial.

I was later sentenced to six months in prison for the drug possession misdemeanor and a $5,000 fine. My sentence was to start in November 1990, around the time of the new elections for mayor. Obviously, I couldn't run for a fourth term for mayor, but I submitted my name on the ballot for an at-large council member seat against incumbent Hilda Mason.

At first, I didn't want to challenge Hilda Mason, who was running for re-election of her at-large post. We had a long-standing relationship. She had helped me to raise money for SNCC when I first arrived in Washington. She supported me when I ran for the president of the school board. She had a lot of love from the community and she had been a strong supporter of my public service as mayor. The people of Washington affectionately called her "The Grandmother of the World." I didn't feel comfortable running against her, but I ran against her anyway and lost; the only loss of my political career. I had a good showing, with over 50,000 votes. I wasn't *supposed* to win that race. I needed to be *humbled*, and I was.

At my sentencing, my attorney, Kenneth Mundy, advocated for community service and no prison time, but the prosecutor advocated for six months, *at least*.

Judge Penfield decided to agree with the prosecutor on jail time. He said, "I think the time away from it all will give you an opportunity to get yourself together, Mr. Barry."

You can't argue with the judge. Sometimes God puts things in our lives to test our faith. I was not yet at the point where I could give it all up to God, but there were a lot of regrets at the courtroom, including my relationship with Rasheeda. Our relationship, however wrong it was, became a tool for the government's takedown of a public official whom they obviously wanted to get rid of. And our story became a classic firebrand for interest around the world.

The biggest problem that I have with it is how Americans love to focus in on the dark. That's just the way it is. You do a million good things for the community, and they try to wipe it all out with the bad things. The media liked to talk about all of the things that we continue to work on instead of the things that we've already solved. They liked to talk about the things that are torn down instead of the things that we build up. They liked to report on my period of womanizing but not how many women I hired to major government positions. They liked to report all of the crimes in D.C., but rarely about the joys of living in Washington, at least not when it comes to blacks.

You never have a rest from fighting all of the negative perceptions out there, because they will always be there. You just have to make sure that you focus your energy on continuing to do the things that are going to help your city to grow and prosper.

The common American perception is that there's always a decline in progress when whites are no longer involved in controlling things. So those individuals liked it when there was no power for the blacks in Washington before I arrived. Blacks were the voiceless citizens who lived there, who were forced to deal with whomever Congress appointed to lead them.

I felt badly that the government had gone to such great lengths to get me and the unintended consequences to people of Washington and the nation. I've learned that you have to be extra careful about our human frailties. I was relieved that this had finally come to an end. I was glad to put this chapter of my life behind me. It was very painful to hear those testimonies—true or untrue. I was overwhelmed with a variety of emotions—sadness and anger. I would often glance at Effi knitting in the courtroom and wonder what she was thinking and feeling. God knows I never meant to bring any harm to her or Christopher, but I did.

CHAPTER 15

PRISON TIME

I was sentenced to six months at a federal correction facility in Petersburg, Virginia about a half hour south of Richmond. I was to begin my sentence in November 1991 to May 1992, but I turned myself in to the authorities in October, where I was able to get out that next April. I had to come to terms with myself and prepare to do the time, and that's what I did.

After my initial trial and sentencing, Effi needed a break from it all and moved out of the house with Christopher and into an apartment on Connecticut Avenue, Northwest. She had been through more than she could take and had held it together throughout the trial, but once the cameras and the media attention was off of us, she chose to find her own space. I can't say that I blamed her. Surely I was upset that I no longer had her and Christopher at the house with me, but I understood. Effi was strong, but personally, it was a lot for any woman and child to take.

While living up on Connecticut Avenue, Christopher went to a school with predominantly black kids. He said he liked it there more than at St. Albans, but then he started to act out with his new friends. For instance, he used to like the rap group NWA. (Niggaz With Attitude), who I thought were disrespectful to everything we had learned during the Civil Rights era. Now these angry young men were calling themselves *"niggas"* on purpose, and were talking about the most negative imagery of Black America on their records. You couldn't even play the music in your car. So Christopher was definitely going through his stages of rebellion. Or at least I thought. Maybe that was the new era of black music, but I didn't like it.

Throughout the separation, Effi and I had conversations about getting back together, but nothing worked out. Then in September 1991, right before I turned myself in, Effi took a job in Hampton, Virginia teaching at the high school level, and she took Christopher with her. At that point, I was ready to serve my time in prison anyway. However, I could no longer count on Effi to support me. So before going to serve my time in prison, I left Cora Masters with about $75,000 to pay my bills and take care of my household while I was away. She did that for me and didn't take a dime of the money for herself.

When I turned myself into the correctional facility in Petersburg, everyone knew what I was there for, so it didn't get any easier for me. I would be reminded of my bad decisions for the rest of my life. But Petersburg was close enough to Washington—about two hours away—where I was able to stay in touch with what was going on in the District by reading the newspapers and hearing things. I even did a few radio broadcasts from jail on the Cathy Hughes WOL radio show. We had a break during the day where we could use the phones, so I was able to stay connected to the people.

Petersburg was a low-level security prison with an open door dorm room and four beds for roommates in a cubicle. The white prisoners were mostly white-collar, but the black prisoners were there for everything, but mostly for drug possession and sales. Generally, when blacks do crimes, they are more easily detected and convicted. Black elected officials were also targeted disproportionately in comparison to white officials, and the prison in Petersburg represented that. There were a lot more black prisoners there even though there were more white men who lived in the Commonwealth of Virginia.

We spent a lot of our time finishing furniture in Petersburg, five nights a week. And they would allow you to wear a new pair of tennis shoes that were comfortable to walk around in. But even though I was close to Effi, who was only an hour away in Hampton, she wanted no part of seeing me in prison. She never came to Petersburg prison to visit me *once*. Again, I never blamed her for it. She took our son, Christopher, to Carlise Davenport, from the Tots School, and allowed her to bring our son down to see me in prison.

One time, Cora Masters brought Christopher there to see me, and she said he was very nervous with all of the gates, barbed wire, prison guards and all of that. As a kid, he was very apprehensive about what all was going on in prison, especially since there was a maximum prison facility that was right across the street from the lower security facility. It was a lot more intimidating next door and he could have easily been confused by the two.

That was a very conflicting time for my son. Up until the Vista, he'd had a very good life. He went to the best schools with the privileged kids of Washington. He got a chance to meet with a lot of the famous—athletes and entertainers, who came to visit us in Washington. He went to sports arenas for the Bullets and Redskins games and music concerts.

Christopher really believed in his *"Cosby* kid" years, where he felt like the privileged black kids on TV. He thought his life was normal for blacks, and Christopher didn't know any better. The world was an oyster. But going from those *Cosby* kid years to having your father talked about on the news, kids teasing you, parents talking about your parents, and all that going on at his school was pretty extreme for him. Then having your father go to jail for six months was a lot to ask from a kid. That only got him into more fights and stress. Imagine what that all could do to a kid's psychology, where he's suddenly uprooted from the world he used to know like that. So my son developed a lot of anger issues that he still had to deal with as a young man and an adult.

Effi had to go through a lot herself. She had been under an amazing amount of pressure. You think about all those who loved and respected her; all of the women who worked for me in the government and the wives of officials and businessmen, and the mothers of the kids that our son went to school with. You can only imagine what Effi had to go through with so many eyes and thoughts and questions about her and how she was making out. She had been forced to handle everything, but Effi was a fighter who kept on going and being supportive. But imagine what she had to explain to the people we had bumped in to and socialized with year after year in more than a decade as the mayor.

I remember coming home one day after being sentenced to prison in 1990, and I found all of Effi's things packed up in the living room.

I said, "What's this? Where are you going?"

She said, "I'm leaving. I can't take this anymore."

She was tired of the media interfering in our personal lives. She was tired of subjecting Christopher to the fights of political enemies.

Effi had been through years of hearing about friends and others breaking up, where you start thinking about the bond of your own relationship. Then you have those trying to give you advice on situations that they aren't able to handle themselves. The fact is, when you're married to the mayor or a public official, you're in a relationship that I lot of outside people get to make comments on. They know more about you and your relationship than they know about their own friends and family.

Effi once told me that, according to everyone else, "We were ready to get divorced from the day we were married." There were always rumors about us breaking up or not getting along at home.

Effi would have friends telling her, "You need to just leave him alone."

In a lot of people's hearts, very few of them are happy about others' marriages. Even at weddings, a lot of people aren't really happy to see you happy if they're not. So we knew what we were up against, and very early in our marriage, Effi accepted it. But I had to admit that it had been a very hard time for her and for Christopher during my time in prison. I had always wished that I could have spent more time with my son as a father. I even wanted to have more children with Effi, but I knew that I had too much going on as a political figure to have the time that I would have needed to be the father that I wanted to be. I was too busy moving around and not able to commit the time to the lifestyle of marriage and fatherhood. Effi wanted me around for more family dinners than I was ever able to make, so I felt guilty about that. I really wanted to be around for my family more as well.

During this whole period of my prison sentence, Effi and Cora remained good friends. There was no animosity on Effi's part that Cora was continuing to do so much to help me. She never snapped and asked about Cora's intentions. Effi was an incredible woman who didn't think that way. She wasn't into that kind of bickering.

People can get it wrong to stereotype black women with the idea that they can't get along. Effi and Cora both understood what the bigger picture was. They both wanted to help me without any of the fighting or arguing that most would consider normal between two women. Both women had great respect for me and for each other, and Cora was able to pick up the torch and continue to help me.

During the trial, Effi had done all that she could do to support me and my career, but I accepted that it was time for her to want to move on and do some things for her own life and career. However, I admit that I was surprised that Effi didn't come to visit me at all in prison. And I had to deal with however she felt about it.

Effi had a way of keeping things to herself, so she would never tell some of her innermost emotions. She would always find ways of doing what she wanted to do in her own space. It wasn't as if I stopped her from doing anything. We were both able to keep the peace at home, but there was nothing I could do about the media. That's why Effi rarely let them into our private lives; she cherished her privacy. I got a chance to think about all of that while in prison. I no longer had the distractions or a busy day *not* to think about it.

At the prison in Petersburg, although I got a chance to stay tuned into the D.C. news and community, I didn't like the prison life. Obviously, you didn't get a chance to do much there but think. And with the maximum security facility in the building right across the street, I was reminded every day of what the next level would look like. They had guards with rifles inside the barbed-wire fence who were ready to shoot you down. But in the lower-level security facility that I was in, we only had a line that separated us from the street. We all knew where the line was and what the boundaries were, and you didn't cross it because we would have been charged with trying to escape.

Despite the low-level security in Petersburg, it was still a prison and I didn't want to be there. Nor did they make anything easy for me. Some inmates even tried to assassinate my character in prison. About three months into my six-month sentence, there was a crazy report that came out with eight white men accusing someone of having oral sex on me inside the visitation room. Now this was a big room with a front door, a back door, tables and chairs and other inmates with visitors and guards all around us, and they accused me of *that*. I had black inmates there who reported that it never happened, but the media ran with this story anyway and it was all over the news; on television, in print and on the talk shows. It was *crazy*, and pure character assassination.

I had a number of supporters who wanted to come visit me during my sentence in Petersburg. There was a limit of ten whom I could put on my visiting list each week, and the list changed depending on who was coming in to visit me. With this one particular person, these white inmates decided to bring up this crazy allegation. Out of privacy, I won't include the visitor's name, but the story and the media attention got me into trouble with Cora Masters, because she wanted to make sure that people knew it was *not her*. So it created another embarrassing mess that I had to clear up for Cora's sake and her reputation.

She said, "Marion, you better clear this thing up and tell them who this woman *is*, because I do *not* want people thinking that *I've* been coming down here to do that."

She said, "I am a *mother*, a professional educator, an active member of the *church*, and I have my own reputation to protect. Now you tell them who this woman *is*, whether she did anything in that room with you or not, because it was *not me!*"

Cora was *pissed* and I couldn't blame her. When people go after your character, they often bring down the good names of those who support you. But to this day, I still can't understand why these white inmates did that. Did someone pay them to say that or promise them something? I don't know. I didn't believe that racism could get that deep. There were a lot of guys there from different walks of life whom had gotten themselves mixed up into trouble. A lot of their cases were not as cut and dried as you would think. And maybe they had deals set up to reduce their time.

After this visitation incident in Petersburg, the prison officials moved me to a place called Loretto in Pennsylvania. I didn't have as much access to the Washington news in Loretto. It was another low-security federal prison, but it was more national with hundreds of different people who had done some major crimes in life. We had one white guy who was the world's best safe cracker. Petersburg was more of a local prison with mostly white-collar crime and a lot less to do. At Loretto, we had a lot more time and freedom to move around. There was also more socializing between the races. I was able to befriend more of the white inmates in there. I worked a lot in the kitchen, preparing and serving food, and they also had a drug and alcohol program.

Obviously, things had slowed down a great deal in my life as a result of me being sent to prison. I couldn't drink, use any drugs or fall to any other temptations in jail, so I was able to clear my mind. I don't want to say it was a good experience for me, but maybe it was all I needed.

At Loretto, I got along with everybody: white guys, Hispanics, blacks. I learned a lot from talking to them and getting to know certain people. We had more leisure time there to read in the prison library and to associate more. We played a lot of handball, ping-pong and talked a lot, especially with the time I spent with the guys who worked in the kitchen with me. Some guys liked to lift weights, read and write letters, and I was constantly doing things to bide my time in there. But you can't count the days too much. That part would drive you crazy because there's too many hours and days that you have to wait to get out. So I only counted my days during the last two weeks or so.

Loretto was more of a transition prison where a lot of the guys were close to being released, so you didn't have too much craziness there. The rules there were much less restrictive, making the guys a lot more easygoing. But that didn't mean you were getting out early or that they would let you do whatever you wanted to do; it was just made for a better set-up.

There was more desperation down in Petersburg, but at Loretto, we had different concerns and daily checks and balances to keep the inmates all in line. Prison was still prison, so no matter how you served your time, you would rather be home with your family and *free*. I didn't lose sight of that; none of us did.

While I was there in Loretto, we had the first Black History Month celebration that the facility ever had. The white guys participated in it, too. That's how Black History Month is supposed to be; it's for everyone to learn and be educated about, like we do with white American history.

On Sundays, we had a prison fellowship where we sat around and talked about things that were going on in our lives. We had some folks who tried to escape, too, but the prison guards usually found them lost in the woods, because there was nowhere out there to go. And we definitely had some sexual assaults that would go down in prison. We had a running joke where we told the new guys not to bend over for the soap in the shower.

I had a couple of guys who tried to hit on me in jail, but you have to stand your ground when that happens. So I told them, "I don't go that way," and they left me alone. But you can't ever forget that you're in prison. Your guard has to be up at all times.

Overall, Loretto was a much better place for me than Petersburg, but it was farther away from Washington. I had to depend on God to make it through those tough times of disconnection. I missed the District *immensely* and all of the good people there. There was no other place that I would rather live. And I just knew that I would have a much better life for myself and my family when I was released. So I did a lot of reflecting, reading books and reading the Bible. I listened to a lot of sermons on tape and was inspired by the journey that could happen with my spirit. I also received hundreds of letters in jail that I read and sometimes responded to.

To call home to our family and loved ones from Loretto, we had a phone and a money limit. If you didn't use your limit of $25 in quarters each month, they would take them away from you. You couldn't keep them in your locker, so the guards would pat you down and have regular checks on all of the inmates.

You couldn't keep food in your room either, or you weren't supposed to. This one guy who worked in the kitchen with me made his own whiskey from raisins until he got caught. That's why they wouldn't let you keep food if you worked in the kitchen. They figured the people we served would not have enough food on a tray to do much with, but if you worked back in the kitchen, you had a lot more access to use the food to your own advantage. So they wouldn't allow us to take anything extra.

The most important four things in prison were your mail, food, phone time and your visits. As the former mayor of Washington, D.C., I got so much mail that I had to start telling people not to write anymore. It was making a lot of the guys jealous in prison, and I didn't want to deal with that. You can get real lonely in prison and start to feel like no one cares about you. So I didn't want the other guys feeling bad about themselves. I even befriended some of the people I spoke to on phone calls from the other inmates. They were always curious about me, and their family members and friends wanted to talk to me and give me encouragement.

Even though I couldn't possibly read all of these letters or even accept them anymore, I was really uplifted to see all of the support from people who still believed me and appreciated all that I had done in the District. Oftentimes, when you're down, that's when folks who used to support you are no longer around, but I didn't find that to be the case with those who continued to support me in Washington. On the contrary, I saw that a lot of people still had hope and could see that I could make a change for the better through my hardships. They could see that I was turning the corner, particularly in having an opportunity to get myself clean from addictions. It was a real blessing that I was able to do that.

I didn't have as many visitors or contact with Washington while I was at Loretto, but every morning I called Cora Masters to talk to her and to update myself on what was going on inside the District. All the while, she continued to pay my mortgage and bills with the help of six contributing pastors.

Rock Newman continued to support me during my stay in prison, and he even called to talk to me one time before a fight card in D.C. I don't remember who was fighting that night, but he put me on the loudspeaker to say hello to the crowd and let them know that I was doing all right in prison and that I hoped to return soon to Washington.

I couldn't hear it clearly through the phone, but Rock Newman said that the crowd went *crazy*. The noise from the receiver was ringing in my ear, but it wasn't the same as being there. I couldn't see or feel the crowd doing it; all I could do was imagine what it looked like.

Rock Newman told me that's when he first started to think that I may be able to make a big return to politics. The emotions of the people were still on my side, and my prison time didn't change their support for me. But I had to get out of jail and get back home first—my home of Washington, D.C.

CHAPTER 16
BACK TO WASHINGTON

On April 22, 1992, I was released from an unfair six-month prison sentence. I knew my release date. We didn't want a media frenzy with me going to prison or being released. Three of my former security people were part of the release. One of them called the prison and disguised his voice and said, "You're being released at eight to eight-thirty a.m." We had arranged for my departure for 4:30 to 5 p.m. From there, I went to the hotel where I met up with Cora and other supporters—four or five. She had brought corn and okra, which is one of my favorite dishes. Rev. Wilson was there and we prayed over my release. I had gained weight and I had worked in the kitchen. Effi and I were still separated at the time. In fact, she had moved to Hampton, VA with Christopher to accept a teaching job. She wanted to be there when I was released.

Reverend Willie Wilson and Cora Masters and others in the community organized a welcome home rally at the Union Temple Baptist Church with a caravan of six or seven buses of 400 to 500 people, who came to Pennsylvania to see my release from jail. It was like the Prodigal Son coming home. They were there to help welcome me back to Washington and to take the trip back home together. These incredible supporters were taking the time out of their lives to ride two and three hours to come get me and return me from being a political prisoner. I was so appreciative and inspired that I can't even put it into words to describe it. I was thanking God for them and for Reverend Willie Wilson and Cora for being so supportive. I didn't know what to expect when I got back out, but the people of Washington were letting me know that I still had a big place in their hearts.

We got back to Washington with our caravan of buses and pulled up to the

Union Temple Baptist Church in Southeast where there were thousands of people waiting outside in the street, cheering, hollering and screaming. The crowd was so thick we couldn't turn the first bus into the lot to park. I was absolutely *overwhelmed* by the people's inspiring show of support. And they were not only from D.C.; I had supporters from Maryland and Virginia. It was *phenomenal!* I must have spent *hours* thanking people, shaking hands, taking pictures, holding and kissing babies, *everything.*

A few weeks later, Rock Newman invited me to a Lorton Prison graduation in May, and the inmates in Lorton were very excited to have me to come speak to them. Fresh out of prison myself, they all knew that I could relate. In Rock's introduction, he hinted that I may have been the *future* mayor of Washington, and the crowd went *crazy!* These were guys who had been arrested and were doing time in prison, but they still had a lot of appreciation for what I had done for the District, and they could all relate to me being forced to serve time in jail. Everyone had a relative, a loved one, a son or a daughter, who was either serving time or connected to someone in the system. So it wasn't that unusual for black folks. It was how the American law had it set up. They expected us to slip up and land in jail, and there were plenty of land mines in poor urban neighborhoods for us to do it.

I didn't add anything in my speech that day to confirm that I would run again for mayor, but I *did* recognize how much support they had for the idea. At the time, I was still trying to figure out what I would do or if I would run for *any* office, let alone the *mayor's* office.

Shortly after the Lorton speech with Cora Masters, Rosetta Bryson, who was the student government president of the University of the District of Columbia, invited me to the campus to speak to the students. She had been teaching political science at UDC for *years*, and she figured it would be a good idea. But I was still a little leery of how they would respond to me. I didn't know if the young people and students there would boo me or what. I simply didn't know. I had my doubts about whether they could relate to me anymore. I thought I may have had more in common with the inmates at Lorton and those who had served time. I told Cora I wasn't going.

She said, "You must go to UDC," and convinced me that I should. She knew a lot better than I did how the students, the staff, and the people of D.C.

still felt about me. So I showed up to speak, and when I arrived at the auditorium, the students gave me a standing ovation. They were clapping and were excited to have me there to speak to them. I couldn't believe the support they were still willing to give me. They even tried to pull together a teaching position there for me. I guess all of the hard work I had done for the people of the District was really coming back to me. The students thought about the hotel and drug set-up from the FBI, and they considered me a hero for having gone through it. Not so much that it happened to me, but that I had survived it and come back.

The support that I was getting was all great, but I was now out of office and had no idea what I would do. I had been in a position where I could help lots of people as a council member and then as the mayor of Washington, but who could really help *me* into a position? I had a few supporters, including Reverend Willie Wilson, who tried to pull together an economic package of $150,000 for me to live off, while I developed my next move. Rev. Wilson even asked Bob Johnson to contribute $50,000, but he turned him down.

He told me, "Bob Johnson said, 'No, I can't do it.'"

I had built up a policy of empowering black people whether it would individually benefit me or not. So Reverend Willie Wilson continued to take up collections for me at his Union Temple Baptist Church. And I really appreciated and *needed* it. At the time, like a lot of black politicians, I thought more about helping others than building up assets for myself.

Without us asking, world-renowned televangelist Reverend Tom Skinner came out to support me with a speech about forgiveness and recovery. He and his wife, Barbara, had come to visit me in prison at Loretto, but we had no idea that he would go public with his support. Visiting me in prison was one thing, but his national support was something else. In reference to what some said about my fall from grace, he spoke about all of the people in the Bible who were able to overcome all of the negative things that they had to go through. And that allowed me to begin to focus on my comeback. I couldn't keep walking around holding on to what had happened to me at the Vista and kicking myself for the past. I had to brush myself off and get back in the fight.

Sharon Pratt Kelly had been elected to the mayor's office by then, so I thought about running for an at-large council member seat. There were two at-large seats open for election that year in 1992, and four ward seats. I started thinking about running for a ward seat as another option. At the time, I still lived in Ward 7 that covered the far Southeast and Northeast areas. But I didn't want to run against my friend H.R. Crawford. I knew I would have beaten him. The polls showed that I was very popular with the middle-class residents of Ward 7.

However, my friend and political ally, Joe Johnson, came up with another suggestion. He said, "Why don't you run in Ward Eight?"

In Ward 8, Wilhelmina Rolark held the council seat and I had been friends with her and her husband, Calvin, for years. But I felt that Rolark's best years had passed and the people weren't responding to her ideas as much. I saw a need and an opportunity for new energy and leadership in Ward 8, so I investigated the idea.

We did a poll survey that asked if it would make a difference if I moved from Ward 7 to Ward 8, and the people said it wouldn't. Based on the polls, the voters in Ward 8 were very appreciative of my efforts while mayor. I knew that I could win an election. I then decided to move farther south to Ward 8 and challenge Rolark for the council member seat.

I found a place called the Washington View Apartments and moved in only fifteen days before petitions were due to run for office. The apartment complex was a large, well-kept place of 200 to 300 units and had a great view back into the city. A lot of Southeast areas had great views, especially from the hills. So I moved in—not to be a politician or anything—but to get settled.

The Washington Post immediately published an article and asked the question, "Marion Barry moves to Ward 8; what does it mean?"

Once I began to set up my office and organize a campaign, Wilhelmina's husband, Calvin, became *pissed*.

He said, "As much as we did for *you*. How could you do this to us?"

Calvin worked with a life insurance agency and was a pretty solid figure in the community. His wife had been in local politics for as long as I had been. She had served sixteen years on the D.C. Council, but I felt the time had passed her by. She had done a great job, but she didn't have the new ideas that I had for Ward 8. She was a lawyer in her seventies at the time. I was fifty-six and full of new ideas.

I didn't feel guilty about running against Rolark. Politics are politics; you win some races and you lose some. I still knew how the city government functioned, and I still knew how to push the right buttons to get what was needed for the citizens in Ward 8. So I wanted to lend my voice and wealth of experience to them. The residents and voters there could forgive you as long as you were still willing to work hard for them.

Ward 8 was also the poorest ward in the city and the most forgotten. But no one would forget about them if I was there as their council member; that's for sure. I could also relate to many of the family members in Ward 8, who had to reestablish their households and lives after loved ones had spent time in prison. Some there started calling me Anwar Amal, the Arabic name for "Bright Hope." I even went back to wearing dashikis with matching kufi hats. It was all about reconnecting to my roots. The dashiki was a part of who I was as a person and the spirit of the community that I had come from.

I told Wilhelmina's husband, Calvin, "I'm on a mission from God," and I left it at that. I really didn't need to say any more. The position wasn't about me or his wife; it was about the *people*. Who would be better for the people of Ward 8?

I really started to believe that I owed my ongoing career to God. I couldn't explain anymore how I was able to rise up from the ashes and continue to be successful in my fights for the community. As a scientist with a master's degree in chemistry, and an ABD (all but dissertation), I had been trained to rely on myself and on the here and now. Surely, I believed in a superior being, but I had relied more on myself to get things done. But after all that I had been through, I felt it was my destiny and a calling to get back involved in politics.

I also felt that I couldn't allow my political career as a public servant to end on a bad note. The "Prodigal Son" had to return back to service, a new and humbled man. So even though I was later offered opportunities to teach and to join other businesses, I turned them all down. I wanted to continue to fight for the people who showed me a tremendous amount of respect and loyalty. To continue to represent and lead the people was what I still felt *blessed* to be able to do. And that's what I did.

Some questioned whether or not I had other opportunities of employment outside of politics, but at the time, I didn't want any, or not anymore. I figured, why would I want to leave elected office if that's where I could help the most?

I found an immense pleasure and purpose in continuing to serve people. So I planned to get back to doing it. My goal was to focus on doing the right thing, while hoping that the people who see it would grab on to it.

Reverend Willie Wilson, his church members, and many others in Ward 8 were very helpful through the whole process. We put our campaign together with the slogan, "Ward 8 Needs a Fighter," and went on to win the Democratic primary for Ward 8 that September of 1992 in a landslide victory with over 70 percent of the vote. The general election was an even bigger win of 90 percent over Republican W. Cardell Shelton. And I was back on the D.C. Council proudly serving the poorest people in the District who needed it the most.

I had a gift of standing up and fighting for the people, and a broader vision of empowerment; that's why I kept getting reelected. A lot of white folks and outsiders didn't understand that. Voters weren't loyal to me for no reason; I had done a lot of things in the city that the residents and people from all over had benefited from.

Every day I continued to meet people who told me, "You helped me get my first job." "Your housing program helped our family to own our first house." "Your leadership program helped my son to attend college and make something of himself." I would hear from seniors about my strong support of them and black businesses that prospered as a result of opportunities that I implemented.

Those are the stories that the pundits never think about. They think it's about the new and empty promises, but it's about the old and established delivery.

The people ask, "What have you done for me to deserve my vote?" And with me, they have an answer. I've done *a lot*.

So I went back to war as the Ward 8 council member and worked with people who still had fight in them. But it wasn't just about politics; it was about the forgotten and disrespected people of Southeast. We wanted to work with the kids, telling them how important it was to go to school, helping their parents to pay rent with more affordable housing—especially in the absence of a man. There were far too many who had rent payments that were dispro-portionate to their income. If you live in an area where your income is only a thousand dollars a month, rent payments of $800 are way too high.

I wanted to get our hands dirty with a fight for reasonable and subsidized housing so that people could afford to live instead of using all of their income just to have somewhere to stay. I wanted to give the people a *reason* to want to vote again. Ward 8 typically had the lowest voter turnout because they didn't believe the city's policies cared about them. I wanted to get in the trenches and show them that I cared. That's the real work of serving the people and touching their hearts and spirits personally. You can't just talk about it; the people have to see you *do it*. You can't just talk about it; you've got to be about it. A lot of folks outside of Washington didn't understand that. They simply didn't *know*. I was never afraid to get my hands dirty as the mayor, as a city council member, or as the school board president. That's what the people respect in a leader.

I had unknowingly duplicated what my parents had done to my siblings and me in Memphis. They were always working, and I had gotten used to the work ethic, but not how to stop, slow down and enjoy my family. Imagine if Effi and I *did* have three or four kids. How would I have been able to deal with that? How would *she* have been able to deal with it?

I remember Effi and I attended Carol Thompson and Curtis Cole's wedding as one of our last events together. This was while I was still in the mayor's office before turning myself in. We danced together and had a good time at the wedding. But I knew that I couldn't expect to hold Effi around anymore. I was looking at a six-month stint in prison, and Effi wanted to establish some career goals of her own in my absence, and she had a right to do so.

We had a bunch of initial talks about getting back together, but once Effi signed that contract in 1991 to teach in Hampton, I knew that it was over. I wasn't moving down there and she was no longer committed to D.C. That was a very emotional process for me.

When Effi and I were separated, while she and Christopher lived on Connecticut Avenue, we could still get together for lunches and dinners and events, and sometimes family events out with Christopher. But when they moved to Hampton, it became impossible to see her and my son regularly. So once I returned to Washington from prison, Effi and I spoke about it and finally agreed to divorce. We started the paperwork in 1992 and were legally divorced by February 1993.

It was a pretty amicable divorce. We settled our debts, split up our assets and set up a fair support plan for her and Christopher. It wasn't anything elaborate to make the news because Effi was never that kind of person, and I had never made that kind of money. Protecting and providing for Christopher was at the top of our list of importance. We considered ourselves to be a role model of a black couple through our public and political struggles, and we continued to be respectful of that idea and imagery in our quiet divorce.

Some found it peculiar that I would move on with Cora Masters, but she and I had been dear friends through the struggle. We had spent so much time together to rebuild my life and career that it was only natural for us to have affections for each other. I had been involved with Cora mentally, spiritually and emotionally, and I wanted an intimate relationship and everything else. We wanted to be able to love, care for and be with each other, so once my divorce was finalized with Effi, Cora and I decided to marry. Many find it unbelievable that Cora and I had been friends since 1971, and never entertained an attraction or a relationship. Effi was never suspicious and she and Cora were friends. People will still have their suspicions, but I've stated my case. Cora and I had decades of friendship, and in a relationship, friendship is even more important than love.

Once Effi and I were officially divorced, I was free to marry whomever I wanted to marry. So I told my son, Christopher, about the marriage to Cora. He later came back to Washington to live with us, and he had no problems with it.

I then decided to sell the house on Suitland Road for an undisclosed amount. The property value in the area is now listed at an average of $450,000. I gave Effi her percentage of the money. I prepared myself to move on.

After I had sold my house on Suitland Road, Cora and I found a place in Ward 8 on Raleigh Street, off of Martin Luther King, Jr. Avenue, that we wanted to renovate and live in together. We had an architect draw up blueprints of the rooms, with new building designs, a kitchen and a back porch, but we had a lot of problems with the black contractors not doing the renovations on time. That was a real concern for me, because I had worked so hard to create opportunities for black companies to get more of the construction, building and renovation jobs in and around the District. I thought the company's work habits and attitude was ungrateful, but that happens sometimes.

Cora and I got married on January 8, 1994 by Reverend Willie Wilson at his Union Temple Baptist Church. The ceremony included Evangelist Tom Skinner; Cora's brother, Thomas Masters, and hundreds of guests, including Maya Angelou, Rock Newman and Dick Gregory.

Cora had two older daughters, Layana and Tamara, from a previous marriage in the wedding, and I had my son, Christopher, in the wedding as my best man. I became a stepfather and Cora became a stepmother when Christopher came to live with us off and on to stay connected to his father. Effi never stopped him from coming, and my son spent his sixth-, seventh- and eighth-grade years of middle school with us in Southeast, D.C.

I didn't have to worry too much about income at the time. I was serving as the new Ward 8 council member and the money I had received from selling my Suitland Road house gave me a little bit of a cushion. Cora and I both shared in the cost of renovating our new family house. During the renovation process, Cora and I and the family stayed at either her house on Loud Place, Southeast, or at my apartment at the Washington View.

After we had moved into the renovated house, *The Washington Post* published reports in the newspapers alleging that someone had helped us to pay for the renovation. It was always something new to take shots at me in the media. I guess they never expected me to rebound and pull my life together. So everything I was able to do—in their eyes—still had to have a backstory or a corrupted catch to it.

There was a front page newspaper article about Yong Yun, an Asian-American businessman who owned a dry cleaners, and the reports were saying that he paid for some of the costs of the renovation. The story even caused the U.S. Attorney's Office to look into it. The U.S. Attorney's Office requested that Cora and I actually had to show our receipts and bank statements on all of the renovations we did because they were trying so bad to find something new to pin on me. *The Washington Post* even ran a diagram of the house and the layout. I issued a statement about it, citing that it was a security risk. It was all a part of my continuous struggle. It seemed like it would never end.

I was sworn in as council member in 1994. While working as a council member on things of interest in the ward, and everywhere I went, people always stopped to tell me what the government wasn't doing—not enough jobs and other complaints, which got me thinking about running for mayor again. Plus, I was tutoring. I would often visit public schools, which was another factor of helping me to decide to run again. I would often visit and tutor students in D.C. Public Schools. By the second and third grade, I could see their lights dimmed and dreams not being achieved. I decided I could do more inside as the mayor than I could outside as the council member.

Shortly after my marriage and plans to settle in with Cora, we started putting together our thoughts on a new campaign to run for mayor. I felt that I had straightened myself up from the drugs and the alcohol, and I had gotten myself back in a good position politically. I had survived my darkest hours, so I felt it was time to rise all the way up from the ashes as a great example to the people. I really thought of myself as the "Prodigal Son," and my story wasn't over with yet. Maybe I was crazy or delusional to think that I could run for mayor again, but Cora didn't think that way. She felt it was doable. She had witnessed the full transition that I had made from the Vista Hotel, to rehab in Florida, the long trial in the courtroom, the loss of my wife and family, and spending prison time in two facilities. Then she had witnessed my ultimate return to Washington, to the people of Ward 8 through public service, with a new marriage, a new family, a new home and a new life. So with all of that on the table already, only by the grace of God, we both figured, *Why not finish the story of Prodigal Son and run for mayor again?*

CHAPTER 17
MAYOR FOR LIFE

The 1994 race was the toughest of my political career. There were two formidable candidates—an incumbent mayor and a popular council member who had run for mayor. I had been out of prison for two years at this point. We campaigned all over the city, but my focus was on the black vote. At first, I didn't go to any forums. People often had their minds made up on their candidate. John Ray and Mayor Kelly stopped going and I started going. If politicians don't come out to see you before the election, they definitely won't come out to see you after the elections. They came to some occasionally, but by then, I had gained momentum. Mayor Kelly thought she had the black middle class on her side, but I knew better. Perception was she was aloof, and she had Jack Kent Cooke, the owner of the Washington Redskins, leave Washington and move the team to Landover, Maryland. Additionally, there was a feeling that she was not in touch or in tune with the black middle class.

In terms of campaigning, we campaigned hard all over the city. I knew the media followed me, so I did everything—putting up posters, walking the neighborhoods, knocking on doors—and the people embraced me. Members of my coalition from 1978 were still intact on their support for me, and I was even stronger in 1994 than in 1978, particularly with the labor unions. Unions had been shifting since 1982, and continued to shift from the candidates. The Washington Teachers Union Local 6 was my strongest supporter. The WTU endorsed me in 1978 and every election that I've had because the Washington Teachers Union and the teachers knew how much I cared about young people, and demonstrated youth jobs. I had been in and out of schools pushing for education reform—pushing for raises, particularly teachers, fire and police. My other strongest union support was the Service Employees International Union (SEIU), AFSCME, as well as Josh Williams, the president of the Central Labor Council, which included over seventy unions in D.C., Maryland and Virginia. He had been a great supporter of mine over the years. Besides, I supported most of the issues important to labor.

Reverend Robert Hamilton, Jr., who was an associate minister at several D.C. churches, wanted to put together a campaign for a new run for mayor in 1994. We did a poll of the three main candidates and found that Sharon Pratt Kelly only had 13 percent of the vote, I had 29 percent and council member John Ray had 35 percent. So we knew we were within reach of winning a fourth election. My wife, Cora, suggested that we register 20,000 new voters in areas where residents typically didn't vote. Usually when you lack hope, you don't vote. So we wanted to give them something hopeful to vote for again and make them thankful that I planned to bring back community politics to Washington. We figured we could get at least 15,000 of the new votes with our campaign.

We called the new campaign "Unfinished Business." In our slogan, we stated, "He may not be perfect, but he's perfect for D.C."

We knew there would be a lot of talk about me serving time in prison for drug possession and all of that, so we decided we would beat the media to the punch and put my past issues out front. There was no sense in us trying to run away from it. I was all cleaned up with no more drinking or drug habits, so I didn't feel vulnerable. I managed to drink a little wine every now and then in moderation, but that was it.

When we began to campaign again for mayor—after already serving twelve years in the position—we had some who wondered why we had not worked to prepare the next wave of Washington, D.C. leadership in the community and in city politics. They said I was holding on too long because I had nothing else to do and was getting in the way of us moving forward. Did the city need new energy and new leadership? *Yes!* I felt so, too. But that new vision simply wasn't there. If the new vision and leadership was there, it would have surfaced and presented itself. I didn't have time to bicker with people calling for new leadership. I wanted to continue the work that I considered myself *born* to do. My public service to the people of the District of Columbia remained a *calling*.

When incumbent Mayor Sharon Pratt Kelly found out that I was running for mayor against her, she was as pissed as Calvin Rolark was when I ran against his wife for the Ward 8 council seat. I guess Mayor Kelly thought I was going to stay out of the way and remain on the council, but I saw new opportunities as the mayor. I believe Sharon Pratt Kelly knew that I still had a lot of love and support from the community, and enough to be elected again.

Some people didn't think I had the tenacity to come back. Others thought I shouldn't. They wanted me to go away and retire from politics. But I wasn't coming back to do the city any harm. I still felt I had a lot of good and a lot of management experience to offer. I had already apologized to the community and taken responsibility for my actions, but I was never taking the responsibility for being set up. I had paid my debt to society and I was no longer plagued by bad decisions or by addictions. I was ready to come back and serve the people with a clear conscience.

I was too knowledgeable and I cared too much about the citizens of Washington *not* to run again for mayor. I was convinced after my short time as the council member of Ward 8. The new business developments, schools, construction and programs for the poor that I had advocated for Southeast in my first two years back on the D.C. City Council had been *phenomenal*. I brought a powerful voice and a lot of experience to Ward 8, and I wanted to bring that same voice and experience back to the core of the government. And by the grace of God, we went on to win the Democratic Primary with 47 percent of the vote to John Ray's 37 percent and Sharon Pratt Kelly's 13 percent. And I was halfway there on my return to office.

My victory in the primaries shocked the nation, but it didn't shock me. After the video of the Vista Hotel, there were still naysayers who believed I would never run again let alone *win*. There were newspaper articles from the *Boston Globe* on the East Coast to the *Los Angeles Times* on the West. After the fallout at the Vista and the following trial, I didn't expect to be able to generate much support from white voters. So I was very surprised to win a large enough percentage of the white vote in the Democratic Primary to carry a victory. That showed that I still had a significant amount of support from many in the white, gay and lesbian communities, as well as the white business community.

I also did very well in Ward 4, the middle-class black community which I expected Sharon Pratt Kelly and John Ray to carry. I did well winning eighteen of nineteen precincts. The only precinct that I didn't win was Mayor Kelly's Precinct 62, where she lived. The black middle class understood how much I had done to open up all levels of employment. I had created job opportunities not only for the poor, but for the higher management and professional workers in the community. In fact, during my three terms, I focused on challenges facing the poor. I focused on strengthening the black middle class including creating job opportunities. I believe my track record for getting things done in office made me feel like a gladiator in Rome. I was that successful at pulling in the people whenever I ran for office. I also received much support from Ward 5, where black retirees lived; some parts of Ward 6, and certainly all of Wards 7 and 8.

But *The Washington Post* no longer endorsed me for a fourth term. It really didn't matter. *The Washington Post* Editorial Board didn't register well in the black community. It helped Carol Schwartz pick up some white Democratic voters. They endorsed Carol, helping her to win 42 percent of the general election. Nevertheless, I won 56 percent and the mayor's office of Washington once again. It was an unbelievable victory, but it was *close*. Carol Schwartz had gained on me. But once again, it showed that *The Washington Post* didn't have much juice in the black community. It was an unbelievable victory. Carol Schwartz had done better than she thought she would.

I understood that in every election, race is a factor. So I was not surprised at how well Carol was able to do in her second run against me. Whites often vote for white candidates and blacks often vote for black candidates. It doesn't make them bad people. We don't have the awareness or trust of other cultures sometimes. But it's not always that predictable. Some whites will vote for black candidates, and some blacks will vote for white candidates.

However, there was no gloating on my part. And when Carol's team and campaign managers continued to talk about me winning the election, I made a comment at a forum after the primary that she needed "to get over it." There was a meeting at a predominantly white civic association, which Carol and I attended. The election was over and it was about doing good for the city. We needed to move on with the work of the city and the community. My statement wasn't meant to be another catchphrase or a slogan, but once the media and the newspapers reported it, the community ran with it and made it a bigger deal than what it really was. It got to the point sometimes where everything I said became quotable.

That fourth campaign and election for mayor gave the people an opportunity to vote again on my behalf and to speak volumes about their unyielding support for me. I not only won the support of Ward 7 and Ward 8—which was expected—I won the votes of the black middle class in Ward 4 and Ward 5. They still showed that they appreciated all that I had done for the black poor, the professional class, the entrepreneurs, the police chief, the fire chief, and in rebuilding so much of the African American community in Washington.

I even had more white votes than I expected against Carol. The people understood that the Vista Hotel was all about a government agenda of entrapment, and they voted to show that they didn't approve of it. That sent the government a final message that the people were not naïve about their attitudes against me.

By me running for mayor again and winning, I was also showing a level of defiance. I was not going to allow the media to determine who I was or what I could or could not do. I refused to allow the white establishment to control me or greatly influence those who believed in and voted for me. Ultimately, I wanted to be an example that we can fall down from great heights and still get back up again to uplift *more* people. I wanted my fourth term as mayor to be inspirational.

The "Mayor for Life" title started with Ken Cummings who was a political reporter at the *Washington City Paper*. But I never liked that name. It reminded me of Papa Doc Duvalier of Haiti, who considered himself a "President for Life," and I didn't want to be known that way or be connected to that style of rule. Everything I did in government in Washington was for the benefit of the common people; that's why they continued to vote for me. I hadn't forced myself on anyone. It was all a democratic process. So I never liked the reference of being the "Mayor for Life." However, once people started using it, over time they were able to bring a positive light to it where I could accept it. I didn't have a choice anyway, because they kept using it.

It took a lot of courage for me to face the entire Washington community again, and Cora had a lot to do with that through her insistence. One thing was certain: I now had a bunch of new and humbling stories that I could tell to relate to everyone. I had been up on the mountaintop and the government tried to bring me down to the dark alleyways of life, giving me an even stronger perspective to fight for the people who couldn't fight for themselves. No one could say that I had been a silver spoon baby, and no one could say that I didn't understand their struggles, because I had been through some of it myself.

But it wasn't easy for me to return to office. There were some people trying to stop me everywhere I turned. A week before the primary election, I parked outside of a building downtown and came out to find a boot on my car with a newspaper cameraman right there on the scene to take pictures. They reported it in the newspapers the next day. You have to ask yourself whether the newspapers had been tipped or whether it was a coincidence for a cameraman to arrive at the same time to take pictures and report it.

There was also a book published around that summer of 1994 called *Dream City* by two white Washington reporters, Tom Sherwood and Harry S. Jaffe. In this book, I was essentially blamed for everything that was wrong with Washington. I was fairly satisfied with Tom's historical reporting of my public service in Washington, but not with Harry's reporting of my current life. It was as if I had done nothing right in the city in my recent years. Of course, that was always the case for some white Americans. Any black man who dared to look out for the progress of his people became an immediate political enemy to some whites.

These reporters were blatant enough to suggest that dark-skinned blacks voted for me as the champion of the poor to resist the middle-class, light-skinned blacks of the District. They actually wrote that in their book.

The television reporters and journalists continued to make money off me, hand and fist. But through the "Amazing Grace" of God, I won the election that year anyway. That's why I chose to quote the "Invictus" poem at my 1995 inauguration speech:

Out of the night that covers me,
Black as the pit from pole to pole,
I thank whatever gods may be
For my unconquerable soul.

...

It matters not how strait the gate,
How charged with punishments the scroll,
I am the master of my fate:
I am the captain of our soul.
—WILLIAM ERNEST HENLEY, 1875

I was determined to do the impossible again in an unprecedented fourth term and rise up out of the darkness to continue to lead the city of Washington, D.C. back into the light. Throughout my life I had been knocked down, but I refused not to get back up. I refused to quit because I didn't know what quitting was. I had learned early on in my life to persevere. Where my friends and other leaders I had known had something to fall back on and stop, I had nothing but God, my faith and my strong will to keep me going. That's the inspirational fuel I used to run and win again as mayor. My strong spirit and tenacity, despite everything that happened to me in the District politically and personally, allowed me to keep pushing forward.

By continuing the fight, I wanted to set another example for the downtrodden that you *all* can get back up and continue to move forward toward progress. If I could do it with the whole world watching, and not be afraid to get back up and succeed again, then what's your excuse not to do the same? I still considered Washington to be a great city, and I still wanted to lead Washington. And the majority of the people still supported me. They understood how strong my spirit was regardless of our dark times together. They realized that I was strong enough to keep up the fight and the hope with the hard work that it took to continue to guide such a great city that still needed great leadership.

In my fourth mayoral address, I expressed all of my heart to the people. I told them not to quit on my leadership, not to quit on D.C., and not to quit on their hopes, dreams and aspirations. More importantly, I told them not to quit on themselves. I still believed in the city and I was still deeply committed to it.

Fighting for the people was my work and my legacy. I felt that I was put on this earth to do it. It was never just a job for me; it was a *calling*. I had been called back to continue doing the duty of the people. I saw much that we still needed to do—providing job opportunities—building public and private rela-

250 Marion Barry, Jr. and Omar Tyree

tionships to create new economic development and opportunities for our citizens, including refurbishing playgrounds, day cares and new school programs for our children. We still needed programs and money for public safety, health care and security for the elderly. We still needed a lot of things that I wanted to help provide.

I thanked the people of Washington for voting for me and for keeping the faith. I recognized Eleanor Holmes Norton and demanded she have a Washington, D.C. vote for Congress. I thanked all of the people who helped us start a new voter registration drive. I made note of the great Dorothy Height, who was in her eighties, and her work with the National Council of Negro Women. I thanked my team, staff members and the D.C. City Council and administration leaders; David Clarke, Michael Rogers, Barry Campbell, Anthony Williams, Steve Halpin. I even thanked Judge Eugene Hamilton and Annice Wagner from the courts.

I was elated and on a new high. I was so proud of everyone. My supportive wife, Cora Masters Barry; my loving mother, Mattie Cummings; and my son, Christopher, were all there beside me. I still got a little nervous when speaking in front of big crowds, especially that one, but I continued to have the willpower to make it through and to express to the people what we all needed to hear. Whether you voted for me or agreed with me or not, you had to respect the message of continued hope from the darkness no matter *who* you were. My message was pure and my heart was righteous. I still felt strength, energy and invigoration to help the people.

We still had too many young black men and Hispanic boys on the news each night going to jail for something, and I still wanted to speak on doing something about helping them to turn their young lives around. I still cared about that. I wanted to remind everyone that we still had good kids who were doing the right things. I felt they ought to have an opportunity and a *right* to get a good enough education and go to college or engage in a career to make something of themselves for their families to be proud of.

I still believed in the Youth Leadership Institute and our summer youth jobs and training. We had a "Hands Without Guns" project that we started to get kids to think about using their creativity in life and not violence. We wanted them to keep dreaming and to realize their dreams. We still had far too many kids who didn't graduate, and far too many children in homeless shelters and foster homes, or in abusive families. I still cared about all of their futures.

It was estimated that $1.5 billion a year went to the consequences of not dealing with children in their earlier years when we could have made a significant difference. I considered the future of my own son, Christopher, in the District, where he needed to have skills and to find necessary work as a young man. And I felt it was a shame that we spent $265 million a year on the Department of Corrections when a great deal of money that could have gone to so many other positive things in the community, like the University of the District of Columbia (UDC).

We had 10,000 students who attended UDC on Connecticut Avenue at its height in the 1980s. We wanted to keep their support going and make sure that the proud graduates who stepped out of UDC each year would have somewhere to earn a living and to practice their trades. But there were several council members at the time who were discussing closing UDC or turning it into a smaller community college.

I said, "No way! We can't do that!"

The local government was willing to spend $265 million a year to incarcerate our young men and women, but they refused to spend the $45 million that we budgeted to educate 10,000 future workers? I found that disparity in budget priorities to be *outrageous*. Those were only *some* of the many reasons why I wanted to be back in a leadership position.

I told them:

Destiny is no matter of chance.
It is a matter of choice.
It is not a thing to be waited for,
it is a thing to be achieved.
—WILLIAM JENNINGS BRYAN, © CIRCA 1900S

It was important to me that I establish all that I had done and had been through to show that I could still come back from it all. To get remarried and run the District government again represented a fresh start. It was incredibly gratifying to have the people's support in my goals and mission. My mother was there to support me, and she stayed in D.C. for a couple of years at the Golden Rule Apartments in Northwest. She helped me to continue to believe in my faith and in the strength of God to keep going.

My mother was still proud and was never down on me. Her iron will and unwavering support helped me continue to carry through. I still had the big visions and the big dreams for Washington, as the nation's "First City" to lead as example of how to overcome. So I introduced our "Vision for America's First City." And we were not only America's capital city, as the capital city of the most important country in the world; I viewed us as the *world's* "First City." We were the home for 165 foreign governments and 20 million visitors each year.

I still had a whole lot of ideas I wanted to implement in D.C. I was never at a loss of ideas about what we needed to do to move the city, the people and the policies forward, but the execution of it all and the money that was needed to carry these ideas out was a whole other ball game. Congress had other plans for the District.

Some things we were able to do, including the restoration of the U Street corridor near the Frank D. Reeves Center on Fourteenth. We improved transportation time and fire prevention. We improved the city sanitation and world-class education standards. We were able to close down the open drug markets in the District. We sent hundreds more of our police force on bikes and on scooters to get closer to the crime.

The murder rate died down due to a decline in the drug culture. A lot of people can look at several different factors, but all murders went down nationally as the drug culture became less prominent. But there was a new rise in murders from the Hispanic population, as they entered into their own drug and gang wars. And we had to deal with that.

There were hundreds of more things for us to do in Washington, more people to thank and more people to include in the plans to help, including George Hednut, vice chair of the Wish List Committee and vice president of BFI Industries. I thanked the Department of Parks and Recreation for ongoing ideas on how to engage the youth with use of D.C.'s recreational facilities. I thanked boxing manager Rock Newman and former Heavyweight

Champion Riddick Bowe for their economic help in supporting our "Funds for Guns" program. I thanked Douglas Kim and the Korean Chamber of Commerce, who provided 100 bicycles for our Metropolitan Police. And Lilia Peterback for her "Adopt-A-Park" program to clean up our public parks. There were so many people who were still willing to be a part of our continued solutions and answers for the District. I was truly blessed to have them.

I closed my final election speech and plans by quoting Langston Hughes:

"We build our temples for tomorrow
strong as we know how
And we stand on top of the mountain
free within ourselves."
—LANGSTON HUGHES, 1926

As I went back to work in office, I hired Raymone Bain as my press secretary. She had worked as well in the offices of President Jimmy Carter from Georgia. Raymone had experience in dealing with entertainers and celebrities, including Michael Jackson and the Jackson family, Kenneth "Babyface" Edmonds, Boyz II Men, and a host of other prominent celebrities and newsmakers. She had worked for Bert Lance at the Office of Management and Budget during the Carter administration. Raymone had vast experience in dealing with the media and crisis management. I met her in the '70s, right after she arrived in Washington to work for Bert Lance. She was bright and articulate, as she is now. Plus, she was a black female. By then I knew that my winning the mayor's office again in Washington had become a national and international story. How could it not be with all that I had gone through and how the government attempted to destroy my career and credibility? There was no way for us to avoid the national media attention or questions about me, so we continued to deal with it head-on.

We had interview requests from all over: Barbara Walters, Montel Williams, Phil Donahue, Ted Koppel, Sally Jessy Raphael. Of course, the late-night show comedians were all over me. Jay Leno, David Letterman and other national comedians did spoofs. Chris Rock was among the worst comedians. It took us almost three years to educate him on Marion Barry. As a matter of fact, I was his main guest on his comedy show in 1998. Chris Rock turned his views around so much so that he wanted to talk to me about producing my life story. There were spoofs on TV, radio and in newspapers and magazines. They all tried to turn the story into an embarrassment, but I continued to hold my head up high and persevere.

On the Sally Jessy Raphael show, they tried to trick me after inviting me on the show to talk about addictions. I figured I was going to talk about alcohol and maybe my drug addictions, which I knew a lot more about after therapy, but they started talking about sex addictions. I answered their questions about sex, power, alcohol and drugs. I explained how they can all go together some-times, but the audience was confused, because they expected me to talk a lot more about sex than what I planned to. I didn't think I had any more of a craving for sex than the average man did, and I said all I had to say about it. Then they had an expert who spoke about it.

Looking back on it, I was being very honest at that period of my life. Sex, power, drugs and alcohol *were* sometimes linked together. They were all vices that could get you into trouble when you made the wrong decisions about them. But you couldn't look at sex individually and say that I had a sex addiction. I had been friends with plenty of women and had hired women, whom I had never had sex with, done any drugs with, or had shared any drinks with. I had a clear separation between my addictive behavior and whom I dealt with. I looked at sex and drugs as being more about my bad *choices* than anything else. That's why I was able to reform from it, where everyone thought that I couldn't.

After the government and the national news media had broadcast my sting and court case all over the world, I had popularity and infamy in London, Japan, Australia, Canada, the Caribbean islands and Latin America. But I wanted to use my life story as an inspiration to the people. I wanted to show the people of Washington and everywhere else that we can get knocked down and then pick ourselves back up again. I had done it all of my life and I was still a fighter.

Raymone told me to tell the truth about my story with articulation and poise. She said, "The straight answers are the best answers."

So I tried to do just that. She considered me to be an iconic figure who transcended politics, race, gender, age, economics and class. In my fourth term, everyone knew about me. My story had been the talk of the country. But my story wasn't over yet.

I still had the most newspaper clippings in *The Washington Post* than anybody because I had *done* more. I said what I wanted to say and the press never failed to publish my comments. Some members of the press refused to publish all of the good that I had done. I think being the Mayor of Washington is not only local, but national news. I really think the city of Washington had a lot more to do with my national popularity. To be a leader in Washington with the programs we had started, the stories that came out of the city, and my overall personality, philosophy and passion all added to it.

At first, I didn't feel comfortable with a lot of the national interviews and all of the attention. Of course, I knew what they all wanted me to talk about. How could I come out of jail and still be the mayor after all I had gone through? But a lot of the national journalists and interview personalities were very respectful to me. They found me to be intelligent and good-spirited about everything. They appreciated me for how I handled it all. You can't be the mayor for more than a dozen years without knowing what you need to know or how to talk to people.

Since everyone wanted a piece of my story of resurrection, I felt it was important to hire Raymone as my press secretary, because she had immense experience in the entertainment and media world arena. So I used the opportunity to turn my charm back on and let the world know all of the wonderful things that I had done in Washington. I couldn't let too much of my personal life grab all of the national headlines. After awhile, I had to let these people know that I was still in charge of a multibillion-dollar budget. However, once I had settled back into office, the budget had definitely gotten out of hand.

The huge deficit led to the government's eventual response of implementing a Financial Control Board to oversee all of our department budgets and affairs in Washington. And money became the biggest issue for everything.

THE FINANCIAL
CONTROL BOARD

n Sharon Pratt Kelly's four years as the mayor of Washington from 1991-1995, she found out how hard the job was. As a result of the District's money problems, the city ended up borrowing more money than what we were taking in. But that put us further into debt, not only with the federal government, but with Wall Street. And by the time I took office, we got a chance to reestablish those Wall Street relationships. Our bond rates had become junk bonds. So the city was cash strapped with not enough money to pay all of our bills and responsibilities or pay down on our deficit.

She didn't realize the enormity of the job because there is no textbook on being the mayor. We had created most of the infrastructure ourselves. A lot of people can talk about it, but to actually do the job is much harder than most people think.

One of the first things I asked Mayor Sharon Pratt Kelly not to do when she took office was allow the budget cutters to slash the summer youth jobs program, because they were always under attack in the budget. I had always protected the program. But as soon as she got into office, the first thing she did was allow the budget cutters to cut funding from the summer jobs program. She was later booed off the stage at Cardoza High School in her own backyard of the Northwest, from hundreds of students who didn't appreciate her priorities. She was not protecting the things that the people cared about the most, and it was bad policy. So when I got back into office, I immediately put the summer youth jobs program back into the budget.

Moreover, I didn't like when Mayor Kelly ordered to remove my name from the Frank D. Reeves Center at Fourteenth and U streets either. I felt it was a misdirection of energy and a shot at my legacy in Washington. You can't remove a person's name like that. There's one argument to disagree with how a person ran the city, but it's another argument to slight a city leader *personally*. I felt that taking my name down from a city project that I was *totally* responsible for developing was blatantly disrespectful. So after she took my name down from the Reeves Center building, when I got back into office, I put my name right back up. I was not going to allow *anyone* to erase my history in the District.

Mayor Kelly also refused to deal with the establishment of the Washington Redskins and owner Jack Kent Cooke. He wanted to build a new stadium in the District and tear down RFK Stadium, which seated only 60,000 people in the Northeast. Bigger and better football stadiums were popping up around the country, and Jack wanted to compete with them here in the District. These football organizations had more seating capacity, better technology and company luxury seats to help pay the bills. Luxury box seats for company employees to enjoy professional sports games were the new wave of business at national stadiums and arenas, and not only for football, but for baseball and basketball as well.

We knew for a *fact* that we could fill *thousands* of additional seats at the football games in the District because the stadium at RFK was always jam-packed with fans, and the Redskins had a long waiting list for season tickets. Jack Kent Cooke didn't want the team to be left behind the times with its old structure, but Mayor Sharon Pratt Kelly refused to talk to him personally. I kept advising Mayor Kelly that Jack Kent Cooke wasn't that kind of guy. He was from the old school and he liked doing his business face to face with the mayor. Mayor Kelly named Clifford Alexander, who ran for mayor in 1994, and had been Secretary of the Army, to be the liaison to the Redskins. I told her earlier, in terms of the Skins, Jack Kent Cooke was insistent on meeting with the mayor personally versus meeting with surrogates.

Jack called me one time while I was still serving Ward 8 as their council member, and he asked, "Marion, what's wrong with your new mayor? How come she won't meet up with me and talk about this?"

When I was mayor, Jack loved talking to me about sports and inviting Effi, Christopher and me out to all of the Redskins games. We also held a lot of concerts and big events at RFK. The stadium was beneficial to all of us. We could have had even bigger concerts at a new District stadium. But I don't know if Mayor Sharon Pratt Kelly even liked football. Maybe it wasn't on her priority list and she didn't know how to talk to Jack about it. Instead, she would send her cabinet members to meet with him and discuss the new stadium, and then she called Jack a "bully" whenever he complained.

All big business owners could be aggressive when they really wanted something done. That's why you have to be a firm mayor. But you can't avoid these people if you want to get the deals done. You have to face them, tell them what you need to tell them, and work it out. There were plenty of white businessmen that I could have called bullies in my first years as the mayor, but they all learned to respect and do business with me. But before I could get back into office and hammer out a new football stadium deal with Jack Kent Cooke, he signed a deal with the State of Maryland. The Cooke family then sold the team when Jack died in the mid-'90s before the new construction, and the Redskins and the State of Maryland built an 85,000-seat stadium in Landover, which was once the largest arena in the National Football League. We could've had it right here in the District.

Instead of investing in a new D.C. stadium and more business for the community, Sharon Pratt Kelly became the mayor and installed a $40,000 fireplace in the mayor's office. I don't know what that was about, but that's what she did. Maybe she really likes fireplaces. She also leased an office building at 441 Fourth Street, which was a $140 million to $150 million Peter Schwartz spec building that had no tenants. Mayor Kelly then installed a bullet-proof glass window to protect a second mayor's office there. Peter Schwartz had tried to get me to do that same deal with this spec building during my term as mayor, but I turned it down because of the cost.

Of course, there were back-and-forth reports of Sharon Pratt Kelly blaming her overspending on an overlapping small deficit from my final year in office. In the last year, the council refused to increase taxes to the point of balancing the budget. I balanced the budget for eleven of the twelve years and she tried to blame it all on that one year. That's why it was so important for the new cabinet and management officials to be able to balance the budgets. You have to hire the right people. The new budgets would always have to factor in any deficits.

I did agree that the District's healthcare costs for Medicaid and welfare had gone up. Without healthy citizens, workers and new employment in Washington, those necessary costs had nowhere to go but up. We had no *choice* but to spend money on the community. We had to take care of the people in the city who still needed it even though they didn't have jobs. That was the burden of any government.

So I was forced to look at different examples of what some of the other major cities had done to decrease their deficits and to manage their increasing budgets. I had to come up with some ideas of what we would be able to do, or at least *try* to do in Washington. Of course, I planned for an uphill battle with every dime that I needed to ask for. That's where the majority of my energy went on my fourth and final term as mayor. I didn't care about what people had to say about us in the District; we still had work to do to return to the promise of excellence in Washington that I still hoped for.

We hired Michael C. Rogers as the new city administrator, and we dug deeper into the books with an audit in February 1995, and found that Mayor Kelly left us with an even bigger deficit than we first thought. The District was over $500 million in the hole! Adding a new budget of $150 million, Sharon Pratt Kelly's administration left the District facing an accumulated $700 million in total deficit. We had a lot of work to do to get the city back on track.

None of our argument back and forth mattered when we had to deal with Congress that year. They didn't care whose fault it was; all they knew was that a $700 million deficit was out of control. By that time, the Republicans were back in power of the House. A lot of the Republicans never liked the idea of D.C.'s "Home Rule" in the first place, unless it benefited them. And if we had to ask for nearly a *billion* dollars to get us out of the hole, clearly Congress wasn't going to like that. So we realized that we were in deep trouble.

There was really no way out of the District's money crisis without asking Congress for help. Congress responded with their idea of the Financial Control Board. The implementation of the control board restricted us from what we wanted to do, but it had to be done to make the budgets acceptable again to Congress. The idea was to allow us to appoint an independent chief operating officer, who would oversee District government spending in all of our major departments. Essentially, the control board would be under the mayor's employ, but it would not be forced to carry out any budget spending that it did not agree with under the provisions set by Congress. So it gave us about ninety days from April to hire the CFO we felt could get the job done, or Congress would pull together its own financial manager to advise the District.

Starting in April 1995, North Carolina Senator Duncan "Lauch" Faircloth, who served on the Appropriations Committee, wrote language that basically allowed the FCB to take over the affairs of much of the government on an economic needs basis. I considered Faircloth a conservative and a pig farmer from North Carolina, who had no business writing anything in reference to people who couldn't vote for him. But he was in a position of authority to do so. Immediately after, I held a press conference and called the control board a "rape of Democracy." But complaining wouldn't change anything. Immediate actions had to be done to save the District.

All five control board members were appointed by President Bill Clinton that April. Andrew Brimmer was appointed as the chairman, Stephen Harlan was appointed the vice chairman, Constance B. Newman, who was a black Republican, was appointed as an executive assistant, and Joyce Ladner and Edward Singletary rounded out the five members.

To more effectively fight it, if we had more members of the control board who were sympathetic to the District, we would have been better off. However, Constance B. Newman advised us to find a CFO based on expertise in accounting and economics to avoid future arguments with Congress. She said it was smarter and more proactive than starting a racial warfare with name-calling. The bottom line was to get it done to balance the budget. At the time, we didn't know how long it would take to do it, but we knew it would be at least a few years. That was the predicament we were in, so we all had to deal with it.

These control board members were later assigned to oversee nine of my major departments in the District government, where we had two separate groups of professionals in our cabinet meetings. They were all respected professionals in their fields, but the general idea of having a control board to overrule my department heads and my own decisions was a mess waiting to happen. They basically had the congressional power to suggest cutting thousands of city jobs and slash millions of dollars on our various social programs and services.

In hindsight, what I should have done in office was develop stronger ties and spend more time with New York Congressman James T. Walsh and his staff, who had a relationship with the House Republicans. Out of New York, James Walsh understood the big city budget and state issues that we were in, and with more planning and anticipation of what we needed to do, I'm sure we could have worked out a better management and payment system than what the control board had in store for us. Nevertheless, I realized that the federal government could still execute a relief plan for the District that I could not. Not only did we have a $700 million deficit, the District had a $3 billion liability unfunded pension for our fire department, our police department and public school teachers.

With the ninety days that we had to hire a CFO to work with the control board, I initially hired Carol O'Cleireacain before I took a vacation in Jamaica. I needed to clear my head a minute. But a couple days after I had arrived in Jamaica, my city administrator, Michael C. Rogers, called and told me that Carol had written a four-page memo about her duties, powers and responsibilities to the chairman of the control board, Andrew Brimmer. Well, she should have written and addressed the letter to *me*. *I* had hired her, not Andrew Brimmer. She had been hired to work for the *District*, not for the control board. It was an immediate show of disrespect and I would not tolerate that type of insubordination in my office. So I told Michael Rogers to let her know that she was *fired*. If you knowingly allow a staff hire or a cabinet member to blatantly disrespect you in office, then you give license to *everyone* to do it. I had not been the mayor of Washington for three terms without knowing how to control my office. And I was not going to *lose* control of it in my fourth term.

Anthony Williams, who was the CFO at the U.S. Department of Agriculture, had been an applicant for the job before we hired Carol and he had dropped out. I told my search team to attempt to get him back in the running for the job—which had been reopened—and the team was successful. I talked to Anthony Williams personally about joining the administration. I later hired

Anthony Williams because of his expertise and background in business. Tony Williams was credible and qualified and I didn't think he would fight against our government budget and debt negotiations. But that decision ended up becoming another headache.

The Financial Control Board was set up to deal with our overspending and deficit issues, and the full team was in place by that September of 1995. Anthony Williams had taken the job as the CFO and John W. Hill was appointed as the executive director of the control board. The first operation of business was to reduce the pay of 10,000 government employees. We needed to make the government more efficient and consolidate some of our departments. I didn't agree with cutting the budget by only downsizing government workers. I believed in "rightsizing," or reorganizing government responsibilities, employees and departments to work correctly.

Well, we got our man Tony Williams, where we were to meet with him and the control board members once a week for our economic council. I set up a meeting on Mondays, Wednesdays and Fridays with the CFO, staff, and Barry Campbell, who had served in various jobs under my administration in 1979 and was respected for his management and respected for the politics of the Mayor's office. Tony, as the CFO, would agree to a decision at a meeting, and then would sometimes follow up with his staff and change his position. I had a real challenge trying to figure out how to accommodate these new positions to get things done. As an elected public official, you want to take care of the people who have the least in the community. I was the jobs czar. I was used to fighting to give the people opportunities to make a living and to make money for themselves and their families. But when budget cuts happen, the least of us are typically forced to feel it the *most*.

For the people who were denied the imagination to believe, my intention in that fourth term was to use my great heights, my deep lows and my perils, and the joys in life to tell the people, "When down and out, don't give up." I was still shocked myself to be able to do so many things and to help the people to uplift. But at the beginning of that fourth term, I really had to control my own emotions and not give the federal government any indication that the control board regulations had resulted in unwise decisions by them. You had to stay strong in that situation, while being stripped of the power that the people had voted you into office to have. That took a lot of political maturity and temperament. But I had to deal with it. The control board was able to do things that needed to be done that I was not able to do. Everything could not be done politically. We needed Congress' approval to spend our own money.

I would do whatever I needed to fit the situation. So I tried to convince myself that the Financial Control Board was only another hurdle to negotiate for the benefit of the people. If I could negotiate with the man and woman out on the street and with businessmen in their offices, then why not negotiate with the control board? That's what I figured a good politician is supposed to do. You are representing *all* of the people; not just the poor or the rich, the educated or the uneducated, the young or the old, but *all* of the people as a group. So I had to humble myself for the greater good, even though I didn't like it.

We also were under a new welfare program from President Bill Clinton. President Clinton wanted to greatly overhaul and reform the welfare system by transitioning people back to work. But it didn't work well. The problem with this "from-welfare-to-work" transition program was that most of the jobs would be minimum-wage positions that didn't pay enough to live on. A major restriction of the program was that no employable man was to be allowed in the house. That rule basically meant that you were dealing with overworked, single mothers with children. That only enslaved more mothers and children to poverty, and further destroyed and denigrated the fabric of the family for poor people. If these families couldn't provide for a household with *two* able workers, then how could they survive with only one?

Then you had the discipline and structure issues within these households. Without fathers involved, you would have more poor households raised by women who could not handle all of the issues that would arise with their children. I have nothing but respect for black mothers who have to endure despite it all. Having two parents to negotiate all of the issues of childrearing is a benefit of the normal family structure. But when you forcibly take the man out of the household, not only do you minimalize his role, but you create situations where the children become used to broken families as the normal structure. That only adds up to more family problems for the next generation, which doesn't even *attempt* to incorporate the fathers.

There was also a time limit of sixty months that you could be on welfare with President Clinton's new plan. They even gave it a new name: Temporary Assistance for Needed Families (TANF). These new welfare plans may make sense for businesspeople who understand how to budget their money with a secure job, but for poor people in low-income jobs, where companies always find ways to fire them, economic planning and a time structure is never foolproof. Even with welfare reform, there's not much emphasis on getting people out of poverty. You have less poverty, but you still have poverty.

I had a meeting during that time in the Oval Office of the White House with President Bill Clinton in person. I met him as the Mayor of the District of Columbia. Even though I had been in the Oval Office before, I was still somewhat nervous. President Clinton evoked that type of excitement from people, and he was very similar to me in a lot of different ways. Who would ever think that a poor Mississippi boy would ever be invited to the Oval Office for a one-on-one talk with the President of the United States of America? But President Clinton was a Southerner like me who was very comfortable and used to being around black people, even dirt-poor ones.

I had been a good friend of the late Ron Brown, who became the first African American Secretary of Commerce and who also chaired the Democratic National Committee. Ron Brown was an original Washingtonian raised in Harlem, New York, and he was the real architect behind Bill Clinton's presidential victory in 1992. He facilitated our meeting because I wanted to meet with the president as the mayor of Washington to discuss how he could be more involved in the District after we had given him 92 percent of our vote. I particularly wanted to talk to the president about our budget and other needs for the District. I planned to include a discussion on my struggles with the five members of the Financial Control Board that he appointed.

We had a very amicable talk, but President Clinton had a lot more going on at the time and we both understood that the control board was a necessary measure for the District to get back to where we needed to be. But it was generous of him to meet me.

I remember I first met Bill Clinton in 1988 at the Democratic National Convention in Atlanta. At that time he was still the governor of Arkansas. Bill Clinton gave a highly inspired two-hour speech, which was way too long.

While he was speaking, the delegates began clapping, not for his speech, but for him to sit down. However, Bill thought they were clapping for him and he kept going on and on with his speech. He was an energetic leader who really believed in his message and had an ability to inspire.

Another time I met with President Bill Clinton was sometime after the Monica Lewinsky incident. His wife, First Lady Hillary Clinton, had an event at one of our local hospitals, and it happened that I was there for something else. I saw President Clinton walking through the hallway with his security team and called out to him.

I said, "Mr. President." He stopped and turned to me, and I asked him what he was there for. He told me that his wife, Hillary, was having an event at the hospital. Later on during that hospital visit, he said he wanted to talk to me more in private.

He took me into a meeting room at the hospital, where as it turned out, he wanted to talk to me about how to handle embarrassing personal situations as a public official. Like everyone else, he knew about my situation at the Vista Hotel, and we ended up talking for a good twenty minutes all about what to do when someone either pushes you in a hole or you put yourself in a hole of controversy.

I said, "The first thing you gotta do is stop digging the hole that put you there in the first place." By that I meant to stop feeling bad about whatever you did and feeling sorry for yourself, while questioning yourself about what would have happened *if*, because you don't know. President Clinton had read about my personal and political issues as the mayor of the District, and I thought it was a great gesture for him to come to me and ask me about how I handled my own situations. He could identify with me. He knew that I had been forced to handle it and had made a great comeback in my political career.

In 1997, President Clinton signed the Economic Revitalization Act, which was created by the Republican House and adopted by the Democratic Senate. This provision made it possible for us to borrow money at affordable rates, but at the same time that the federal government would take over $3 billion pension liability and take control over our prison system—the Department of Corrections. With the feds taking over, pension liability improved our ratings on Wall Street. Without it, we couldn't have been able to borrow money from anyone. At the same time, we had to allow the Financial Control Board to put us back in good standing with Congress, where we would qualify to borrow money again to pay off all of our debts and bills as a successful city operation. I was only concerned about the overuse of power with the control board and the officials that we were forced to deal with.

The way it all worked was that the District department heads would carry out their normal operations and then report back to the control board members. There were nine major departments. Every major department was included in the FCB review. They left some of the day-to-day operations with me—the smaller departments like parks and recreation, public libraries, the Corporation Counsel, and tourism to be run without control board supervision. The government didn't care anything about those departments, and the budgets were not large enough to hurt anything. Tourism didn't mean anything to the feds, but it meant a lot to us in the District. It was good for us economically that thousands of people from around the country were visiting the nation's capital. As far as the libraries, black people weren't allowed to read before the Civil War, and the federal government still didn't think we read, so they didn't see the libraries as a real priority in the District either.

When you're used to being the mayor, you consult with people on your decisions, but technically they all work for you. It was the same with the control board, but the difference was that I couldn't tell them what to do. During a number of early morning meetings with the Control Board, many instances became a dispute.

I went on a two-week spiritual retreat to St. Louis during these disputes to replenish my reserve and energy. This fourth term in office as the mayor was physically exhausting from all of the struggles with the control board, and those fights had almost depleted me. So in St. Louis, I read the Bible, I relaxed, I ate healthy food, and I got a lot of my energy back. There were several people in Washington, including Rock Newman, who had advised me of this wonderful place in St. Louis in a peaceful environment that was operated by a Catholic church. And the short break was right on time.

Usually, I liked to go to Jamaica and other Caribbean islands to get away. I loved the food, the sunshine, the water and the people in the islands. But they had problems with race and class in the islands as well. I used to stay on a resort near the water in Jamaica, where whites owned most if not *all* of the best beachfront property and housing. I allegedly was the first black person, along with my wife, Mary Treadwell, to stay at a place, which was an exclusive white-owned-and-operated resort. I was invited to stay there by a Jewish couple, Joyce and Marvin.

The second day there, the management of the resort called Marvin in and told him, "You and your black guests have to leave."

Marvin refused to leave because he had already paid for the week. So Mary and I stayed there with him and his wife for that entire week without the club management removing us. I remember baseball player Henry "Hank" Aaron was the second one to integrate that same beachfront property. White people had million-dollar villas there on prime beachfront property in Jamaica that they were *not* giving up.

These vacations and retreats away from Washington allowed me to keep things in proper perspective. It allowed me to understand how important my position was in the District to continue to fight for black people with no power, because white people would *surely* fight to keep theirs. So maintaining my energy and a clear head was very important.

Through all of my disputes with the Financial Control Board, I continued to provide the needed services for the people. We still worked on fairness and pushed for a government that worked for blacks, the poor and for the middle class. We were still fighting for fair contracts and providing hope and community resources to the people who had lost hope. At the end of the day, we still wanted to deliver for the people of Washington, so we continued to work with Congress to advocate fair budgets and fair policies for the District.

I also remained involved in the private sector developments. In the early part of my fourth term, Abe Pollin, who was the owner of the Washington Bullets, first came to me about moving his basketball team out of Maryland and into downtown Washington. As part of his move, he wanted the city to pay for construction to build a basketball arena downtown.

I told him, "We can't do that with city money just for you to make more off of your team in the District."

He said, "Well, I want to sit down and talk to you about it." So we started having face-to-face meetings on it, like I always did with big businessmen. I wanted them to *know* who they were dealing with.

First of all, I agreed that the city would like the Washington Bullets to move into an arena downtown. However, when we met, I repeated to Mr. Pollin that the District would *not* pay for the construction of the arena, but that we *would* agree to pay for the infrastructure and preparation of the site, including tearing down two city-leased buildings. My staff estimated that the preparation would cost about $50 million. However, Mr. Pollin insisted on the city paying for the construction of the downtown arena. And that's how the meeting ended; we were at an impasse.

A week or two later, Bob Johnson of BET made it public that he would pay for the construction of an arena downtown and bring a basketball team to Washington. That forced Mr. Pollin to rethink his position. As a result, we came to a new deal where Abe Pollin would pay for the construction costs and the city would still pay to prepare the site. Well, Mr. Pollin didn't have to look for a new team; he already had one. So the deal made sense to move forward with him.

Abe Pollin and I also agreed that we wanted this downtown arena built on schedule and on budget. In order for that to happen, he appointed Peter O'Malley, a longtime big wheel in Maryland politics, to help assure that this project would move forward according as planned, and I appointed Robert Moore, the former housing director, as my point man. The two of them remained in constant conversation to address any problems with the end result of us finishing the construction on budget and on time. But Washington's new downtown arena would not have been built if Mr. Pollin and I had not worked *personally* on the details of the project.

Well, immediately, we all believed that this 20,000-seat arena downtown, along with the Seventh Street Metro stop, could serve as a new business anchor. With an on-schedule completion of the arena and the construction of Gallery Place in that same Seventh Street area in Northwest, the whole corridor exploded, creating many more retail businesses. Douglas Jamal, a big developer in the District, participated in buying and remodeling many of the Seventh Street storefronts to attract and retain the new customers. That was the type of explosive and innovative business deals that I was known for in the District that outsiders didn't know about and couldn't appreciate.

However, despite my continued successes in business with friendships and influence in the private sector, it all had no effect on the control board. I was still not allowed to fully run the D.C. government as I did when I had full powers in the 1980s.

We continued our weekly meetings with the CFO, Tony Williams; my chief of staff, Barry Campbell; the city's top lawyer, Judge John W. Ferron; and others as needed. Tony Williams had been known on occasion to agree to one thing in the meetings and then later change his mind.

Around the same time, a friend of mine introduced me to Republican House Speaker Newton "Newt" Gingrich, who wanted to help figure out how he and the Republican House could assist the city. He and I then worked together on a number of projects to help the city, and we became known as the "Odd Couple." *The Washington Post* published our picture and story on the front page of the newspaper, and we were also featured on the front page of the *New York Times Magazine*. But over time, Newt Gingrich could not get things done that we wanted to execute for the city, and our relationship slowly diminished.

Newt Gingrich said he could relate to my struggles as a Democrat in battles with a Republican-run control board. He was a Republican House Speaker during the Democratic term of President Bill Clinton, so he had a lot of speaking events where he was booed, while trying to negotiate terms with the Democrats. Bipartisan negotiations between the two parties were that tough.

I remember African American Secretary of Agriculture Mike Espy resigned from the congressional pressures that he was under in 1994 after only serving a year in office. Years later, he was indicted on a bunch of trumped-up charges for allegedly taking sports tickets and benefits; charges that were all thrown out of court. It was reported that millions of dollars were spent on his case, only for it all to be dismissed. So being a black official in America was very hard. The government officials still don't give us the benefit of the doubt, and America will spend more money to hurt or discredit us than they will to help us. But I was battle tested enough to continue on in the fight as a fourth-term mayor. I had no time to run out of gas.

During the control board budgeting years, Tom Davis, a Republican from Northern Virginia, headed the authorizing committee for the city's money, and James T. Walsh from New York was the committee chairman who appropriated it. We had to deal with these two congressmen on a regular basis. In fact, Tom Davis was the official who had introduced the legislation to establish the control board. And with some modifications, his legislation for the Control Board passed through Congress. He had become Chair of our House District Committee. Looking in retrospect, I should have gotten to know him better and privately discussed the finances of the city, then wait for the House meetings. Tom had come to one of my inauguration parties, and I had attended his. I don't know if this would have changed Tom's attitude, but I should have tried it.

Not only did I have a hard time adjusting to this new period of compromised power, my son, Christopher, continued to have a difficult time adjusting. Although I had returned to the mayor's office to govern Washington, it wasn't the same for Christopher. His mother and I were no longer together in our house with family like old times, so it made him miss the early years even more. Nothing can take a child back to the joys that he used to have as a little boy.

As a black man and a leader of the Civil Rights Movement, who understood the long years of toil and struggles of our people, I tried to explain to Christopher that we had to continue on and fight. It wasn't over with simply because things had changed from the earlier years. I was unwavering in my approach and my service to the District in the 1990s, just as I had been in the 1980s when my son was much younger. But as a teenager, he could see the difference. Christopher was old enough to witness for himself the continuous attacks on my character, my style of rule, and all of the accusations and attacks that continued to be made against me.

When the reelection year came up in 1998, I had become tired, weary and exhausted. I was *tired* of all of it. So I made the decision not to run for office and to do something else with my life. The control board had tried to wear me down. But while I served my final term, Anthony Williams told me that he would never run against me if I was to run for mayor again. He was that confident that I would win. But he didn't have to worry about that, because I wasn't going to run.

I held a press conference in May 1998 to take my name and all speculation out of the race. I said I would not run for reelection and I meant it. I had to step away from politics. I was finally at that point. And *The Washington Post* reported it on the front page: "The mayor will not seek reelection." That closed the book on my long run as the mayor and leader of Washington.

I then took a consultant job with the black-owned, investment banking firm of Bernard Beal & Associates. My assignment was to travel around the country and speak to other mayors and city officials about bond deals and how they all worked. Since I had gone through the process with the District government and Wall Street, the bankers saw me as the best man for the job. I would basically explain how cash-strapped cities could borrow money against city bonds and pay the loan back with interest over "X" amount of years. I was offered several jobs, and since I had experience with the city bonds, it was a natural for me. I was very successful with mayors and city council members, particularly black mayors, using Bernard Beal in assisting to put together bond deals. And I worked there from January 2, 1999 until I decided to run for the Ward 8 council seat in 2004.

CHAPTER 18
BACK TO SERVICE

The Financial Control Board process took about six total years to pull the District's deficit and budgets back in order before Congress suspended it. By that time it was 2001, and I had been out of office for two years. My former CFO, Anthony Williams, had been elected as mayor.

I was still working for the investment banking firm of Bernard Beal & Associates and I had made a considerable amount of commission money from millions of dollars in bond contracts. I would travel to different cities around the country to discuss the bond process with city officials and bring them up to a certain level to deal with Wall Street. I made good money doing it, well over six figures. That's when I got into trouble with my taxes. I procrastinated on filing them.

I didn't refuse to file my taxes by intent or maliciously; I just didn't do them. When I worked in the D.C. government, I had staff members who would prepare my taxes for me, so I had gotten out of practice. But once I had to do them myself or pay an accountant to do them, I continued to put the process off and not file. Before I knew it, I was behind on my taxes by a few years.

The IRS took me to court where my lawyer arranged for me to plead guilty to one account of failing to file my taxes. I took responsibility for it. The U.S. Attorney's Office wanted me to do jail time, but Judge Deborah Robinson gave me a two-year probation, where I had to check in with a probation officer.

This IRS tax case was reported all over the news as another career embarrassment that I had to deal with. I had created the problem on my own and I didn't make any excuses about it. I accepted my terms of probation and went on to make amends with my next tax filing. I didn't like the idea of having to check in with a probation officer, but it was better than going back to prison. Then I missed the next filing date by two days and had to hire a new accountant.

For that, I got two more years of probation and no jail time. I continued to catch more scrutiny with my taxes because I was a public official with a target on my back. But it wasn't like I didn't have to pay them, because I still did. And when you're late, you pay the extra penalties.

It seemed like my whole life was about overcoming one thing after another. In the meantime, I was still being mobbed by people who wanted me back in politics. Every time I went to buy groceries at the local Safeway in Southeast, it took me two hours to get out of there from people complaining about their problems with the government and urging me to run for office again. And these community conditions began to weigh heavily on my heart.

I had started tutoring young children through the Savoy Elementary School. I was tutoring students in the Southeast on the second- and third-grade level on Tuesdays and Thursdays. They could barely read. On Mondays, Wednesdays and Fridays, I took on a whole class of students and found more of them who couldn't read. I then decided to answer the call to return to public office and serve as a council member.

At the time in 2004, Sandy Allen held the council seat in Ward 8. So I ran to unseat her in the 2004 council elections. She didn't want to give up her seat, so I told her, "May the best person win." But I had only lost an election once.

I went on to win the Democratic primary for Ward 8 with 58 percent of the vote, followed by 91 percent in the general election. A bunch of people were shocked that I was still willing to step up instead of step down, especially in Ward 8. The population of the poor in the area was 98 percent black. But I still had it in me to lead, and leading the people who needed it the most was part of my philosophy. It was all about uplifting people with policies that I thought were still important. I still wanted to give the people there a sense of hope and help put Ward 8 back on the map with government policies.

I set up my new office at Melon Street and Martin Luther King, Jr. Avenue in Southeast, one block down from Malcolm X Boulevard. MLK Avenue and Malcolm X Boulevard in Southeast was one of the few places in America were MX meets MLK. And on January 2, 2005, the announcement was made that "Marion Barry is back in politics!"

I jumped right back in the fold with budget proposals for 10,000 new units of housing in Ward 8, and better education facilities and more jobs for the people in the area. I was elected for a four-year seat instead of a two-year seat; the issues that I was prepared to attack were constant. If you don't have any jobs, you can't live in new housing because you can't pay the rent. Then you end up selling drugs to make a living, which sends you to prison. And once you return from prison, people can use your criminal record as another excuse not to hire you. All of those issues needed time to address, so I needed a four-year term.

It was a hard cycle of poverty that we needed to break in Ward 8, but it was hard to get people there to see the straight-and-narrow path to success. For so many who didn't know where their next meal or dollar was coming from, they were more liable to commit an armed robbery. Like I continued to state: if you don't inherit money, and you can't make any money, then you'll end up *taking* money. Either that or you'll start selling something illegal.

Some people didn't think that certain kids and young men in impoverished communities would ever do right. But I thought it was all a part of a system of inequality, a lack of care and a strategy to deal with the underprivileged. The way I saw it, far too many people thought about Ward 8 and the community of the Southeast as being filled with dope dealers and prostitutes, hopeless mothers and people that had been abused. They couldn't see the thousands of families who lived there like normal people—working, paying bills, going to church, laughing, living, dreaming and going off to school every day. I knew because I had tutored many of their kids. So I was ready to fight to advocate more money and programs for the poorest people of Washington who needed it to keep striving.

I later set up an office on the third floor of the government's social services building, right across the Southeast Bridge on Martin Luther King, Jr. Avenue, across from the Big Chair, a landmark in Anacostia and Ward 8. The fifteen-to twenty-year-old building was spearheaded by Don Peebles, who became a very successful African American developer of real estate. He had worked in my cabinet on the taxing and appeals board in the 1980s. His mother had introduced him to real estate at a young age. In fact, I think he was only around fourteen when I first met him. But once he got off the government tax board, he started getting into major real estate development.

So when Don Peebles came up with the idea to develop an office building in the heart of Southeast, I personally signed for the government to lease the building during my third and final term as the mayor. Mr. Peebles told me that my decision to have the District government to lease the building was his first big contract, and he became yet another story of success that my innovative leadership had spearheaded.

Typically, it's very hard to develop anything as a black man in America, including development in the political town of Washington. When you're black, you can't get anything done, except when I was the mayor. Sometimes the financial institutions would turn you down solely based on the ZIP code that you wanted to build or develop in. But the National Bank of Washington, led by Luther Hodges, gave Don Peebles a minority business loan to finance the construction of the building that put Peebles on the map.

Don Peebles later moved to Miami, where he was part of a major project to develop the first black-owned hotel in Miami and in the nation. He then moved up to New York to develop more projects. And he was on his way to become one of the most successful business developers in the country. However, he left Washington, D.C. to do it, because it was hard to get deals done in the city without me being there to help. So ask Mr. Peebles how valuable I was at giving him the opportunity he needed to become the very successful man that he is today.

Closed doors happen to a lot of young black minds with big visions and big ideas. You can have the creativity for new business, but you can never get the finances to start it or to keep it going. That's how a lot of new businesses start only to fold. Black entrepreneurs end up spending so much money to build something new that they don't have enough left over to run it properly. So I was there to make sure Don Peebles' idea for an office building in Southeast didn't run out of operational capital before it started. The building has been operating now for more than twenty years.

We didn't even have a name for the building. Some people called it the Welfare Building. Other people started calling it the Effi Barry Building, out of respect for the "First Lady of D.C." Effi will always have that title as far as I'm concerned. And we use the building for all kinds of social services, community programs, job internships and career planning. We use it for poor people who need different kinds of help, and they are all delighted that it's still there. The building is open and jampacked with people seeking services five days a week, in sunshine, rain, snow or sleet.

Of course, when I returned to public office as a council member for Ward 8, some people didn't like it, but I didn't care if they liked it. It made some of the council members and politicians nervous because of my voice and experience. But I didn't care whether or not I made them nervous. I had a job to do for the people I represented in Ward 8. I viewed it as more unfinished business. I knew more and spoke up more than any other council members in office, but that was to be expected. I advised the other council members to use me by leaning on my experience. I wasn't there to get in the way but to help provide guidance and more productivity around the District.

After serving the District in office as the mayor for sixteen years, some people found it hypocritical for me to criticize the city government about so many inequalities in Ward 8. Some of these detractors claimed that the same inequalities occurred for Ward 8 when I was the mayor. But I didn't see the problem with me instigating and advocating changes at all. I had done a lot in my four terms as the mayor—more than anyone else had done—but as the council member for Ward 8, I could do even *more* to fight specifically to provide for the people who needed it most.

I felt I was closer to the people in Ward 8 as a council member. They were my direct constituency in the underserved neighborhoods of the Southeast. It was always the *least* that needed the most help anyway. So it made more sense for me to be in Ward 8 than anywhere else in the District. And the people in Ward 8 saw it the same way. They knew that I would fight for them harder than anyone.

We got right to work and established tremendous progress in Ward 8, not only with housing, jobs and education, but in the physical development with new buildings, schools and centers of entrepreneurship. Compared to what was in development in Ward 8 prior to 2003, it was night and day the things we were able to do.

We also started a new policy of transparency in the council for open meetings with the press, but I believed that stopped us from making the hard decisions we needed in order to get things done. Some members of the press were not interested in simply reporting the news but in creating news and conflict where they could sell newspapers. I didn't like that, because it stopped certain members of the council from speaking out. I would speak out anyway, but I didn't want the other members on the council feeling intimidated by the media reporters trying to make disparaging news.

In my personal life, Cora and I had bonded during a time where we both felt a need to support each other, but as our relationship and marriage moved on, that need for support was no longer as strong as it had been in the past. We still loved and cared for each other, but it wasn't the same as those initial years of rebuilding my life and career. We found that we were no longer clicking right.

I remember Cora up and left the house for about two to three weeks during the early 2000s. I had no idea where she went. She didn't call me or anything. I was going crazy, calling around and looking for her. I didn't know if she had been kidnapped or what.

When Cora finally called me back, she said, "We can't continue on like this."

Cora was her own woman with her own opinions, activities and her own ideas about how she wanted to live and what she wanted to do. She was not as tolerant as Effi had been, and I didn't expect her or want her to be. However, Effi's understanding was what had allowed us to be married through so many different issues. I couldn't expect that from Cora. So we decided to separate around 2002. Cora had been consistently involved in my life since the early 1970s, and she had participated in everything I did, starting with my first political campaign. We remain good friends and allies in life, but the dedicated marriage part became too much to handle for both of us.

As a man in need of companionship, I got involved with women who sometimes were not good for me. They were more bad personal decisions on my part. Effi had always told me that I was not a great judge of character. A lot of times I put myself in bad situations by not choosing to be around the right kinds of people. But as a man, you get involved with women anyway because you still have human needs: emotional, physical, spiritual, intellectual. And you still want to feel the love and care of a woman. So I have to forgive myself, even in my older age, from being a normal man with feelings for a woman.

Then I found out in 2006 that Effi was sick. She had moved back to the District after ten years of teaching at Hampton University, and she had an apartment in Northeast D.C., where Christopher was staying with her at the time. Our son was grown and out of school by then, but he would drop by to see me sometimes and he would tell me that his mother didn't look so good, or at least compared to what he was used to. Effi had always been a good-looking and classy woman.

Well, she went up to Howard University Hospital's emergency room with what she thought was a bad sinus infection and found out that it was much worse. The doctors at Howard diagnosed her with acute myeloid leukemia. Leukemia is a cancer of white blood cells that damage your bone marrow. After the diagnosis of leukemia, Effi became lethargic, she was not eating, and soon she lost a lot of weight and didn't have her normal energy.

Once I found out about it, I wanted her to go to Johns Hopkins University Hospital in Baltimore. I liked Howard University Hospital and went there myself, but I had to admit that Johns Hopkins was the best, and I wanted nothing but the best for Effi. But she was admitted at Howard for treatment, where Christopher and I went to visit her. Sometimes we went to the hospital to see her together and sometimes separately.

At the time, Christopher was twenty-six, Effi was sixty-two and I was seventy. After all we had been through, Effi and I held hands and professed our love for each other at her bedside. Although we had not been married for years, I still cared a great deal about her. I had also been separated from Cora for a few years and showed up to see Effi at the hospital every day, or as often as I could make it. It was an awful feeling to see her like that. My stomach was in knots from anxiety and regret, but I remained strong for her.

Effi went into remission for a period, and we all thought that she would make it through. She was released from the hospital and capable of caring for herself. She was taking outpatient chemotherapy and appeared to be on the road to a successful recovery. But during her remission, Effi told me that she wanted me to take care of Christopher, as if she knew she didn't have much time. Even though Christopher was grown, she was still worried and concerned about his well-being, as most mothers would be. And it was understandable. Christopher was her only baby.

Before we knew it, cancerous cells got back into Effi's system and wreaked havoc. When these cancerous cells returned, I again recommended that she go to John Hopkins in Baltimore. In fact, I was *adamant* about her being seen there because I still knew that they were the *best*. Effi's health decreased rapidly, and she agreed to see a specialist at John Hopkins Hospital. She was seen there on an outpatient basis by Dr. Bernardine Lacey, who had extraordinary credentials. Dr. Lacey was also one of Effi's fellow sorority sisters with the Deltas. Dr. Lacey and Effi even worked together at Children's National Medical Center together for a period of time in their early careers, when Effi was working in outreach. So it was a perfect situation for her.

After evaluating Effi's condition and treatment needs, Dr. Lacey suggested that she move in with her. So Effi lived with Dr. Lacey on Maryland's Eastern Shore for six weeks and returned to Johns Hopkins Hospital often for treatment. But the commute became exhausting for her. Also, in the house where the doctor lived, Effi had to walk up and down a lot of stairs, which drained more of her energy.

During this live-in period, Dr. Lacey would treat Effi a lot at her home as well, administering chemotheraphy through a portal in her arm and her chest. Effi received pain medication for severe back soreness and was given medicine for nausea and vomiting, which grew progressively worse.

Eventually, Effi reached a point where she was at peace with dying. She wasn't afraid to die and she grew to accept it. That was how she was with most things; she was very peaceful.

The Monday before she passed, she asked to have her cell phone turned off. She only wanted to speak to me, Christopher and her mother. So Christopher and I drove to the Eastern Shore in Maryland to visit with her that day. Effi was very happy to see us, and we were delighted to see her. She was still beautiful, even through her illness. Dr. Lacey cooked dinner for all of us at her house that evening, and she told us that Effi had been excited all day that we were coming. She even asked the doctor to lay out her clothes for her to wear because she wanted to look pretty for us.

Christopher and I visited for several hours that evening with Effi and we didn't want to leave. Although she was weak and tired, she talked and laughed with us up until the last minute. But we realized that she needed her rest and we didn't want to exhaust her.

A few days after that, I flew out to Memphis to see my mother and to talk about everything I had been through, including my marriage to Effi and raising Christopher. I even cried while visiting my mother in Memphis, which I needed to do to release a lot of the pain and sorrow that I felt.

Linda Greene, who was like a sister to Effi and a dear friend to both of us, was at the hospital at Anne Arundel Medical Center when Effi went in and passed away. Linda called and told me while I was still out in Memphis that it didn't look good. I was still expecting Effi to pull through. I figured I could get back to Baltimore and see her again at the hospital before anything happened. In the meantime, I asked Linda to call me every fifteen minutes to let me know all of the details. So Linda called me to report and she said that Effi's blood pressure was dropping fast.

"She's sinking fast, Marion. She's sinking."

I could hear the pain and despair in Linda's voice. It made me anxious over the phone, but there was nothing I could do about it. I was still out in Memphis.

On Linda's next call from the hospital, she told me through tears that Effi was gone. It was September 6, 2007 and Effi was sixty-three years old. My stomach dropped and a cold chill rushed up my back like a ghost ride. It was totally unexpected to lose Effi like that. It was only a year from her first diagnosis at Howard. If I had known that she was going to leave us that fast, I would have never flown out to Memphis. But I guess it happened the way it was supposed to.

That next morning on September 7, I took a 6 a.m. flight back to D.C. to return to Effi. And our son, Christopher, took it badly. His mother meant *everything* to him. He had been there with her through all of her struggles, and Effi had been there through all of his. And he did a great job with speaking at her funeral service that next week. We had a huge funeral at the Washington National Cathedral, where Christopher gave his mother a very emotional tribute. He spoke of how she meant the *world* to him and to the Washington community. He compared his mother, and Washington D.C.'s First Lady, to Queen Nefertiti, and everyone was very impressed with his speech. Effi Slaughter Barry was a great loss to all of us. She was the epitome of love, loyalty, support, elegance and class. And there will never be another First Lady like her.

Naturally, Christopher had been through a great deal of pain and discontent in his life, so I understood it when he had his own bout with substance abuse after his mother's death and funeral. Since I had dealt with it myself, I was able to understand the process and address some of his needs. So we were able to deal with it head-on and get him some immediate help.

Christopher was also forced to adjust to people's expectations of him. Children are not cookie-cutters of their parents; they have their own strengths, weaknesses and ideas about how they want to live their own lives. But when you're the son or daughter of popular officials, businesspeople, athletes, entertainers, or parents who have created a legacy for you and your family, a lot of time it's much harder for the children to find their own niche.

Christopher wanted to be his own person, but everyone around him expected something different based on what I had done. He had spent a lot of time trying to find himself and to become who he wanted to be. He had to figure out what he wanted to do with his own life and not worry about what I, or someone, wanted for him. I could continue to support him as a loving father and parent, but Christopher had to become his own man.

He did a year of college at Hampton University—his mother's alma mater—before finding work in construction and other entrepreneurial building services. Christopher has remained involved in construction services for the past decade, a hard-working black man trying to pull all of the pieces of life together.

Because of my highly public life, my son had been forced to overcome many of his own struggles, a lot of which stemmed from the hectic position he was put in as a child. My life in politics took a heavy toll on me personally, and it took a toll on my family. It also affected my friends and loved ones, all of the people who worked with me on my campaigns, in my cabinets, and all those who supported me in my sixteen years as mayor. They all realized that I was willing to do whatever was needed for the thousands of mothers, fathers, grandparents and children in the District, despite my personal demons. And if I had any regrets, I would probably think about the pain that my life decisions caused every one of them, and in particular, how my life impacted my wife, Effi, and my son, Christopher.

While wrestling with Effi's illness, I continued to serve as the council member for Ward 8, dealing with pressing issues impacting the ward. Meanwhile, there was an important mayoral race taking place in the city in 2006 between Linda Cropp and Adrian Fenty. Many people expected me to endorse candidate Linda Cropp over Adrian Fenty. Mayor Anthony Williams announced on September 29, 2005 that he would not seek a second term, which left the field wide open. It only made sense that Council Chair Linda Cropp would consider the position, and Adrian Fenty had made his intentions obvious two years prior to throwing his hat in the race. I had known Linda and her husband, Dwight, for more than twenty-five years, ever since she served on the D.C. school board. Dwight was part of my first team for the transformation of the city. He was the Secretary of the District and held the official seal. Out of loyalty, most of my political friends supported Linda Cropp for mayor. But I planned to meet with both candidates before I made my final decision. For me, the mayor's office was more about who would be best for the people, and not about my personal loyalties. And I knew that I still had a ton of influence and know-how to offer around the District.

I told both of the candidates, "If you're elected, I want to be a part of your close advisers' inner circle."

I felt it would be respectable to utilize my political experience and connections to get all that they would need done during their term. Well, they were both receptive to my support and were wooing me by taking me out to breakfast and lunches and calling me up regularly for my endorsement. But what it came down to was Adrian Fenty's aggressiveness and sense of urgency.

Adrian had become very popular around the city. He was young, bright, athletic, aggressive and an activist, who garnered a lot of notoriety around the city for walking literally door to door pleading his case for why the city needed his leadership. He had big ideas for the Office of the Mayor to take over the D.C. Public Schools system—which had not been up-to-par for a long time. He had visions for modernized schools and increased test scores. Some years back, council member Bill Lightfoot and I tried the same thing, but the climate was not right for it. He announced his intentions two years prior to his run. He raised over $800,000 and ultimately $4 million. During his run, everywhere you looked, there was a sea of green-and-white lawn signs, posters and door knockers. In a lot of ways, he reminded me of myself when I first got involved in activism and politics. The difference was, I knew that I could have never achieved as many accomplishments without the help of others. That's a big lesson that everyone needs to understand. To become successful, you can't do it alone.

In one of my many meetings and discussions with Adrian about my support, *The Washington City Paper* was riding him over his connection to Sinclair Skinner, his campaign adviser. They published an article, "Why is Adrian Fenty Hiding Sinclair Skinner?" Mr. Skinner was a Ward 1 activist who had characterized D.C. Council member Jim Graham as a racist. Jim Graham was an openly gay white man who had represented Ward 1 in the District since the late 1990s whom I had known and worked with for many years, particularly around the issue of the AIDS epidemic. He had been reelected several times. But Skinner made an accusation that Graham had been helping to drive African American businesses out of the Columbia Heights, Shaw and U Street corridors. So the editors at *The Washington City Paper* were raising this issue to stir up a controversy for Fenty and to see how he would respond to it.

Adrian told me when we sat down to meet, "I'm not getting rid of my right-hand man, Skinner."

He could see what they were trying to do in the media, and I immediately respected him for that. I felt he needed to have that defiant attitude to create new accomplishments in Washington. A political leader cannot be a pushover. Professional politics is a tough task and a strong demeanor is an essential trait of city leadership. Different groups of people will always pull you in separate directions, but you have to learn how to keep the course and steady your ship.

So I told Adrian Fenty, "Not only do I want to be in on the take-off, I want to be in on the landing, and I expect to play a major, programmatic role in the administration once elected. After sixteen years as the mayor, I decided not to run again, but I still want to be intricately involved with city politics. I'm gonna get behind your run for mayor." I felt that he had some new ideas that were workable, so I helped him to win the primary with 57 percent of the Democratic vote.

With council support Adrian Fenty worked toward controlling the school budget. I led efforts on the council to approve it. When Adrian sent his budget proposal over, he only had about four votes. The Board of Education had previously made the budget decisions over the mayor and the superintendent, but in Fenty's term, he placed the educational budget under mayoral control, where his staff could prepare the educational budget and make it more responsive and specific to Washington's schoolchildren and our overall community needs.

On the other hand, I didn't think Linda Cropp, notwithstanding all of her great work in the past, would put in the tremendous amount of effort to move the city forward. She still had a lot of old school philosophies that I didn't think would push the government forward fast enough. I believe that she needed to have a bigger and better vision. And I felt that Linda's ideas were not as aggressive or did not give off a sense of urgency. Even though she was running for mayor, as the chairman, she was advocating a new $500 million major league baseball stadium. I wanted her to push more for economic development around the District, which we were able to do on the council, including the new Washington Nationals baseball arena in the Southeast corridor.

When Linda served as the chairman of the D.C. Council in the early 2000s, she and three other council members were the only four voters for the stadium out of thirteen. When I joined the council with council member Kwame Brown and Vincent Gray, the idea of a Washington, D.C. baseball team was *hot*. However, for the three of us all to vote and tip the scales forward to build the new stadium, I *insisted* for economic development, businesses and new housing around the stadium. Linda Cropp picked up on this and outlined that to the mayor.

At first, my group was opposed to the idea of a new baseball stadium. We didn't agree with the city spending a bunch of our tax money on it. But we decided that if we could get an economic package to surround the stadium, then the Nationals could work for everyone as a win-win situation. And that's what we did. We joined Linda Cropp's group, along with another council member, and we won the vote 8-5 for the new Washington Nationals team and stadium.

Because of new city development that we pushed in the deal, the Southeast District area around the Nationals stadium was transformed from strip clubs, bars and warehouses into condos, apartment complexes, retail stores and new public housing. The baseball stadium started off as a hot and controversial issue, mostly because of arguments about who would pay for it. We wanted the owner to bear some of the responsibilities. But eventually, we got the economic development that we wanted.

Those were the kind of big development deals that I needed Linda Cropp to envision and push for to gain my confidence in her as the mayor. But she was willing to give her vote for the stadium without getting much more for the people of Washington. That was just not progressive enough of her government deal-making. So after losing the election for mayor, Linda Cropp retired from her many years of public service. Those of us who lived and worked in the District will forever be grateful for her service.

However, once Adrian Fenty was elected to office, he did some things right, but he wasn't able to hold his ground with the many different decisions he had to make with the guidance of the advisers who were around him. Victor MacFarlane, another sports owner and businessman, wanted to build a new soccer stadium for the D.C. United during Mayor Fenty's term. His soccer team had been playing at the old RFK Stadium, and he wanted a new stadium deal. I thought it would create another District property that could change the shape of the city's economy. So I strongly supported the stadium to bring more new economic development to the District. Even Eleanor Holmes Norton tried to step in and help the progress as a nonvoting congresswoman. But ultimately, Mayor Fenty wasn't interested enough to get the deal done.

A lot of disconnect on various deals and government business policies had to do with the mayor's office and a new cabinet of officials. But the new elected mayors who took office after the control board, including Anthony Williams, Adrian Fenty and Vincent Gray, had a lot of the leftovers from the control board. I felt the federal government had a lot to do with that. They were still too involved with the local office through certain checks and balances that were set in place during and after the control board.

The first two years I worked well with Adrian, but then he turned into a different person—his actions. He became more arrogant and not as cooperative with the council as he had been. He lost a lot of his touch with the community.

Enough about the mayor's race. Moving ahead. There was a bigger race, and a movement across the country, and that was the selection of Barack Obama as our Democratic nominee. I remember sitting in the audience in Boston in 2004 when Obama delivered the keynote speech. I was immediately intrigued. He was young, handsome, intelligent, and his oratory skills were incredible, but what captivated me even more was his ability to connect with the people. Tears streamed down the faces of attendees as he delivered this electrifying speech based on hope. He represented where hope can lead. He was an underdog in the Illinois Senate race and had risen to the top unexpectedly—reminding me of my first run for mayor of the District.

Fast forward to 2008. Obama was set to accept the Democratic nomination for the United States presidency. Watching him make that acceptance speech took me back to my days at SNCC, when we were just fighting for more seats at the Democratic Convention in Atlantic City. And the Civil Rights Movement, as we fought for equality and voting rights. Then let's not forget 1984, more than two decades earlier, I had backed Rev. Jesse Jackson for president and now a black man stood before the world on the fast track to the White House. It was extremely emotional for me. It was surreal.

The year 2008 also led me to make another difficult decision. I had been longtime friends with President Bill and Hillary Clinton. I was an early supporter of Bill Clinton in 1992 and was close to endorsing Hillary for the party's nomination, but as I watched the race closer, I felt that Clinton represented older and less flexible forces in the party. And, I must admit, it would have been difficult based on my own history and personal journey to not endorse a strong African American candidate for president. I'm not saying that I would have endorsed *any* black candidate for the presidency, but in this case, the movement throughout the country was almost magical. Watching the results from Iowa come in—a predominantly white state, in support of, was amazing. I listened to Obama and I felt that he represented a fresh start and a new direction. His candidacy was a breath of fresh air.

When the results came in that Obama had been elected, like most blacks around the country, possibly around the world, I was overwhelmed with emotion and I cried. Tears of joy and a whirlwind of emotions built up inside of me watching this black man standing there with a striking black sister by his side, and two beautiful little girls knowing that they were moments away from residing in the most powerful house in the nation, built on the backs of black folks. I can only imagine that the spirits of the slaves were dancing through the halls of the White House. The slogan "Yes We Can" was real. All of the hard work and sacrifices that we had made during the Civil Rights Movement had paved the way for Barack Obama to become the first black president of the United States of America. Quite frankly, I'm getting emotional just thinking about it.

Some use the election of Obama as an excuse to not do more for black people. Some believe that racism is dead because a black man was elected to the White House. Well, I'm here to tell you, racism is still very much alive, and the racial divide may have become even greater. Further, the black community still has a myriad of issues—high unemployment, increased school dropout rates, and families living below the poverty line. And for those of us in D.C., statehood was still a huge issue that hadn't been addressed. I'll talk more about that during the reelection of Obama, but before we can get there, the District was facing another controversial election—the mayor's race of 2010.

Mayor Fenty was up for reelection, and after two years, I had concluded that he had become quite unpopular in the black community. He was up against Council Chairman Vincent Gray, whom I had been friends with for over thirty-five years. We worked together to depopulate Forest Haven, a place for the mentally challenged that was miles away in Maryland, and were elected to the council together in 2004.

I supported Adrian Fenty's 2006 run against Linda Cropp. He wined me, dined me, impressed me; I even made robocalls on his behalf.

But Mayor Fenty had become arrogant and a great disappointment, indulging in cronyism. Therefore, I decided to use my power and influence to help those who were in need, and in this instance, it was Vincent Gray. I supported Gray because in my view, he was more personable and cared for the District's vulnerable citizens.

I made a huge media splash when I appeared at an event wearing a "Gray for Mayor" campaign shirt. I hadn't officially endorsed him yet, but when an aide to Fenty saw me with that shirt on, they immediately forwarded it to all of the reporters and political bloggers.

Some were scared of Fenty's backlash, should he have been reelected. Of course, I'm not one for running scared. I'm the champion of the people. I will always work on behalf of the most vulnerable. Period. And it didn't matter to me whether it was Fenty or anyone else. If you're not serving the people and doing the good will of those who put you in office, then you've gotta go. Race was also a factor in this campaign. Whites heavily supported Fenty, and blacks heavily supported Gray. Fenty raised $4 million over the course of the campaign. Gray finally raised almost $2 million. The money came by love, meaning that the people love you. I had been talking to Gray over a year about running for mayor. A number of us were ready to support him, but he wouldn't make up his mind.

A good friend, Joe Johnson, and I decided to spend some time with Don Peebles; in fact, a lot of time. After a while, it was very clear that Don Peebles would have made a great candidate for mayor, except for any reason or another, he seemed to be a little afraid to lose. My own philosophy is that nothing in politics is guaranteed that you're going to win all the time. Same in sports, you're not going to win all the time. You work as hard as you can to win. And winning is not the only thing; it's being able to be of assistance to help the largest number of people.

This 2010 campaign was run mostly like campaigns run—polling—putting together your team citywide. Fenty had to build a citywide organization. Each of them attended many, many debates and straw polls, including Ward 8.

Ward 8 appeared to be a test of how Mayor Adrian M. Fenty could mobilize his support. Despite getting booed during a Ward 8 debate, Fenty toppled Gray 69 to 61, which was a shock to almost everyone. It was a good thing, though. If Gray were to carry Ward 8, he would have needed a tremendous amount of support from my supporters and me.

The most memorable was the Ward 4 straw poll, because it was in the heart of the black middle class, with a minority of white people. Since this was Adrian Fenty's home turf, it was very important that Vincent Gray win the Ward 4 straw poll. The church was packed with over a thousand Ward 4 residents and supporters on both sides. It was heated to say the least. The room was tension filled, and rush-hour traffic was backed up on Sixteenth Street for blocks and blocks. If you wanted to attend, you had to maneuver through side streets to make your way.

Both Adrian and Vince pulled out all the stops. Most people had to wait until after the debate to vote. It was the same debate when Sulaimon Brown attacked Adrian Fenty. Sulaimon Brown was a minor candidate for mayor. He wasn't as popular as the front-runners, of course, but he was colorful, and got a lot of press, which he shouldn't have. Sulaimon had a catchy pitch to voters as he would wrap up a campaign event: "If you can't vote Brown, vote Gray, but whatever you do, don't vote green."

Fenty's delivery was monotone, without much energy. On the other hand, Gray was energetic, enthusiastic and convincing. Many of us had worked hard to get people out and because Gray was far more effective than Fenty, he won the straw poll 581-401. In politics, it's rare that a nonincumbent Vincent Gray would beat an incumbent Adrian Fenty in his own ward.

With all the controversy, Gray continued to campaign. He invited a number of supporters to a restaurant called Eatonville to celebrate the Ward 4 victory. Sulaimon Brown came also.

By the end of August 2010, I had made a decision to formally endorse Vincent Gray for mayor. I told reporters there are all kinds of ways to endorse candidates. I attended the Ward 5 straw poll just days after the heated Ward 4 straw poll, and Ward 5 turned out big. Vincent Orange, who is a Ward 5 resident and lived next to the church where the straw poll took place, had the barbecue grill out in the front yard. It was like a victory party on Taylor Street. Gray's supporters were ecstatic at the large turnout. I came decked out in a Gray campaign hat, a T-shirt touting Ward 5 incumbent Harry Thomas, Jr. and stickers advertising Kwame Brown for chair.

Adrian Fenty continued to try to get me to support him and had at least six emissaries approach me about supporting him, but my decision was final. There was no way I could support Adrian Fenty. I would have been run out of my community. Adrian was really a good guy, but his politics and his attitude became an impediment after his first two years as mayor.

Election Day—September 14, 2010—The Gray campaign and his Ward 8 campaign, headed by me, did the usual. The night before, we blanketed the ward with Gray signs and made sure that all seventeen precincts had Gray signs—plenty of literature for the workers. We had a food person that made sure we had coffee and Danishes in the morning, sandwiches for lunch, plenty of water and sodas and chairs that workers could sit in and take a break. The polls opened at 8 a.m., and they were all covered with three to four people, sometimes five to six. Fenty's poll workers were not as plentiful as ours. A significant amount of his workers didn't live in Ward 8. In D.C., since Home Rule, we find that the city is very divided politically, racially, and a number of other issues. On Election Day, blacks could vote late, and whites vote early. Usually always when the morning boxes are counted, predominantly white precincts have already voted at a higher rate than black precincts—which served true in the Gray campaign. During the Gray campaign tracking polls, we knew that Vincent Gray, when all was said and done, would win the primaries. We were more organized citywide and more passionate and more skillful than Fenty's campaign. As a result, Ward 4 helped Vincent with Wards 1 and 2 and a little of Ward 3. The big votes were Wards 5 and 7.

When you analyze the vote, there was a tremendous turnout in Ward 8 that got Gray over the top. In the final analysis, Vincent Gray won with 83 percent of the black vote, and 17 percent of the white vote. Fenty got 83 percent of the white vote and 15 to 17 percent of the black vote. This town is truly polarized. Regardless of our best efforts, Washington, the nation's capital, has become a city of the haves and have-nots. As Charles Dickens said it best....these are the "best of times," and these are the "worst of times." Just look at our school system. There are 47,000 students, with 32,230 families living in poverty (two-thirds).

The economic gap between black and white is wider than ever before. In fact, in D.C., one-third (200,000 out of 600,000 people) of our citizens are living at or below poverty level, one of the highest of major urban cities. More about that in the last chapter.

Most mayors, and Vincent Gray is no exception, put together transition teams to help their administration to get off to a great start. As I told Gray from the very beginning, there's no textbook on being the mayor or chairman. You have to learn from those who did it. Vincent Gray was pulled on by everyone who supported him. Many wanted jobs. Others wanted programs funded. Looking back on it, I don't think Gray had a structure to deal with that many requests that were coming in fast and furious. I think by and large, he appointed good people to cochair his transition efforts. When you looked at the overall picture, you didn't see a large number of supporter types heading transitions. The other thing that he did that I think was a mistake was that he had five personnel search firms that did pro-bono work for him. Most of them were all national searches. I wouldn't have done it quite that way, and I told Vince he should have mostly department heads that he knew or knew something about and who had a good professional reputation. If you had them in the government, keep them in the government. He made some good selections for department heads—particularly those departments that Fenty had loaded up with white leadership. There's nothing wrong with having white department heads, but blacks are very leery about having white department heads with ample black talent around from right here in the D.C. area.

During the Christmas season, Vincent Gray did what most mayors do. He visited various constituencies and Christmas parties, and continued to work on his transition. Gray is a workaholic. He stays up until one or two a.m.

On January 2, 2011, I awakened all excited about the dawning of a new day. Mayor Vincent C. Gray was being sworn in as the sixth black elected mayor of the District. I was the second. He was the first chairman of the City Council to be elected mayor of the District. Gray had defeated *The Washington Post*'s fair-haired opponent. Council member Kwame Brown, whom I had known since he was a kid, was also being sworn in as the City Council chairman. Kwame's father, Marshall, and I had been friends for over forty years. Marshall had worked with me in all of my mayoral campaigns and in my administration as an aide, as well as a ward organizer in my campaigns. He was a political operative around the city. Watching his son Kwame being sworn in added to the excitement that change was coming to the District.

As I watched Vincent Gray being sworn in as the mayor, I thought to myself that we have two black men at the helm of leadership in this city—President Obama and Mayor Gray, working only blocks from each other. As I continued to listen, I reflected back to my swearing-ins as mayor and the excitement and anticipation around the inaugurations—hungry for something more, something better, something different. I listened intently as Gray delivered his speech and discussed the budget deficit that he was inheriting.

"Since the inception of Home Rule, five people before me have raised their hand and taken this sacred oath. Each has left a unique mark on the office. They served in times of prosperity as our city flourished. And they served in times of challenge and hardship. But all have benefited mightily from the strength and optimism of the people of the District of Columbia."

I'd overseen the city during its most challenging times, and delivered the city out of hardships. I thought back to the deficit that I inherited when I defeated Sharon Pratt Kelly. That's one of the greatest challenges to face any mayor—balancing the books. He spoke of his "One City" vision, which was new to all of us, especially when the divide in the city was so wide. In my view, it should be called "the tale of two cities" indicating the vast differences between life west of the park versus life east of the river.

"Today, we begin a new chapter in the history of our city…one defined by a sense of common purpose, shared sacrifice, and communities united. A chapter written not by a single author, but with the pens of six hundred thousand residents from all eight wards and all walks of life, committed to a vision of one city—our city."

Gray, like any mayor, was going to have quite a job on his hands. There were unparalleled expectations from those who were disappointed with Fenty. And again, there's no textbook or guidebook that explains how to be an effective mayor. You can only meet with other mayors, choose advisers with great expertise and reputations, and the rest is truly trial and error.

What I also noticed during the swearing-in was that Gray was surrounded by his children, Carlos and Jonice. Gray was a widower. His wife, Loretta, a schoolteacher, had passed away in 1988 from cancer. Though I'm not a widower, and had remarried prior to Effi's passing, I still found myself thinking of Effi at that moment. I could picture us walking down Fourteenth Street in the cold air. We didn't even feel how cold it was because we were so pumped up with excitement.

Politics can be a very challenging job. Grueling even. Your skin has to be tough, while having a heart to serve those who are most vulnerable. You also have to have courage and make tough decisions that may make some feel less favorable toward you, but those are the breaks! It's just what comes with the territory. As a leader, I've learned that you'll never make everyone happy, but you try to broker the best deals possible where everyone at the table walks away with something.

Back to the point, because you're always at the beck and call of the people, it's important to have an understanding life partner by your side who truly has your back and your best interests at heart. You need someone whom you can confide in about your frustrations, anger, fears and hurt. Without it, this can be a very lonely job. Even in a room full of people who are talking to you, engaging you in conversation and jokes, it can still be very lonely. The old saying is true—it's lonely at the top. I know. I've been there and done that.

Looking at Jonice and Carlos made me think of Christopher. They had no idea that once their father took the oath of office, their lives would no longer be their own either. Being an elected official is not only about you and the position, nor the people whom you serve. It's also about your family and how their lives will be affected by every decision that you make. The decisions that you make as the mayor can ultimately affect how people treat your children. Christopher had a tough time at St. Albans simply because his classmates' parents were predominantly wealthy white men who didn't necessarily agree with all of my decisions and policies. As a result, their children would overhear their conversations, and in their own way, the kids would take it out on Christopher. There are many privileges to being the offspring of power, but with the perks comes a unique set of challenges as well. Though Jonice and Carlos were adults, they still would be judged because of their father's decisions.

Normally, the first year in office is a honeymoon period. There's a love affair between you and the public, as well as the press. This administration, however, went sour very quickly. Quite frankly, I've never seen anything like it in all my years in politics. Within the first ninety days, the wheels on the wagon flew completely off. Mayor Gray found himself making unwise decisions with personnel. The media began reporting allegations of cronyism.

My dear friend Lorraine Green had served as the campaign chair for Vincent Gray's mayoral campaign. She and I have been friends for at least twenty-five years, perhaps more. She rose from a GS-2, which is an entry-level job in the federal government, to the highest ranks of government. I had appointed her head of the Lottery Board, among other senior-level positions. She was one of three close advisers to Gray during his mayoral campaign. After Gray was elected, Lorraine didn't seek to become a part of the administration, and chose to remain a close friend, confidante, and adviser to Mayor Gray. By then, she was a vice president at Amtrak, and had years of local and federal government expertise under her belt. There was no reason to give all of that up. Lorraine still found herself in the hot seat. Allegations began to fly that Lorraine had promised a government job to rival candidate Sulaimon Brown in exchange for attacks on the then-incumbent Adrian Fenty.

Sulaimon claimed that Mayor Vince Gray got him his job as an auditor for the Department of Health Care Finance, making $110,000 annually.

I'll never forget the day that Mayor Gray was addressing the press and Sulaimon came inside the press briefing room and took a seat after being released from his position and escorted from the office by the D.C. Protective Services. Once the mayor concluded his press briefing, what should have been the end instead became the beginning of The Sulaimon Brown Show! I began to think to myself, *what the hell kind of circus was this??!!* The press surrounded Sulaimon, who began by praising Gray as an "excellent mayor" and expressed disappointment that he'd been unfairly fired "without respect and without dignity."

The next thing I knew, it looked like Sulaimon was about to cry, while talking about working his way through school and having a "very hard life."

Lorraine denied those accusations by Sulaimon Brown that she or Mayor Gray promised a government job to Sulaimon. What made matters worse, Sulaimon claimed that he was offered payments and a job by Green and another Gray campaign aide in exchange for leveling attacks on then-Mayor Fenty.

But wait. There's more. Yep…more. This was like watching a snowball speeding down a hill that kept growing and growing in size. More allegations would follow, including the children of Lorraine; Gerri Mason Hall, who was serving as the mayor's Chief of Staff; Linda Wharton Boyd, who served as the Director of Communications to the Executive Office of the Mayor and had worked as my Communications Director during one of my terms as mayor, and a couple of others had all been placed in positions within the government—some were even holding senior-level positions. This was really spinning out of control, and all of this could have been avoided, had Mayor Gray consulted with other mayors and me, especially on personnel decisions.

A special council committee was formed to look into these allegations. I, along with council members Mary Cheh, Harry Thomas, Jr., and Council Chair Kwame Brown, were tasked with getting to the bottom of this catastrophe. My job was to get to the truth without being ruthless. Thinking people are guilty until proven innocent is not how the American justice system operates. I made it my business to protect the women who were involved in this mess, and show that their children were qualified for the positions that they held. It was an unfortunate circumstance that not only were these women being scrutinized, but their kids' lives were being unraveled, and that to me was totally unfair. It only brought me back to the unfair scrutiny that my own son, Christopher, has endured over the years. What made this even more unfortunate was that all of this could have been avoided if Mayor Gray had only consulted other mayors and me. This was a poor personnel judgment, and so many lives were being turned upside down as a result.

Unfortunately, Lorraine's daughter was the only one whom could be saved. Her qualifications and credentials supported her keeping her job, but the others were relieved of their positions.

The Special Committee was also tasked with holding a hearing with Sulaimon. Lord have mercy is all I have to say!!!! That had to be the biggest three-ring circus that I've seen in a long time. Sulaimon is a master at attracting media attention, and this was his moment to shine. I had already schooled council member Cheh to not feed into his antics, but Sulaimon sucked her in almost immediately. Sulaimon walked into the hearing wearing dark-tinted sunglasses, looking like a missing member of *Men in Black*. I could see the irritation on council member Cheh's face, and I kept whispering to her, "Do not let him get to you." Well, what was the first thing she did? She asked him to remove his sunglasses, which he refused to remove, justifying his behavior by saying that he had stayed up late preparing for his testimony and didn't want the press to snap photos of his tired eyes. His behavior was belligerent and extremely disrespectful. He called both Cheh and citywide council member David Catania "delusional." And then, he had the audacity to try me! I knew he was crazy then! No doubt in my mind! I still can't believe that he brought up my arrest involving the Vista. That was over twenty years ago! I told him that he must have been out of his goddamn mind! He was just antagonizing us to no end, and we allowed ourselves to get sucked down the rabbit hole!

Later, council member Cheh released a committee report saying the Gray administration's hiring practices caused "deep harm" to the District's reputation, including what we already knew…senior-level staffers' children improperly hired; senior-level staff overly paid; Sulaimon allegedly promised a job; and that a Gray campaign aide allegedly gave Sulaimon money.

Among the findings included the fact that one of former Mayor Adrian Fenty's last acts in office was to give City Administrator Allen Lew a $69,000 bonus, apparently by circumventing council rules. The Gray administration later signed off on the bonus. Another finding stated that the hiring of Leroy Ellis for a job he wasn't qualified for was straight-up "cronyism."

Council member Cheh's report dings the mayor for being the top dog when all these shenanigans were taking place, but also says there is "scant" evidence that he knew of or approved of illegal acts. "The blame for the many personnel errors committed by the Gray administration falls squarely on the trio whom Mayor Gray directed to manage the selection and placement of political appointees in his administration," the report says. That trio, of course, was who we already knew—Lorraine Green; her protégé and the mayor's former chief of staff, Gerri Mason Hall; and Gray's former human resources director Judy Banks.

It's been close to three years now, and here we are in 2014, and none of these statements have proven to be true; even the U.S. Attorney's Office is not collaborating the story at this time.

As for my own election, we campaigned hard. My team passed out a lot of literature, I shook a lot of hands and didn't want the people to feel as if we took them for granted.

I always encourage people to run against me because in a democracy, competition is good. It helps to keep me on my toes and focus on going forward versus standing still. We had about four to five opponents. Even if I run unopposed, I still believe in campaigning hard and demonstrating to the people whom I represent that I'm still fighting hard for resources and opportunities for the vulnerable and the poor. Because of people's longtime faith in me, I campaigned hard and won the 2012 primary with 73 percent of the vote, with four other candidates combining for 27 percent.

OBAMA'S 2012 RACE

The highly anticipated reelection campaign for President Obama was underway. I was a big supporter of President Obama in 2008, and continued to support him in his reelection aspirations.

Like any politician, he hasn't done everything I wanted him to do, but he's done more than anyone else has done. I would have liked for him to have taken a more active role on D.C. statehood, but when you have two wars, a recession and are attempting to provide the country with affordable health care, despite your health conditions, well…I could give him a pass until his second term. I mean, what is our alternative? Mitt Romney? Not me. And I took that stance with me all the way to Charlotte, N.C., where I served as a delegate for the 2012 Democratic National Convention.

Racism, no matter how much we wanted to make the case that it doesn't exist, was even more prevalent—especially since the election of President Obama. Many like to make the argument that this country is no longer divided by race because an African American was elected to the highest office in the land. Well, I'm here to tell you that's simply not true. As a matter of fact, the divide grew even wider because so many believed in that nonsense. We still only comprise 10 percent of Congress. There are still not enough African Americans in the executive offices at our news stations controlling the images of black people. Even on the talk show circuit, there are still very few black opinions and analyses of current events.

We're still not making a dent on Wall Street and at Fortune 500 companies, so anyone who thought 2008 changed the game needs to quit drinking the Kool-Aid. Barack Obama was elected because he had the best vision for where this country needed to go, and after eight years of Bush, the country was excited to have new leadership and a different vision. The fact that he's black is simply icing on the cake.

I knew that President Obama would be reelected, but I also understood the challenges that he would face. And Lord knows, when Obama messed up that first debate, I felt like climbing through the TV and asking him what the problem was myself. We all remember that infamous debate. He wasn't confident. He wasn't poised. It was as if he left Barack Obama at home and had an unknown stand-in debating Mitt Romney. It was horrible. But, we have to give any leader the benefit of the doubt. We have good days and bad days, too. And, not to mention, he wore two hats—President Obama and Barack Obama, candidate for the presidency. Trying to juggle those two roles while still trying to balance marriage and fatherhood is unfathomable. Mitt Romney had a field day during that first debate, which gave him a lot of momentum. Did Romney forget what President Obama inherited? Somebody had short-term memory. He sho nuff thought he had this all wrapped up with a pretty little bow on it. Well…that's before he remembered his controversial comments about the 48 percent. Yep, he thought he was going to slide his behind into the White House already separating and dividing folks. Well, as the young people say, he had it twisted!!!! Nobody was in a position to be left out, and people, even Republicans, could not rally behind that type of talk. So thank you, Mitt Romney, for giving us a gift that kept on giving all the way to the polls.

There's no way that Mitt Romney could have even come close to as much as President Obama has done for the black community, and we weren't going to support Mitt Romney. His philosophy was out of tune—not just with black folks, but with America.

I was in the middle of my own campaign once again, and I was out there campaigning just as hard as I had in my first campaign—riding through the communities with a bullhorn encouraging the community to get out and vote for me, Trayon White for the school board, and of course, President

Obama. We wore our campaign colors of green and white. We not only talked to the people, but we got them excited about the election. We blared go-go music and the Wobble through the bullhorns that made people dance all the way to the polls. You see, you have to entice the people, so you give them things that they can relate to. Once you have their attention, then you equip them with the information that they need to make informed decisions. And that's what we did.

On election night, my team and I gathered at the Players Lounge on Martin Luther King, Jr. Avenue, which is in the heart of Ward 8. The establishment was donned with green and white balloons and streamers. There was a green-and-white cake ready for cutting as soon as the results came in. And of course, the night wasn't complete without some down-home blues. We were ready to celebrate. As I was onstage addressing the crowd, the results came in declaring President Obama's victory, and the restaurant went bananas!!!!! We all jumped up, screaming with happiness, and listened as the commentators gave their analysis. We began playing music and cutting the cake. Trayon had been elected to the school board, and I had been reelected to serve the great Ward 8 once more. It was an incredible night of victory, excitement and anticipation.

On January 19, 2013, President Obama was inaugurated. This time, instead of going to the Hill, the mayor and members of the council hosted an open house in our individual suites. For months, construction took place outside of the Wilson Building where an enclosed, heated viewing suite was built for the mayor, the council and our guests to view the inaugural parade. The Wilson Building is located at Thirteenth Street and Pennsylvania Avenue, and the White House is located at 1600 Pennsylvania Avenue, so we had the best seat in the house.

My good friend Dick Gregory was the first to greet me when I arrived at my suite, which was full of invited guests and a vast array of hors d'oeuvres and desserts. I sat in front of the television and watched President Obama being sworn in surrounded by friends and community supporters, and I must admit, I still felt the overwhelming emotions that I felt viewing the first swearing-in. It probably meant more to Dick Gregory and me than it meant to anyone else in my suite because of our history as Civil Rights leaders and game changers. For every march, racial slur, and confrontation that I endured over my many years as an activist, organizer and a Civil Rights leader, watching this day made every sacrifice worthwhile.

CHAPTER 20
STILL STANDING

I didn't want to write this story of my life while the wounds were still fresh, so I had to wait until I was healed, confident and comfortable enough to say it all. I kept putting it off and putting it off and putting it off, like I did with my taxes. But eventually you have to pay them, and eventually I wanted to write this book. That means that I would have to deal with those dark and embarrassing parts of my life that I didn't want everyone to judge me or remember me by. Sometimes, when bad things happen to good people, you can end up spending so much time running away from the bad that you forget to accentuate the good. I've been able to ignore the bad and do a bunch of good in my professional life, where I continue to serve the community as an experienced and passionate council member. But writing a book about all of my life was another mountain to overcome.

Yet, I've had an incredible life and I have traveled on an amazing journey, where I've cared enough about the people to stand up and fight, organize, lead, change polices, hire thousands of good and worthy people and serve the community from sunup to sundown, just like my mother and father did in the cotton fields of Mississippi. And I should never be ashamed of that. Nor should I be ashamed of my life and work as an activist, a council member and ultimately, the mayor of Washington. So I had to get over all of my bad decisions and embarrassments and trust that people will still judge me based on what I fought to do for *them*, rather than emphasize my personal struggles.

We all have our personal struggles, embarrassments and things that we may not be proud of, but on every man's or woman's obituary, it should read about all of the things that they were able to give or do for *others*, and I did and gave a *lot*, when I could have done a lot more for myself. I understood that my service for others was ultimately more important of a legacy. So this book is one of truth, courage and gratitude for all of the people who remember the great things that I was able to do in the city of Washington as a poor farm boy from Itta Bena, Mississippi and Memphis, Tennessee. In my lifetime, I've been able to bring a whole lot of hope to the people, and I want to be able to give them all a fuller idea of what they may all *think* they know about me.

A lot of times people react without knowing all of the information. There was a time, not too long ago, when certain information was kept away from black people. When certain accomplishments, lifestyles, religions, facts of life and basic details are withheld from a person, it makes it difficult for them to come to a knowledgeable assessment. White people also suffer from not knowing. But sometimes they *do* know and they stop *you* from knowing. That's why some people warn, "Don't judge too fast. You don't know the whole situation, and you could find yourself next."

No matter what, I still love the city of Washington and I still love the *people* of Washington. I don't think there's any other city like it. I had a chance to build this place from the ground up and turn a political vision into a reality for the majority of the citizens who live here in the District, not only for blacks, but for whites, Hispanics, Jews, Asians, immigrants, gays, lesbians; *everyone*. I saw this great city as much more than a stomping ground for the president and for the federal government. I saw the promise and the hope in Washington when I first moved to the city, and I still see greatness moving forward.

Once I began to run the city, I never thought about *not* running it. But so many things had changed that it made it impossible for me to continue to lead. I had to give up some things that I would have never thought about giving up when I first became the mayor. I fought hard to gain control of the budget in Washington; we just needed help to balance it. But prior to the Control Board, for a decade I led a $2 billion government industry, and I will forever be proud of that fact. However, new policies and budget restrictions made fixing some of the things that still need to be fixed in the city of Washington a long shot. With the federal government involved, the less and least continue to be overlooked. Nevertheless, as there is still blood in my body and oxygen in my lungs, I will continue to fight for those things that the left-out people of Washington still need. For that reason, I chose to continue my service in Ward 8 and to be an active and strong voice in the political climate of the District.

I was even part of a poll to see what public figures the people of Washington would want to have enshrined at Madame Tussauds wax museum. I was up against Denzel Washington, Halle Berry, baseball player Cal Ripken, Nancy Reagan, Oprah Winfrey and more. And I won the vote to be immortalized in wax. That may seem like a small achievement or incidental to some, but the main point to me was that the people of *Washington* chose me over everyone else. They did it because they understand the value of my history here in the District. We also figured the wax museum statue would create a great tourist attraction for visitors.

In 2008, not only did I win the Ward 8 council seat, I also found out that my kidney functions were weak and to the point of urgency. Over twenty years I had been diabetic with high blood pressure. Diabetes can be a hereditary issue as well as a lifestyle concern from drinking, obesity and hypertension, or high blood pressure. In my family, my grandmother and my sisters had it.

Black people call diabetes "having sugar" when you have an abnormal breakdown of the glucose in your blood. You tend to crave sweets more because with an abnormal level of glucose that is high in the bloodstream is not getting to the cells. The body then tells you that you need more sugar in your system even when you already have it. Much of the glucose is not in the right place. But I didn't feel sick or anything of that nature.

I had just gone in for a regular medical check-up at Howard University with Dr. Robert Williams, who was my primary care physician for over twenty-five years. He found that my urine sample showed high creatinine levels. Creatinine levels are what they test to see how well your kidneys are working. A low level is good, but a high level means that you may need dialysis to help clean and flush out your system.

The doctor said that my kidney function was so bad that I would need dialysis immediately. A perfect kidney function is a one, but I had a three or a four. Well, I didn't want to go on dialysis right before taking another term as the Ward 8 council member. Dialysis was a hell of a process that could take up to two hours a day and three days a week, with a machine and all of that. Normal kidneys are working twenty-four hours a day. I had done it briefly before and didn't like it. And I didn't want to have to do all of that while trying to serve as a council member, so I asked the doctor about the possibility of finding a kidney donor instead.

The doctor said it's an option, but that the process could take anywhere from four to five years to find a living donor to match my blood type with a healthy kidney that they were willing to give up. My kidneys were so bad that I had to find the perfect donor for an operation to replace them. He said that a live kidney is better than a donor from a dead person, so I had to find someone with a live kidney to donate.

We started the search for a donor, and I happened to ask a beautiful young woman that I had known for a long time in the healthcare department.

I said, "Kim Dickens, I need a live kidney donor."

Kim had worked in my Ward 8 council campaign. She had perfect health in her forties and had been a twenty-year vegetarian, who was in excellent shape. She went jogging, worked out regularly and had two beautiful daughters. I didn't really know all of that when I first asked her. I thought Kim had a great positive spirit and that she could help me to spread the word to find somebody, especially since she worked in the healthcare department.

Kim said, "I'll do it," just like that. She wasn't talking about trying to help me to find someone; she wanted to be the donor *herself*. I couldn't believe it! But first we had to see if her blood type matched mine. So we went in to be tested, and sure enough, Kim and I both had B-negative blood types. That was *amazing!* It was only by the grace of *God* that I had found someone that soon. It only took seven weeks.

We had the operation on February 20, 2009, with Dr. Clive Callender, one of the foremost African American transplant doctors in the country, and I was able to begin my third council term for Ward 8 without needing dialysis.

However, I did need to take about a dozen pills a day, including a diuretic pill, a cholesterol regulator and immunosuppressant pills. The immunosuppressant pills allow the body to reduce the levels of natural defense that it creates to protect you from various ailments. Whenever the body recognizes a foreign object, it naturally wants to protect you and defend itself. So it attacks it. I have to take these pills every day for the rest of my life. But it's better than the alternative. The alternative is much worse: the graveyard. I've been taking my pills ever since, and they have greatly improved my quality of life.

I still see Kim Dickens every so often. Sometimes she'll call me up and joke, "Hey, Mr. Barry, my right kidney misses my left kidney. We need to get together sometimes and hang out. I feel like my kidney misses me."

Kim has such a great spirit. She has been one of the *many* true blessings that God has bestowed upon me. I've had a really blessed *life*; that's why I continue to serve the people of the community so diligently. Service is what I was *born* to do. And as I continue to bless the people around me, I continue to be blessed.

I even wanted a bill to provide funding for programs to test more people for diabetes. You have some people in communities walking around for twenty years and living with it without ever knowing. I wanted a bill to provide massive testing for different cancers, HIV, diabetes, high blood pressure, ailments that lead to strokes, and then make sure that we have compliance for treatment once people are diagnosed. But ultimately, it would cost too much.

We had health programs in Washington, where people on Medicaid were only getting 50 percent of their benefits instead of the normal 70 percent that other jurisdictions were getting. We were far away from getting any uniformed testing. But I keep up the fight for massive improvements for the quality of life of the citizens in Ward 8 and across the District regardless. And as I have my health issues to deal with and to correct, I fight for everyone else's.

I remember in 1995, I was also diagnosed with prostate cancer. I was on a general check-up at the doctor's office at George Washington Hospital. The doctor called me back in to discuss the cancer, and Cora explained how important it was for me to follow up. Prostate cancer kills 40,000 men a year, and a large percentage of them are black men. In fact, a lot of times, when you find out you have prostate cancer, it can be too late. But when the doctor said that he wanted to operate on me, at first I said no. I wanted to find out more about it to see if I had any other options.

Once I made it public that I was seeking other options, I had offers from all over the country to cure me. However, all of these other options had not proven to be effective and therefore, they had no use to me. I then had a choice between surgery and seed radiation. But I eventually chose to have the surgery at Johns Hopkins Bayview Medical Center in Baltimore. The operation was performed by Dr. John Walsh, one the foremost prostate cancer surgeons in the country. He told me that there were two nerves on both sides of the prostate for continence and potency, and during the operation, he saved three of my four nerves for a successful procedure.

As a man in his late seventies with a long history of running around and overworking myself, I can no longer expect to have a bill of perfect health. However, I'm still making it along and doing what I need to do to keep living, serving and inspiring the people. I still get a lot of people who go out of their way to recognize me, speak to me and offer me thanks and kind words, too. And I kindly appreciate it. But if I didn't have more controversy in my life to overcome, my name wouldn't be Marion Barry, Jr. So over the past few years, no matter how small or big, my name continued to pop up in the newspapers and in the television media.

After all of the work I had done with the gay and lesbian community for their rights, political power, economic development, health concerns and everything else, I caused some flack a few years ago with gay rights activists and the media when I dissented on a vote for a bill supporting same-sex marriages. I had told gay rights activists a year earlier that I was not opposed to same-sex marriages. I personally believed that they should be able to do what they want, but in context of the bill, my constituency in Ward 8 didn't support it. There were ministers and families in the African American community of Southeast Washington who were extremely opposed to the bill. So I chose to vote in line with my constituency.

Had I still been the mayor, it would have been totally different. I would have had a much larger pool of citizens to poll from on how they felt. But my personal views and how I voted as a council member, who represented the community of Ward 8, had to be taken into consideration. You couldn't go against your constituency that way, especially when they were so strongly against it. My advice at the council hearings was that we needed to move more slowly on the issue of same-sex marriages as it became more acceptable in certain communities, and at that time, it wasn't supported in Ward 8.

I was then called out for "flip-flopping," but I found it unfair and unknowledgeable for those who said I no longer supported the gay community. When I served as the president of the District School Board in 1971, I stepped up to stop the firing of a gay schoolteacher at McKinley Tech High School in Northeast. And as the mayor of Washington, I was the first politician to recognize the gay and lesbian community and to address their issues, as well as hire gays and lesbians in many of my cabinet and campaign positions. My track record spoke for itself. I had done a hell of a lot more than *anyone* to champion gay and lesbian rights and causes.

When I first arrived in Washington, the gay and lesbian community was very much under wraps and not that involved in the D.C. government. But my inclusive campaigns helped them to find the confidence they needed to speak out and to become more actively involved in the city's politics. My acceptance and inclusion also opened up the gay and lesbian communities to a lot of Washingtonian business, and I was very proud of that. The gay and lesbian community loved my courage and how I readily came out to support their issues. They showed me a lot of loyalty, and they had been some of my most *staunch* supporters.

However, in Ward 8, there were a lot of other issues that we were dealing with, and going against the grain of your constituency could only get you so far. This same-sex marriage bill created a very emotional debate. The pastors and preachers in Ward 8 were also outspoken about any connection that a lot of people made between civil rights and gay rights. They believed that the rights of black people and their families, who were enslaved, killed, sold and denied the basic freedoms that many gays and lesbians were afforded, should not be in the same conversation.

Baptist, Catholic, AME, Mt. Zion and nondenominational churches all felt the same way, and some of these church leaders were very outspoken. The argument from the African American community was a serious issue that I felt needed more time to address, so I reserved the right to dissent. I looked at the issue of same-sex marriage as a pro or a con, and at the moment—from the seat that I held in Ward 8—I chose to vote no.

A lot of gays were upset about that, but I had addressed the LGBT organization (Lesbian, Gay, Bisexual and Transgender) a year earlier and told them that a vote on a bill for same-sex marriages should not be a litmus test as to whether or not I support their causes, because I *do* support them on a number of other major issues. However, *in* the community of Southeast Washington that I represented as a council member, they were more concerned with jobs, education, housing, economic development and healthcare. And those are the issues that I needed to focus on.

Politics are hard that way. You could have a dozen bills on your desk, where different communities feel one way or the other, and you have to use your better judgment and the results of the polls to help make an informed decision on them. There were many different issues that the communities of Washington failed to agree on, and the support of same-sex marriages was one of them.

But as I continued to work for the community needs of Ward 8, *The Washington Post* continued to report everything I did. Everyone above the line at *The Washington Post*, including most of the key editors, had benefited from covering my life over the years as the mayor of Washington, and apparently, they were still milking the cow.

I had been pulled over a few times by overzealous police officers, who were mostly white guys. Most of the time they recognized me, and they were always suspicious. I was guilty behind the wheel until proven *innocent*. They knew who I was and what I had been through from the Vista Hotel, and it seemed like these police officers were right back in the 1960s with harassment all over again. That's all that my traffic charges and accusations of alcohol and drugs were all about. The judge was forced to throw out several traffic charges and tickets that had been issued to me.

As the mayor of Washington, I had been chauffeured with drivers for sixteen years, but once I went back to driving my own car, I continued to be harassed by the police, who were looking for reasons to arrest me. I was charged with DWB: "Driving While Black." One white cop tried to give me a ticket for driving too *slow*.

I said, "I always drive slow. I'd rather be safe than sorry."

The D.C. traffic court reviewed the ticket and threw out the case.

Another time when a police officer stopped me, he purposefully tried to insinuate drug use.

The officer asked me, "What's inside the car?"

I said, "Nothing's inside the car."

He looked around inside the back of my car and said that I had some white powder substance in the back. He was trying to hint that it was cocaine, but it wasn't, unless he had *planted* it there. The harassment was what many black drivers were still going through in America, particularly black men. But most of these police officers knew me.

These petty accusations and innuendos had come about because—by and large—the white establishment was still pissed off at me for being in a position of power for so long, where they had spent all this money to set me up and get me out of office, only for me to win again. And it all started when I began to give black folks so many opportunities in business.

Another time I was arrested by the Secret Service near the White House. I had Constance Johnson, the Oklahoma City senator, in town for the Black Legislative Conference. She was a bright, young African American woman who wanted me to give her a tour of Washington. So I drove her down to the White House, and after we passed it, I made a turn on H Street to head down Fifteenth Street before we were pulled over by a white Secret Service officer.

He walked up and said really nastily, "Get out of the car."

At the time, I was driving a real low Corvette.

I said, "For what?"

"You don't look right."

"What do you mean, I 'don't look right'? We just drove down here to see the White House area. That's all I did."

He made it sound as if I was planning to do something wrong. I believe I was far too old for that. Then he asked if I was impaired and told me to take a breathalyzer test.

I said, "I'm not taking anything." I hadn't been drinking in *years*. And I definitely would have never done that with a young senator in the car with me on a tour to the White House.

Senator Constance Johnson was outraged. I was upset about it, too, but I was used to it and she wasn't. I had been harassed by whites in positions of authority all of my life. Now the senator had a chance to see what I had been going through.

So I called up my lawyers, Fred Cooke, Jr. and David Wilmot, and that ticket for "driving while impaired" became another inconvenience that was thrown out of court, but only *after* the newspapers had already reported the incident.

The Secret Service officer even told the judge in the courtroom that he suspected I was driving while impaired because of how I climbed out of the car. But I was over seventy-years old and stepping out of a real low car.

The judge asked him, "Do you ever see how a *normal* person climbs out of a car? Is there a certain way you're supposed to do it?"

It was *crazy!* But the police don't bother me anymore. They're used to seeing me drive around slowly. Everybody knows I drive slow. I'm still getting used to driving. Now they go out of their way to speak to me.

"Hey, Mr. Barry, how are you doing? Your tail light is out, but I won't give you a ticket. Just remember to get it fixed."

They don't even ask for my driver's license anymore. If anything, these petty traffic reports only made me more popular with the people, especially in the Southeast. They could relate to their own run-ins with the police and being pulled over for dubious reasons. These bogus stories also let the people know that I was still around and that *The Washington Post* was still reporting on me. And I was still standing

I may be much older now, but I've never stopped my fight for the people. That got me in the news and into trouble recently with the Asian community as well. After a third consecutive victory for the Ward 8 Democratic primary seat in 2012, during my victory party, I made a speech about cleaning up the community. I put Asian business owners on notice, because they don't live in the community. Besides that, a lot of their stores were not up to par on cleanliness. And I didn't want that to be one of my final memories, but as a representative of Ward 8, I had to bring it up. My constituency was concerned about it.

If you don't live in the Southeast, but you own a shop there, where you're taking money out of the community's hands, but you're not providing any jobs to the people who you take money from, then I felt very strongly about that. It was the same way I felt as the mayor when out-of-towners were taking income, employment, property and business away from the Washington, D.C. community citywide. That's why I had advocated for a commuter tax. So my ideas were consistent.

I felt the same way about Asians taking money away, not only in the Southeast, but all around the District. If you have a business in Washington, then employ the people who live there or become a part of the community. It's as simple as that. But my comments about it mainly got a lot of attention because I called their stores "nasty and dirty."

I never meant or intended to identify or label *all* Asian-American business owners as bad people or bad businessmen, so I elaborated on my speech and explained it to a group of Asian-American business owners at a meeting a week later at the Matthews Memorial Baptist Church, up the street from my office on Martin Luther King, Jr. Avenue. We were all able to come to agreeable solutions, where they learned to respect my views and I learned to respect theirs. Overall, it was a good meeting that needed to be held, and they came away with the understanding that they needed to hire people from the community.

In February 2013, we learned that the city government had $400 million in excess that was not spent in the budget to affect the needs of the people. I pulled together a press conference immediately and conducted several media interviews to bring the needs of Ward 8 and the rest of Washington into focus in the hope of spending at least $100 million of that money for the benefit of the people.

I discovered that there was a law that was passed in 2009 that allowed the D.C. Council to spend up to $100 million. I advocated that *all* $100 million be used for those in *need* rather than to keep that money for the Wall Street brokers. I spoke to several media outlets, including NBC-4, FOX-5 DC, *The Washington Post, The Washington Times, The Washington Examiner,* WUSA-9 CBS and WOL Radio. I did all of that to educate the people and to put pressure on the council members to act on behalf of the citizens.

However, Mayor Vincent Gray and Council Chairman Phil Mendelson opposed the measure, which fell short by two votes in the council. Yet, we were able to approve $50 million of the money for the fiscal year of 2014. And once again, that's what my strong advocating and fighting for the people can do.

That's the man that I am, and the man that the people voted for to lead in Washington. I never claimed to be perfect, nor will I ever be. I'll have my cross to bear before the Lord when it's my time like everyone else. But one thing I *can* say about myself that no one can ever take away from me is that, "Marion Barry Junior put it all on the line; his ups, his downs, his courage and fears for *all* of the people."

The seniors' lives in D.C. were remarkably changed because of my ideas and respect for my elders. In me, the young people had a champion who consistently advocated for them and provided summer jobs for 100,000 youth. African American businesses had an incredible $2.8 billion increase in opportunities. And these opportunities increased the black middle class not only in D.C., but in Maryland and in Virginia, with a significant number of highly paid D.C. government employees and professionals who lived in Maryland and Northern Virginia.

We had great programs to help give ex-offenders a second chance. Washington, D.C. was one of the few jurisdictions that allowed ex-offenders the right to vote and to seek employment without prejudice of their records. We had the strongest human rights laws in America, with eighteen groups of people who were protected under the law, including our monumental programs for the homeless, where we provided them with food and shelter.

I was able to create some remarkable years in the District, and I will be forever proud of that. I was the mayor of Washington for an unpredicted sixteen years with God giving me the vision, the courage, the tenacity, the resilience and my strong love of people and belief in *Him*. And with the way I ran the city, creating the most opportunities for black *and* white people, it will unlikely ever happen again.

CHAPTER 21
THE STRUGGLE CONTINUES

"No Struggle, No Progress"
The whole history of progress of human liberty
Shows that all concessions
Yet made to her august claims
Have been born of earnest struggle.
If there is no struggle
There is no progress.
Those who profess to favor freedom,
And yet deprecate agitation,
Are men [and women] who want crops
Without plowing up the ground,
They want rain
Without thunder and lightning.
They want the ocean
Without the awful roar of its waters.
This struggle may be a moral one;
Or it may be a physical one;
Or it may be both moral and physical;
But it must be a struggle.
Power concedes nothing without a demand.
It never did, and it never will.
—FREDERICK DOUGLASS, 1857

"Strong Men"
You sang: Walk togedder, chillen, Dontcha git weary....
The strong men keep a-comin' on; The strong men git stronger.
—STERLING A. BROWN, 1931

"Mother to Son"
And life for me ain't been no crystal stair.
Don't you fall now—
For I'se still goin', honey,
I'se still climbin',
And life for me ain't been no crystal stair.
—LANGSTON HUGHES, 1922

Some people may wonder why I began this chapter with these poems. Let me tell you why. Too many people believe that racism is dead. Well, I'm here to inform you that it's alive in a different form. It went from the streets to the suites. That's right...the streets to the suites. It's not like segregation at the lunch counter or even our schools. In most urban cities, including Washington, D.C., it's the tale of two cities—the Haves and the Have-Nots. Therefore, our struggle today must be individual empowerment and collective economic empowerment. Our struggle must be about closing the achievement and economic gaps.

If you don't believe me that racism is still very real in corporate America, just look at all of the industries, and tell me how many black faces that you see at the top. How many blacks do you see on the board of directors? Take Forbes 500 Companies, for instance. There are only a handful of blacks who sit on the board.

Look at the demise of black-owned banks. At one point in time there were over a hundred black-owned banks. Now, we're down to seven or eight. You can count them on two hands. You can't find ANY blacks who are chairman of the board or president of publicly traded or white-owned banks.

What about black lawyers? The number of blacks in law school is dwindling.

Many scholarships that used to be available to blacks have dried up, which is the major reason why the dropout rate is so high.

Look at Silicon Valley. Although John W. Thompson was appointed chairman for Microsoft, when was the last time you saw a black CEO in the world of technology?

How about sports…sure you see us on the field and on the court, but what about in the owner's suite? With the exception of Bob Johnson, and a few minority owners such as Jay-Z, who else do you have?

Have you checked the management at major broadcasting networks? Blacks in the boardroom are far and few—even black anchors are scarce. Talk shows may have one or two blacks. Don Lemon, Fredricka Whitfield, Melissa Harris Perry, Al Sharpton, the late Max Robinson, Al Roker, Robin Roberts—local anchors, including Bruce Johnson, Leon Harris, Tony Perkins, Maureen Bunyan, Pat Lawson Muse, Jim Vance, J.C. Hayward, Shawn Yancy, Karen Gray Houston, Allison Seymour, Andrea Roane, Derek McGinty, Barbara Harrison, Lesli Foster, Wisdom Martin and Kendis Gibson…the fact that you can name them demonstrates that there's simply not enough.

Publishing, brokerage firms, the New York Stock Exchange…there's only a handful of us on the floor of the New York Stock Exchange, but not nearly enough. How many of us are on Wall Street? How many of us hold major, decision-making roles on Wall Street—not just window dressing?

In the healthcare industry, there are very few African Americans who are physicians in allied health or own major health clinics.

There's not nearly enough black legislators. We currently comprise 10 percent of Congress. We aren't even discussing local or statewide seats.

What about black farmers? We remember the struggle of blacks in the South who were trying to hold on to their land. Do the research and you'll find that black farmers are scarce.

The billion-dollar beauty industry… Blacks account for a large percentage of consumers, but very few are the manufacturers of these products. Black-owned companies produce very little. There's Fashion Fair, and perhaps a couple of others, but again, not nearly enough for what we consume. And the hair industry…we won't even go there.

In the world of media, which controls our images, only Cathy Hughes of

TV One and Radio One is an owner. BET is no longer owned by African Americans, and Oprah Winfrey is a programmer for OWN. Cathy Hughes owns the hardware and the wires. Magic Johnson owns ASPIRE. Media is one of the main industries where we need more African Americans in decision-making roles. We need more African Americans behind the camera, as well as in front of the camera. Black producers, filmmakers, writers…we need more at the top of major motion picture companies. This is the only way that we can change the negative depiction of African Americans.

Take a look at the major airlines. As much as we fly the friendly skies, blacks are not the chairman of the board of a major airline, or even on the board of directors, yet we're stacking up those frequent flyer miles. We've got to do better and demand so much more.

Hospitality and tourism…we own only a handful of hotels and a few travel agencies.

Movie theaters, retail chains, architectural firms, construction, pharmaceuticals, automotives. You name the industry, and you'll find that very few of us are at the top, if any.

We lack ownership and positions of leadership and power, and we MUST change that. We MUST demand representation from the top to the bottom.

Economics is the new silver rights. I guess you're asking what silver rights are? Silver Rights is the unspoken, modern-day civil rights movement involving financial literacy.

There's no way to defend it. There's a glass ceiling all around when it comes to blacks, and it's time that we shatter the ceiling. We are underrepresented or not represented at all.

Some of you may be asking, *what about those who aren't black who are reading this book?* Well, let me tell you. I'm black, and my life has been about uplifting black folks. Don't get me wrong, there's a place for whites in our struggle, and quite frankly, I believe that we need white allies. This book is written by a black man, who lived to uplift blacks and Hispanics, as well as those who've been left out of history books.

Unfortunately, though slavery ended centuries ago, many of us are still enslaved psychologically. Many are still in bondage. We've got to change our mindsets and unify.

Sure, we've made tremendous progress, but we still have a long road ahead of us. Don't take my word for it. Look at the facts and the record. Look at all the industries and tell me how many people of color that you see at the top.

Unfortunately, in my view, blacks do not have the same opportunities or a level playing field as other segments of the population. Contrary to popular belief, we've never been given an equal chance.

Once we're given the opportunity, however, we flourish. We know it. Take sports, for instance. For many years, sports was segregated. Once we were in, we fought our way straight to the top. Muhammad Ali, Jackie Robinson, Michael Jordan, Tiger Woods, the Williams sisters, and many, many more star athletes are just a few shining examples.

When we're given the same opportunities, there's nothing we can't do. Sure, there are many blacks who have achieved much, but, as Dick Gregory says, "They're still a nigga."

You'll notice in the beginning of this chapter that I quoted Frederick Douglass. I used him as an example of what we MUST do. This is modern-day silver rights in a capitalistic society, and it's difficult to operate without capital.

We also know, if left unchecked, capitalism requires there be a permanent underclass. Presently, the underclass is poor blacks and Hispanics. Unless we engage in major economic development, blacks and Hispanics will remain the permanent underclass. Our goal must be to change that and not let us become the permanent underclass.

Blacks are the only group that was brought to this country in chains. We had no capital, and we never received forty acres and a mule when slavery ended.

I believe that blacks have never been close to the top of the pyramid, unlike other immigrants who have been able to move rapidly up the ladder of success.

There's not another group of people who've been discriminated against as much as blacks. Look at our communities. Most businesses in the black community are not owned and operated by blacks. We must keep our focus on ownership, economics and stock purchases. Most of us spend money before we hardly get our hands on it. A good example of community solidarity is the Jewish community. Not only did they produce and manufacture to benefit the Jewish community, but all communities. Jews produced luxury items, such as furs and diamonds, and also assumed professional positions, such as bankers and doctors.

Each of us ought to be committed to building assets, even if they are meager. With homeownership, you can build equity. In my ward, only 75 percent are renters, where in other neighborhoods, the homeownership rate is 70 percent. Usually most people's first asset is a home. Homeownership has to be an economic priority.

We must keep our focus on economics. We need savings clubs. We spend money before we save it. There used to be a time when we had savings clubs. If we save 10 percent of what we earn, look at how much we would amass.

We need to consult with investment bankers on the best way to use our money. We should be acquiring Initial Public Offerings (IPOs) from the very beginning.

We have to demand better-paying jobs—jobs that offer high five-figure and six-figure salaries. We have to make demands, and it's ass backward if we don't think that we have a right to demand. You don't get put in a corner and take it. You make demands. In order to demand better-paying jobs, we must enhance our skills. Skill development must be a priority. You never get too old to learn.

We worship in our churches every Sunday, and give our tithes and offerings. The black churches deposit millions in the bank every Monday, yet those same banks won't lend to parishioners nor patrons.

Blacks and Hispanics and our white allies should be picketing the World Bank and the International Monetary Fund to demand that black countries get the same loans that other countries are receiving.

Just imagine if we picketed one bank that discriminated against making loans to blacks, and we picketed across the country simultaneously the same way we did Woolworth during the Civil Rights Movement. We need to take direct action. In many instances, you can borrow money for a car without a job, yet banks give us difficulty in providing us loans for houses and small businesses.

We must buy stock, even if it's only one share, and sit in those stockholders meetings and demand that blacks have a real seat at the decision-making table...not just as window dressers.

For those sports enthusiasts, when you attend the games, instead of tailgating in the parking lot, how about picketing during the games and demanding ownership. As a matter of fact, the athletes should pool their money and buy part of the ownership in major sports franchises, and then give back to the disenfranchised.

Nonviolent, direct action has no time limit on it.

We've got to start teaching our children as soon as they learn the three "Rs"–reading, 'riting, and 'rithmetic—the importance of saving money, as well as amassing assets, skill development and entrepreneurship. In this capitalist economy, it's not enough to be smart or have a degree. Each of us has to begin creating our own wealth. This is an area I personally regret not putting an emphasis on: creating my own wealth. We've got to teach them the importance of creating legacy and generational wealth. The days of job security in the government are no longer sufficient in building wealth. Job security is null and void. The only job security that you have is the job that you create. Nobody can hire or fire you when it belongs to you. When you create your own wealth, not only do you create a unique opportunity for yourself, you also establish something that can benefit your entire family for generations to come. Let me make it plain. If you don't do it yourself, you're a part of the problem, not the solution.

Just think about what Donald Trump established for his family. His vision led to an international brand where his children are not only the beneficiaries, but are decision-makers. I've met with Donald Trump on numerous occasions, and clearly, his daughter, Ivana, is not just there for window dressing. She's making decisions. His sons, Eric and Don, Jr., are also spearheading the direction of the company. The Trump name will carry on for generations to come. His great-great grandchildren will never have to work for anyone else. The Trump name has enough entities for all of the generations of Trumps to put their passion and skills to great use. There are a number of black families similar to the Trumps, who are making a way for their families and communities.

The Marriotts are another great example of a family that creates generational wealth. And there are hundreds and hundreds of other white families who are doing the same thing.

I applaud those who own barbershops and beauty salons. But we've got to think BIGGER than our neighborhood. We've got to develop the mindset of ownership and brand building. Our names are just as marketable internationally as anyone else's.

On top of everything else, we live in a technology era. You can create things that can be sold online. We need to begin to learn how to create Internet-based businesses that we can do right from our homes. It will not be easy, but definitely necessary. Our kids will LOVE creating their own online businesses. It will be easy, and they can begin developing their minds to think like an entrepreneur, and not just an employee. We need lots of people to accomplish a task, but we also need major leadership stepping up as visionaries.

This mindset, however, begins at home with our youth at a very early age. Kids need piggy banks where they are taught to save money. If they're not allowed to have little neighborhood-based jobs to earn money, at least give them an opportunity to earn money doing household chores. And make them SPEND their own money when it's something that they want, so they understand the value of a dollar, and will appreciate whatever they purchase because they had to pay for it.

Earlier in the chapter, I mentioned the importance of buying stock or other investment opportunities. Well, it's also important to teach your children about investing. There's no better way to teach them this lesson than to buy them a piece of stock in something that they can relate to—such as Nike or X-box. The next time they start badgering you about buying them a pair of Jordans or the new game station, tell them you will do something better than that. When they get to school and encounter the kids who are bragging about their new shoes, your child can come back and say, "Oh, you may have the shoe, but I have stock in the company." *Touché!*

If we get our kids to begin thinking BIG, despite their current environment, then every generation after that will develop the same mindset, and the cycle will continue.

If the slavery mentality still exists four centuries later, clearly, we can instill this mindset the same way.

For those who patronize black businesses, continue. And for those who don't, you need to start. We MUST patronize black-owned businesses so black business owners can flourish and build generational wealth. Black-owned businesses must also produce a product worthy of patronizing.

Also, in order to make these demands, we must be trained. Therefore, a quality school system in our neighborhoods is essential. We must demand quality education in our neighborhoods. There was a time in the black community, no matter how uneducated you were, we made education a high, high priority. Many don't see education as relevant to them, resulting in low graduation rates and high dropout rates. The leadership in black communities must make quality education for our children the highest form of business.

FAMILY VALUES = ECONOMICS

Now here's the really hard part. Now it's time to look at the man in the mirror and have a frank discussion with yourself, and areas that you need to change.

Now fellas, here's a BIG problem. We need more of you to step up and be MEN.

We need more of you to truly be the head of the household. We need you to be active fathers. You need to start marrying these beautiful women who are making it on their own, but still need the support of the strong, black man in the home. Don't be intimidated. She still needs you, no matter how many zeros she has in the bank. Even if you choose an alternative lifestyle, two is better than one.

Just think about it economically: if you hone all of your attention on one person and the two of you build together, consider what you can do, because it's a team effort. That house you keep riding past thinking about the Sunday dinners you'll host…guess what?? You can afford to buy it now because you have support. Think about the difference that you will make in your lives and the lives of your children when both partners are in the home. There's nothing but advantages to making your home life better. So, when I say that it all starts at home, don't think that I'm just referring to our young people. I'm talking to you, too! I would suggest that if that doesn't work, don't get discouraged. Find another partner and try it again.

If you notice, I didn't talk much about Africa in the previous chapters. I wanted to save that until the end to include in our current struggles.

We have been brainwashed about Africa—that the people are a bunch of heathens. We have been brainwashed to believe that there's no reason to connect with Africa and the Caribbean. Africa is our ancestral homeland. Other nations, such as Israel, have a strong relationship with the American Jewish community. The Irish…and the list goes on with those who have relationships with their ancestral homeland. Why should African Americans be any different? Therefore, in order to continue the struggle, in America, there are people who can strengthen our relationship with African countries. I've visited and met with the presidents of more than twenty African countries who are eager to have political, business and social relationships. I want to thank those early pioneers who tried to forge a relationship—organizations such as TransAfrica and the Back-to-Africa movement and the Leaders of the Student Nonviolent Coordinating Committee and many, many other groups. There are countless business opportunities in Africa, and many, many ways that we can help African countries politically. Africa is rich with minerals and oil. Part of the solution for those of us who have skills is not only to build in America, but to build up in Africa.

We need to take American technology to Africa. The African American labor movement has joined with the African labor movement under Bill Lucy's leadership. We need to develop more tourist opportunities with Africa and the Caribbean. Black America should continue to develop tourism opportunities with Africa and the Caribbean.

I personally would like to thank the late Dr. Leon Sullivan for helping forge relationships with African heads of state and African Americans through the Sullivan Foundation.

Black mayors should do more to establish sister-city relationships with African cities.

In closing, you can't lead where you won't go, and you can't teach what you don't know. That's a Barryism. I have been an inspiration to a number of people, but also some people have been afraid to take the same steps that I took. This may be the final chapter of the book, but not the final chapter of my life or yours. For some, it can be the beginning of moving beyond just being here, but also having the vision, courage and tenacity to lead. The struggle continues.

ABOUT THE AUTHORS

Marion Barry, Jr., a four-term mayor of Washington, D.C., has dedicated forty years of his life to public service, living by the motto "always fighting for the people." The son of a sharecropper and born in Mississippi, he joined the Civil Rights Movement and was elected the first chairman of the Student Nonviolent Coordinating Committee (SNCC). His elected career in Washington, D.C., has spanned from 1971 to the present. He currently serves as a council member for the District of Columbia, and lives in Washington, D.C., with his only son, Christopher.

New York Times bestselling author Omar Tyree is the winner of the 2001 NAACP Image Award for Outstanding Literary Work—Fiction, and the 2006 Phillis Wheatley Literary Award for Body of Work in Urban Fiction. He has published more than twenty books on African American people and culture, including five *New York Times* bestselling novels. He is a popular national speaker, and a strong advocate of urban literacy. Born and raised in Philadelphia, he lives in Charlotte, North Carolina. Learn more at OmarTyree.com.